CRUX

CRUX

A Cross-Border Memoir

Jean Guerrero

ONE WORLD

NEW YORK

Copyright © 2018 by Jean Guerrero
Map copyright © 2018 by David Lindroth Inc.

Published in the United States by One World, an imprint of Random House,
a division of Penguin Random House LLC, New York.

ONE WORLD is a registered trademark and its colophon is a
trademark of Penguin Random House LLC.

Library of Congress Cataloging-in-Publication Data
Names: Guerrero, Jean, author.
Title: Crux : a cross-border memoir / By Jean Guerrero.
Description: First edition. | New York : One World, [2018]
Identifiers: LCCN 2017035196 | ISBN 9780399592393 | ISBN 0399592393 |
ISBN 9780399592409 (ebook)
Subjects: LCSH: Adult children of drug addicts—Biography. | Adult children of
immigrants—Biography. | Adult children of alcoholics—Biography. | Schizophrenics—
Biography. Classification: LCC HV5132 .G84 2018 | DDC 362.29/13092 [B]—dc23
LC record available at https://lccn.loc.gov/2017035196

Printed in the United States of America on acid-free paper

Map enhancements (location markers) by Michelle Ruby Guerrero

oneworldlit.com
randomhousebooks.com

2 4 6 8 9 7 5 3 1

First Edition

Book design by Jo Anne Metsch

FRONTISPIECE: *My father tosses me in the suburbs of San Diego, California, in May 1989.*

For Papi, who gave me a story
For my mother, who gave me earth
Para Abuelita Carolina, por las semillas

I heard my blood, singing in its prison,
and the sea sang with a murmur of light,
one by one the walls gave way. . . .

OCTAVIO PAZ, Piedra de Sol

"They shall worship you first. Your name shall not be forgotten. Thus be it so," they said to their father when they comforted his heart. "We are merely the avengers of your death and your loss, for the affliction and misfortune that were done to you." Thus was their counsel when they had defeated all Xibalba.

Popol Vuh, ALLEN J. CHRISTENSON translation

It is important to be on the lookout for the occurrence of positive synchronicities, for they are the signals that power is working to produce effects far beyond the normal bounds of probability.

MICHAEL HARNER, The Way of the Shaman

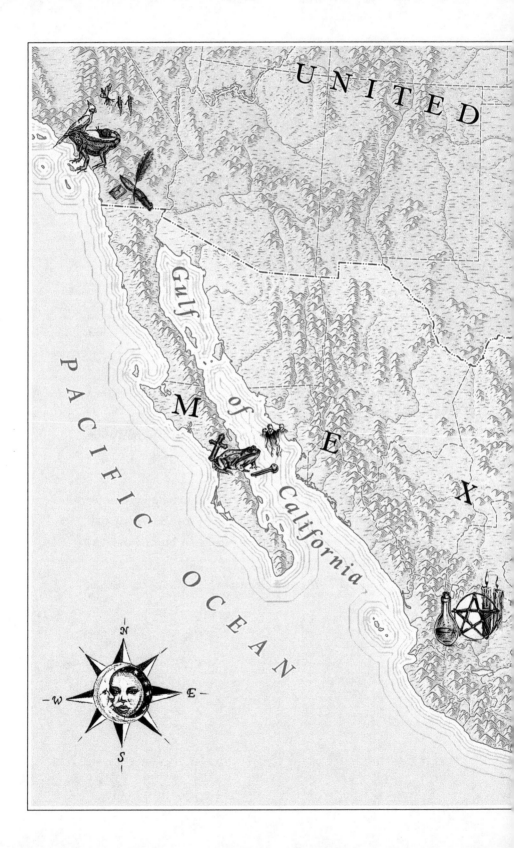

CONTENTS

AUTHOR'S NOTE

This book is divided into seven segments, corresponding to different parts of the ancient K'iche' Maya creation story in the *Popol Vuh*. The legend tells of two twins, the Sun and the Moon, who venture into the underworld, Xibalba, where their father has been trapped. They overcome several challenges and resurrect him.

This is a work of nonfiction. Parallels with the *Popol Vuh* are coincidences. I used memories, interviews, videotapes, diaries, immigration documents, prison records, baptismal files, history books and more to re-create the past. Dialogue with quotation marks is from audio recordings or notes; dialogue in italics comes from recollections.

LA NADA

I'm sorry, Papi. *Perdóname.* I know how much you hate to be pursued. You've spent your whole life running. Now the footsteps chasing you are mine.

¿Papi, dónde estás?

I lost myself searching for you. Trees sprout from the vaulted ceiling. The sky stretches far beyond my feet. The wind sounds human when it whispers. The roads are cobblestone, conch and *caracol.* Everything is shape-shifting.

You say spies or spirits pursue you. My mother, a physician, blames schizophrenia. I'm a journalist. I value the objective, the verifiable. In college, I minored in neuroscience. I studied the labyrinthine patterns of brain cortices, the chemical bases of hallucinations and delusions of persecution. But I am also your daughter, Papi. In Mexico, I discovered a *mundo mágico:* of corpses, *chupacabras, curanderos.* I learned that your great-grandmother was a *clarividente.* They called her *La Adivina*—the diviner. She was paid to commune with the dead.

¿Papi, quién eres?

A cursed *curandero,* a schizophrenic, a victim of the mind-control experiments you describe? I look into the mirror seeking clues. Your quests and questions consumed me, even though you were never there. The last time I saw you was the year the world was meant to end. When I close my eyes, Papi, all the clocks rewind to then.

•

You kick off your boots in the dark. You slip off your beanie, your leather jacket. We're in a double room at the San Francisco Grand Hyatt hotel. I'm already in bed. You stretch and sigh by yours. I'm twenty-four years old. It's the spring of 2012. Earlier in the day, we watched my sister graduate from San Francisco's Academy of Art University. I flew in from Mexico City, your birthplace, where I'm working as a foreign correspondent and investigating your history. Months ago, a psychologist diagnosed me with post-traumatic stress disorder tied to a near-death experience south of the border.

My nervous system thunders. I can't stop thinking about the last time we shared a room. I was eleven, in Autlán de Navarro, Jalisco. It was my first visit to the interior of your country. My mother told me to be careful—Mexico was a perilous place, and you were "not normal." As I tried to sleep, I felt the danger of your country thrusting itself through the thin walls of our rural pueblo room, into you. Your skin was clammy and see-through. Your veins were vines snaking down your neck. Your eyes were protuberant and black. You had been smoking crack.

We're in the United States, in a nice hotel. You haven't smoked crack in nearly a decade. In your fifties, you have a shamanic air, with a *pimienta* beard and long gray-black hair. Your eyes are chameleonic, shifting between shades of ochre. Your face is striking—cheekbones high and prominent, like plump *aguacates,* causing your eyes to crinkle with each smile. Your skin is copper-colored. A self-taught expert in natural medicine, you cultivate curative plants such as comfrey and ashitaba in the Mexican beach town of Rosarito. Some potions you concocted eradicated your mother's arthritis and restored vision to her once-blind Chihuahua, if Abuelita is to be believed.

'They 'symptomized' me."). You didn't seem crazy. What you
sounded similar to Project MKUltra, an actual covert CIA
rol experiment that began in the 1950s. They targeted drug
legal immigrants, prostitutes and other minorities who
dibility or influence so that nobody would believe them if
plained. Those documents have been declassified. For the
Papi, I wondered if you had in fact been the victim of secret
nt torture. I felt it was my duty, as a journalist and as your
to pursue every conceivable line of inquiry.

•

to your knees. Search beneath your bed. Search beneath
np to your feet and dash into the bathroom. You swing open
ets.
hear 'em," you cry.
who?" I ask.
lash to the room door. Throw it open. Step into the hallway.
Inspect the bathroom again. No one. The closet. *Nada.* You
stare at me.
i, you must have been dreaming. There's nobody here," I say,
afraid you might hallucinate that I'm a government spy. "You
hearing someone upstairs. Or downstairs. Or next door. We're
el."
eech you to go to sleep. You march back and forth. Inhale. Ex-
u crawl back into bed. I realize I'm holding my breath.
ost as soon as my body unclenches from consciousness, you
your feet with a howl. "What?" I cry. You sprint to the door,
d jiggle the knob. Once more, you search: beneath the beds,
he bathroom, behind the curtains, the closet. You pace. Remove
veat-soaked shirt. When you collapse again, I know I won't fall
sleep this time. My body quakes with an apocalyptic pulse. You
nd whimper, shifting under the blankets. All night, I hear you
s you dream.
the morning, you rise, wearing only white boxer briefs. Pale

You are still troubled: you binge
can't describe, you are sometimes s
cently, requesting that I bury you '
single blanket so as to decompose
mountains, hidden, perhaps in the Si
don't cry." You're convinced you ha
can detect. Your bones feel heavier th
hardly take a step. But you're a differ

I watch your shadow by your bed
it off. Slide off your jeans, sprawl out
you fall asleep. I notice your peaceful
dreamed in your arms. I remember th
cheek. A tranquil blackness consumes
asleep.

You leap from bed with a cry. I jolt
wall. You're gasping. Hyperventilating.
switch. Scan the room with terrified ey
you say. "Someone's in here with us."

•

At the turn of the millennium, after Au
eral years. We thought you were dead.
Thailand, Malaysia, Vietnam, Cambodia,
lands, Belgium and Mexico, fleeing alleg
ments. You believed the government was
electromagnetic or radio-wave technolog
skull and painful electric shocks into your l
believed, was to demonstrate the technolo
human behavior by eradicating your addict
quit. You came home and buried healing se

On my twentieth birthday, in 2008, you
had never told anyone. Your stories were
Spanglish, with the vocabulary of a voraciou
sprinkled with startling mispronunciations ('

visations (
described
mind-cont
addicts, il
lacked cre
they com
first time,
governme
daughter,

You drop
mine. Ju
the cabir
"I car
"Hea
You
Nothing
stop and
"Pap
suddenl
must be
in a hot
I bes
hale. Yo
Alm
jump t
twist a
inside
your s
back to
shout
suffer
In

light pours into the room and illuminates you. The sight inhibits my speech. The last time I saw you shirtless, Papi, I was a child. You were strength personified, flesh invulnerable as the *tezontle* of ancient Mexica pyramids. Here you are now: mortal, mutilated, marred. A large, gruesome *cicatriz* protrudes from your chest. Two lines of white skin intersect in the shape of a cross. A pale halo of skin surrounds the top of the scar. Creases of skin blur and bend inside, like the curving grooves of brain coral. Your secrets are scrawled on your skin.

●

¿Papi, quién eres? I grasp your shoulders and search your yellow eyes. But the light in them flickers and recedes. You are always running away from me.

I drowned while chasing you. My soul floats bloated in the Gulf of Mexico, strangled by starfish and squid. *Hechizos* haunt my hollow flesh. It has become cliché to talk about your country as if it were cursed. But Mexico's own citizens proclaim it. A kind of fairy-tale physics operates. The only way to escape El Monstruo is to move constantly. Surviving becomes another way to die. Either way, you disappear.

You are the ultimate migrant, Papi. You traveled across countries fleeing shadows that chased you. You visited the future in dreams, migrated back and forth between the United States and Mexico, died and came back from the dead. You lost your mind and recovered it. You abandoned me, returned to me, spoke all your secrets, then fell back into silence and sleep. How often the theme of crossings comes up in your story. Border crossings. Crossings between madness and sanity. Crossings into parallel worlds. A cross-shaped *cicatriz*. What secret do these crossings spell? Where have they led us?

For so long I followed your footsteps that I forgot the route back to earth. But I still have my notebook; I still have my pen. I am a reporter, after all. I have not forgotten the tools of my trade: fact-based research, the quest for primary documents, formal interviews. I will retrace time until I find the place where you became lost—and where I, in pursuit of you, lost my own way. By clarifying the basis of our suffering, I believe I can find a cure. Is it neurochemical, otherworldly, technological?

I will start with my mother, the M.D., the expert in diagnoses. She fell in love with you when you were on top of the world. She can help me locate the crossroads. I will follow the thread through my memories, searching for you in the negative spaces of my childhood. I will plunge into your past, your mother's and great-grandmother's, creating a trail of factual paragraphs. Did you lose yourself looking for your own father? I'll find him for you. With the ropes of letters and the chains of ink, perhaps I can pull us out of these depths. I cannot escape this place without you. Our fates are tangled up. But you are so deep inside this world. I can hear your voice in the breeze. *I am in the place without borders,* you say. *You'll never find me here.* My mother raised me to believe I can do anything, so long as I am sure of my objective, so long as I take step after step in its direction. And so I venture deeper—to the time before I was born, to the time before you were born.

Octavio Paz says the Mexican is the son of "nothingness." He comes of contradictions coalesced, of crucifixes and demons, of *conquistadores* and priests, of Cortés and Cuauhtémoc. The modern Mexican is masked mobility, fleeing from and searching for his ouroboros roots. If you succeed in catching him, you'll find a fiction. Unmask him and you'll find time stretching back a thousand years.

I'm sorry, Papi. *Perdóname.* I know how much you hate to be pursued. But the past has swallowed me. All roads before me lead straight back to you.

Part I

THE ROAD TO XIBALBA

My parents ride horses near Cascada de la Tzaráracua, Michoacán, in September 1987.

THE SUMMONS

Interstate 5 slices north–south and serpentine along the West Coast of the United States, parallel to the Pacific Ocean for more than a thousand miles. In the south, it curves into one of the world's busiest border crossings—the San Ysidro Port of Entry, where San Diego and Tijuana touch. A green sign hangs over the highway: "Mexico Only."

In the summer of 1986, a young Puerto Rican physician drove on a southbound lane just north of the juncture. She sought an exit called Bonita Road. But there is no such exit on I-5, and never was. It exists on I-805, to the east. The woman who would become my mother had just arrived in San Diego, in quest of the American dream, and her suitcase-stuffed rental vehicle was on a straight course to Mexico.

·

Jeannette Del Valle grew up on the western tip of Puerto Rico, suffering asthma her father blamed on the sugarcane pollen of their pueblo, Aguadilla. She had big, startled eyes that struggled to see—diagnosed with myopia at age twelve—and curly ash-blonde hair her mother did not let her cut, so that it grew long and thick to her thighs, a heavy cloak on her bony limbs. Her classmates called her *Esqueleto,* or Skeleton. From her earliest memories, her throat constricted against her will. She tried to pull oxygen into her convulsing lungs; she could not. Raised Catholic, she prayed to God for help. It came in the form of Doctor Mendoza, a chubby, gray-haired man who gave her shots of epinephrine and steroids, consoling her with a competent, bespectacled gaze. At night, she was alone in her battles against death. Her father purchased a nebulizer and an oxygen tank. Blind in the blackness, she sucked air into her esophagus. She survived each time to see the dawn.

Her father, Luis, was a studious, brown-skinned mechanic with thick glasses that hung low on his broad nose. Despite his five-foot stature, Jeannette's father had a towering, storybook tale. He became a provider for his two younger siblings as a teenager, when his mother died of tuberculosis. His father, a police officer married to another woman, refused to recognize him as his son until later in life. Luis shined shoes in the street. He learned to build and install central air-conditioning units. On the hot island, his skills were in high demand. He helped establish the Colegio de Técnicos Refrigeración y Aire Acondicionado de Puerto Rico, to give the island's previously informal cool-temperature trades a licensing structure. He married Luz, a lean blonde with skin like *carne de noni.*

Jeannette was the third of their four children, the most delicate in complexion and size—the skinniest, the fairest, the most prone to sickness. A verdant tangle of plants and *panapen* trees separated their house from Playa Crash Boat, with its peach-colored sands and reaching blue waters. Jeannette's hardy siblings spent much of their time there, imitating the coqui frog's song, kicking coconuts, chasing crabs in the mud. Jeannette liked the ocean from an aesthetic point of view, but she preferred the indoors and its comfortable, controlled environments. Her favorite pastime was reading—medical literature, for the most part, which she checked out from the local library, dreaming of discovering a cure for the asthma that asphyxiated her almost every day. Naturally, her goal was to become a doctor. Even with all the doors and windows of their little Aguadilla house shut, Jeannette suffered. Even after the sugarcane harvests, when the fields were clean, the attacks came. One day, as she doodled unicorn intestines in an anatomy text, it occurred to her that maybe the sugarcane pollen was not the sole cause of her asthma. *Posiblemente,* she thought, it was also the creatures in the attic next door. Every evening she saw the bats emerging in droves. She wondered if spores from their dung or dander clung to the ubiquitous humidity and floated into her breathing space, irritating her lungs. When her family moved to a nearby house for unrelated reasons, her asthma attacks abated, and she remembered her hypothesis. She had a gift.

Luz nurtured it. *It is humiliating to have to ask a man for everything— even underwear,* her mother whispered in Spanish. In her adolescence, Luz had been known in her neighborhood as *La Rubia Peligrosa*—the dangerous blonde. The attention had planted vague dreams of grandeur in Luz's teenage mind: perhaps she would be a movie star someday, or a powerful *curandera.* Now she was a devoted wife and mother, linked forever to the whims, worries and wanderings of the man to whom she had committed. Luz did not know how to read, write or drive a car. She rarely left the house without her husband. She had been eclipsed by her man and feared the same fate for her daughters. She poured her passion into things she made for the family, food like savory *sorullitos de maíz* and *pasteles de yuque.* Luz also made the girls' clothing, expressing her rebellion in bright colors and bold cuts.

Luis was old-fashioned, and didn't believe women should aspire beyond domesticity. When he hired a painting tutor for his daughters, it was to increase their desirability as housewives. But on the walls of their Caribbean home, Jeannette painted murals of an indecorous medical nature—for example, a grinning feline with a sinewy esophagus visible through a slit in its throat. The oldest daughter, Irma, expressed plans to attend law school. The youngest, Myriam, announced she would be a professional painter. Luz's nocturnal whispers had worked like magic on the girls. The three would make their way to the mainland in pursuit of their ambitions. Only their brother established himself in Aguadilla.

My mother was the first to leave. As valedictorian of her high school class, she secured a full scholarship to pursue a bachelor's in biology in Mayagüez. There, she applied to the U.S. Air Force for a medical school scholarship. But she had worn thick glasses since she was twelve, and at the time, the Air Force required 20/20 vision. She applied to the Coast Guard and the Navy. She was underweight. Jeannette told herself it was for the best; it was hard enough to breathe on land. Despite living footsteps from the ocean, Jeannette had never learned to swim. A rip current had sucked her out to sea once, endowing her with a permanent terror of *el mar*. She had been splashing waist-deep on the shore, clasping her sisters' hands, when a swell of water buoyed the girls and separated their fingers. Jeannette alone lost her balance. Disoriented, she watched as her rooted sisters shrank, and the palm trees on the white beach became farther away. She sought a place to rest her feet, in vain. A tall wave crashed around her, knocking off her glasses and plunging her into the deep. She saw the blurry sun cracked to golden pieces by turbulent undulations. She was accustomed to mortal terror, thanks to her asthma—and as water filled her throat, she mentally chanted *traga, traga, traga*, like a magic spell, swallow, swallow, swallow. She resolved to imbibe the whole sea if necessary . . . *traga, traga, traga, don't let water into your pulmones* . . . Even as her lungs screamed for air, Jeannette refused to succumb to irrational impulses. So many times in the course of her life, she would be imperiled by invisible forces like the rip current over which she lacked control—or like Interstate 5, which would push her straight into my father's arms. Her will to survive was always militant. She sank, her hair floating upward like Medusa's snakes, eyes wide open, respiratory system secured. Her uncle dove in and saved her.

After rejections from the Navy and Coast Guard, Jeannette applied to the Army. The recruiter looked at her with pitying eyes and advised her to try the National Health Service Corps: she could remain a civilian and repay her debts as a primary-care provider in an underserved community. She applied. The Service Corps notified her she would be going to medical school, all expenses paid. She completed her bachelor's in three years and moved to San Juan. She specialized in internal medicine: the treatment, prevention and diagnosis of adult illness.

For a year, in anatomy class, she familiarized herself with the innards of an unclaimed corpse. Having studied mutations, protrusions, rashes, gashes, warts, wounds and putrefactions in books since she was a child, Jeannette was not a queasy person. She was fascinated by the labyrinth of tubes inside this human. She sliced open the gray-haired man with scalpels, planting labeled flags in his arteries, muscles and organs. She removed his heart and held it in her hands, imagining the limp, defective organ in its last moments, its once-moist coronary arteries clotted and trembling. When Irma moved into Jeannette's apartment to study law, she was aghast to discover that Jeannette placed her textbooks on the dead man daily and brought them home to study on the kitchen table. *The corpse is sterile,* Jeannette thought, shrugging. *They keep it cold.*

Living on their own was liberating. Jeannette cut her hair short, bleached it and styled it voluminous and layered like the actress Farrah Fawcett's. She had the same wide-open eyes and pale, delicate lips. She weighed ninety-five pounds. She was a top student, but her adventurous wardrobe, inspired by her mother—thick belts, audacious colors, tall boots—meant she was also named Most Fashionable in the yearbook.

A medical student named Carlos proposed to Jeannette. Like her, he was spindly and half blind. Thick-rimmed glasses hid the small eyes on his prodigious head. They were engaged for about a year. But as they neared graduation in 1983, Carlos realized he wanted a housewife. He begged Jeannette to give up medicine. She refused. Carlos asked her to return his engagement ring. For a few weeks, Jeanette's grades slipped.

Heartbroken, Jeannette flew to New York for an interview at the Brookdale University Hospital and Medical Center. She took in the shining, metallic skyscrapers, an alternate universe compared with the ripe green Eden of her home. The silver city beckoned her. When the cutting-edge trauma center offered her a residency, she said good-bye to her relatives and moved to the mainland.

Jeannette sent her family money and gifts, writing letters that focused on the positive aspects of her new life, such as the hospital's ethnic diversity—*I feel like I live all over the world!*—and her improving English. She described the workload—thirty-six hours of emergency-room duty every three nights—in cheerful cursive Spanish: *I find a way to sleep one or two hours, it's enough.*

She said nothing about the dead who plagued her dreams, the patients she failed to save, such as the man whose skull was splintered by a bullet, whose heart she kept beating for nearly an hour. She made no mention of her romantic anxiety, her fear that she might never love again. Although she cloaked her insecurities in her letters, I detect them in her praise for Myriam, the artist, whom she called the smartest of the sisters for pursuing a passion she saw as less exhausting. *Career is not everything in life,* Jeannette wrote. *I hope God blesses you all and helps me keep going forward with . . . a whole life in service of health.* She ended her letters on playful notes. *P.S. They've changed my name a little bit; they call me Jeannette D'val. As if I were French. Americans—or Gringos—don't know how to pronounce my beautiful last name Del Valle . . .*

The winter of the East Coast sank into her tropical bones like teeth. Gargantuan, grimy rats wriggled into her apartment. She slept with her inhaler under her pillow and scattered glue traps. In the mornings, her landlord stopped by to toss their sticky tombs from her window. Once or twice, she passed their twitching tails protruding from the snow like stems of animate flowers.

In the emergency room one night, Dr. Del Valle admitted two drowned bodies as blue as icicles. The corpses had been pulled from a frozen river and transported by helicopter. For hours, Jeannette warmed these dead lovers with blankets, intravenous injections of warm fluids and the aggressive motions of cardiopulmonary resuscitation. She watched as the woman's cheeks regained color and she took a sudden breath of air. The man did not awaken again, but the woman's recovery was remarkable. Miracles such as this, and the role she played in them, allowed her uncertainties about prioritizing her career to dissolve with the snow. Spring came.

She befriended an aspiring radiologist starting his residency at a nearby hospital. Mark Anthony had a thick brown beard, vulnerable brown eyes and a contrasting conspiratorial air that gave him an edgy charm. In Puerto Rico, men had not preferred Jeannette because of her thinness and her ambition, perceived as masculine traits. In New York, with its multicultural range of ideals, she was a desirable Twiggy, with a sexy, superior mind, and Mark Anthony was infatuated with her. They went dancing. He lifted her petite body, spinning her as others looked on with envy. They spent hours conversing about their fields. They both felt that familiar tug of the heart, but they resisted it. They wanted to be realistic. Mark Anthony was younger than Jeannette, and would not finish his residency for another two years. Jeannette planned to establish herself in a more habitable climate, ideally in the Golden State.

She was accepted at several Service Corps facilities, including her top choice: the San Ysidro Health Center in San Diego, California. She picked up her residency diploma and hired a moving van. *Maybe you can follow me someday,* she told Mark Anthony. *Maybe I will,* he said. Then she got on a plane and flew to California.

San Diego, she knew, had the weather of paradise: sun-drenched like Puerto Rico, without the sticky humidity. When she stepped out of the airport, a cool breeze from the west carried the fresh smell of the salty sea. The skyscrapers of downtown San Diego shimmered. This paradisiacal metropolis would be her home—modern and urban like New York, minus the crippling cold and rodents. Dr. Del Valle, the first professional in a lineage of housewives, was euphoric. She was driving to her hotel when she got lost on I-5. Her travel agent had scribbled the wrong freeway in his directions.

Passing exit after exit in a doomed search for Bonita Road, Jeannette grew nervous. The landscape was changing up ahead. Tall mountains covered in incongruously colored houses on foundations of car tires were in stark contrast to the orderly suburbs along the highway. She saw a colossal Mexican flag. A large green sign loomed ahead: "Mexico Only." She gasped. She hit the brakes, checked her rearview mirror and swerved.

She almost didn't make it. At the stoplight of the last U.S. exit, her hands shook on the steering wheel. She couldn't believe the mistake she had nearly made. She knew nothing about Mexico. She had never been to a foreign country. What if she had crossed the border by accident? What if she had gotten stuck on the other side? She was a U.S. citizen, like all Puerto Ricans, but her citizenship felt questionable on the mainland: she had an accent and no passport.

She pulled into the nearest gas station. A tall Mexican man with ink-black hair was leaning over his engine. He wore faded jeans and a white undershirt. His car had overheated and he was pouring water over the radiator with a plastic gallon jug. Jeannette rolled down her window. *Excuse me,* she called.

The man turned around. His eyes were golden, squinting against an afternoon light that seemed to swirl and spring in his irises like fire. She had never seen eyes like his.

Papi smiled as if he knew her, as if he had been waiting for her. He wiped his oil-blackened hands on a rag hanging on the hood of his car. *Yeah?*

The wind entered her window, entangling in her hair. The wind whipped her hair across her eyes. She was blind only for a second, but one second was enough. She asked him for directions.

LA MISIÓN

Papi says I was conceived on a Mexican beach called La Misión. My parents pitched a tent there in the summer of 1987. They caught a squid and cooked it over a campfire. Then they crawled into their tent and made me.

"That's why you're the outdoorsy one," my father claims.

My sister, he says, was conceived at a New Year's Eve celebration. "That's why Ruby's a party girl." He adds a cartoonish chuckle: "Heh, heh, heh."

Years later, I am flipping through my mother's photo albums. I come across a picture of my mother on a beach at night. A campfire illuminates her. She is surrounded by darkness that emerges from the sea. The darkness has a flame-like quality of its own, leaping and slanting at my mother. I pull the photo from behind its plastic covering. On the back, in my mother's handwriting, reads "Summer 1987, La Misión."

I bring the picture to my mother and ask her my question. She nods. Moments after my father took this photograph, the two entered the tent behind her to mix the witch's brew of me. I search for myself in the sinister blackness lurching toward my mother from the direction of the sea.

•

In the summer of 1986, the man who would become my father often drove across the U.S.-Mexico border on I-5. He owned a Honda CX650 Turbo motorcycle and an Oldsmobile Cutlass. He liked the feel of the wind on his face, of speeding back and forth between two countries. He sought challenging coastal rock faces to free-climb and cliffs from which to dive into the Pacific Ocean.

Marco Antonio Guerrero had just been laid off from the National Steel and Shipbuilding Company, NASSCO, where he'd built oil tankers and cargo carriers for a decade. He cut shapes out of steel plates with a torch. He leaned into shards of scattering flame, removing welts, beveling seams and dodging molten metal. He worked quickly, doing in one hour what others did in three or four. His coworkers laughed at him, reminding him that idle workers earned the same as busy ones. But Marco enjoyed efficiency. Physical work was something his body took pleasure in doing—like eating or drinking or having sex. Cigarette dangling from his lips, he reveled in the agility of his limbs. As the *Exxon Valdez* neared completion, the company decided to downsize by a thousand workers. His position, one of many burners, was expendable.

Marco took advantage of the unexpected free time. He visited the library for books about world wars, quantum mechanics, economics, Arthurian legends, mammalian biology, electrical engineering. He read voraciously. He wanted to know everything. He felt the whole world was within his mind's grasp, despite the heaviness in his chest when certain recollections came: his crushed dreams of attending medical school, the abuse of his stepfather, the deaths of his best friends, the nightmares that felt prophetic. He had migrated to the United States at the age of eighteen, to transcend the past. He rarely thought of his childhood or adolescence in Mexico.

Within weeks of the NASSCO layoffs, his stepfather, Jesus, asked him for a favor. Jesus owned a meat-packaging plant called the Butcher Block, which had amassed unprecedented wealth for the Guerreros that decade. In Mexico, they had lived without electricity or running water. Now they owned an ocean-view house in San Diego.

The idea for the Butcher Block had come a few years before, while Jesus was chopping meat at a San Diego grocery store, Miller's Market. A fellow immigrant, Roberto Robledo, came to the meat counter regularly to buy shredded beef for his Mexican drive-through restaurant, Roberto's. He doused the meat in red salsa for burritos. Roberto told Jesus he was losing faith in his American dream. He feared gringos were never going to like Mexican food as much as burgers and French fries. Jesus protested. He recalled seeing long lines of American tourists at a place in Baja California that sold burritos stuffed with roasted steak, salsa *fresca* and guacamole. *They call it "the carne asada burrito,"* he said. *Why don't you try adding that to the menu?* The tip proved useful, to say the least. Roberto's expanded north and east, metamorphosing into one of the largest Mexican fast-food chains in the state, then in the Southwest. The *carne asada* burrito hooked gringos on Mexican food. As Don Roberto came by to double, then triple his meat orders, he urged Don Jesus to start his own *carnicería,* and promised to buy his meat from him. Jesus launched the Butcher Block. The sales of the two businesses exploded in tandem. Copycat chains inspired by Roberto's (Alberto's, Filiberto's, Gilberto's, Humberto's) sourced their meat from the Butcher Block, eager to achieve Roberto's taste. Several times, an inspector from the U.S. Department of Agriculture told Don Jesus he needed to make changes to comply with federal food safety standards. When he went on as usual, the government shut down the plant.

Jesus didn't speak English well and didn't understand what the USDA required. Marco was the oldest and most responsible of his six children: his English was fluent, he read books, he listened to National Public Radio, he had purchased his own house in Lemon Grove. More important, he had worked in *carnicerías* alongside his stepfather since he was ten. Jesus asked Marco to oversee the launch of a law-abiding version of the Butcher Block. He promised Marco the managerial position of the company.

Marco sold his house in Lemon Grove and made a down payment on a plot of land overlooking I-5. He called the USDA to obtain copies of their requirements. He scoured the documents, highlighting, underlining. He made phone calls, interviewing officials and architects. He obtained building permits and supervised the blueprints. He ordered the most efficient cutting machines on the market. He wanted to do a perfect job for his stepfather. He didn't harbor any hard feelings about the past. Marco kept his eyes on the future. And the future looked great. He wondered if it might be time to start a family. He couldn't imagine anything more fulfilling than bringing life into the world.

One summer day after overseeing construction at the Butcher Block, he was driving to Tijuana to fix a leak in the radiator of his Cutlass and then spend a day on the Baja California coast. Suddenly, he noticed the car's temperature gauge touching red. He pulled off I-5 onto the last U.S. exit.

As Marco leaned over his engine at a gas station, a woman pulled in and asked him for directions. He would have thought she was a gringa, if not for her Puerto Rican accent. She was skinnier than he usually liked, noting her bony arms on the steering wheel. But the paradox of her appearance—a pale, blonde *caribeña*—was magnetic. Marco offered to take her to the hotel she sought. *It's too hard to explain,* he lied. *I need to go with you. Just bring me back here.* She acquiesced, as if she saw nothing strange in his proposition. He jumped into her passenger's seat and introduced himself. Jeannette Del Valle told him she was a doctor. For a plummeting moment, he recalled his dead dream. He quickly boasted about the Butcher Block. They were both twenty-nine years old.

As they spoke, a strange conviction welled up inside him. This woman, he felt, was *the one.* He had never had such a strange idea—his fickleness had motivated at least one *norteña* to threaten him with black magic. But Jeannette was different. It was as if her smile had roots in her throat, and harnessed every word she spoke. She used charming hand gestures and goofy expressions. She made him feel comfortable. The hard authority of her profession, combined with her soft femininity, was unlike anything he had ever perceived. He thought: *She'd be a great mother.*

•

The next day, he found her hotel's phone number in the yellow pages. My mother was highlighting apartment listings in a San Diego newspaper. A little surprised but also charmed by his call, she explained she was browsing rentals in the upscale La Jolla neighborhood. Marco argued. La Jolla was thirty minutes north of her San Ysidro clinic, not counting traffic. It was needlessly expensive. He told her he knew of a new complex, Beacon Cove, only two minutes from I-805 in the city of Chula Vista. He offered to take her to see it on his motorcycle. She agreed to have a look. A real estate agent gave the two a tour of a one-bedroom that was affordable and attractive, with air-conditioning and central heating. Jeannette signed a lease the next day.

Marco's parents lived a few blocks from Beacon Cove. He invited Jeannette to their house, a two-story McMansion on a hill overlooking the Pacific Ocean. Jeannette met his mother, Carolina, a regal beauty with the lips of Michelangelo's *Delphic Sibyl*. She and her son had the same symmetrical, attractive face, with a majesty amplified by the sadness that lingered in the corners of their mouths. *How young you are,* Jeannette told Carolina, who looked like she was in her thirties at the age of forty-eight. Carolina was coy and deliberate in her manner, unlike Jeannette, who was frank and casual. But the two women had a natural affinity. Carolina was impressed by Jeannette's profession and her uncomplicated friendliness. Jeannette could see in Marco's mother the same strength and self-possession she nurtured in herself.

Marco regularly showed up at Jeannette's place unannounced to make himself useful. He offered to buy furniture. He brought groceries from organic produce stores: carrot juice, wheatgrass shots, extra virgin olive oil. Often, he cooked for her. His meals were healthy and delicious, with a marine focus—*sopa de mariscos, tostadas de ceviche, paella*—and an immaculate presentation, topped with avocado slices and cilantro sprigs. He invited her on trips to his favorite Mexican beaches, packing meticulously, crowding his Cutlass with sleeping bags, flashlights, a gas-powered grill, toilet paper, a propane stove, fishing rods, foldable chairs, pots, pans, napkins, utensils, dishwashing soap, a heavy-duty camping tent and a rain fly.

He was determined to impress her. And Jeannette found his unbridled resolve alluring; it was a fraternal twin to her own neurotic studiousness. Marco always wore light colors: faded blue or white jeans with gaps in the knees. He was the most resourceful man Jeannette had ever met. He saw through to the mechanics of everything. It was as if he had X-ray vision. He could make batteries, align breaks, fix broken pipes, start a fire from scratch. He knew how to cook and clean and carpenter. Whenever he found a blind spot in his vision, he worked actively to fill it, reading or observing or inquiring. He had amassed a collection of pliers, wrenches, padlocks, nuts, bolts, grips, spark plugs, rubber gloves, screwdrivers, safety glasses. Although he had no college degree, he intimidated Jeannette with his intelligence. He could recite the day's news headlines. He retained full episodes of wildlife programming.

Like her, he was a self-made outsider. Their native language was Spanish. He loved and respected his mother. Jeannette couldn't help falling for this strange, determined man. His only perceivable faults: he smoked a pack of Marlboro Reds a day, and occasionally snorted a line of cocaine or smoked a joint of marijuana. But Jeannette didn't mind. He was experimental. He could control himself. Marco courteously stepped outside each time he craved a cigarette; he knew the smoke provoked her asthma. With her permission, he moved into her Beacon Cove apartment.

When she got pregnant, she wanted to get married. Marco didn't believe in marriage; it seemed a pointless social construct. But he said he was willing to stomach a wedding in Unión de Guadalupe, a rural

Mexico pueblo where he had family and had spent summers as a child. He bought Jeannette a diamond ring. She bought a long-sleeved beige silk dress and a white bouquet. They purchased plane tickets.

Then Mark Anthony called. Mark Anthony, the radiologist Jeannette had almost forgotten, had decided they were soul mates. He regretted having let her go. *I'm coming to see you. We'll go to Vegas together to get married,* he said. My mother laughed. *You can't be serious,* she said. *It's been more than a year.* It should have ended when she hung up the phone. But Marco was recording my mother's phone calls. He had tapped her telephone line and, when she wasn't home, pressed Play on his recording device.

•

Nearly thirty years later, when I ask my mother for the first clear sign of the man my father would become—wrapping his body in aluminum foil, rambling about government tormentors—she recalls this incident and cries.

•

While my mother was at work, my father climbed into their attic and found the telephone line. He cut it into a Y-connection, attaching an induction coil to another cable he maneuvered through a wall to the bathroom. He taped a recorder under the bathroom sink behind the cabinet doors. He drilled a hole in the wall, tugged on the cable from the attic and plugged it into the hidden recorder. He had two recorders, which he alternated as their batteries died. He listened to the tapes in his car.

When I ask Papi *why* he did this, he says he can't recall a specific reason. Perhaps he overheard her having a conversation he didn't like. Perhaps it was simply a symptom of his desire to know everything. He recounts the episode with shrugs and a chuckle, as if discussing slightly embarrassing eccentricities.

My father doesn't remember the content of the phone conversation he heard clandestinely. He just remembers going crazy with jealousy. It confirmed his belief he had something to fear. He wondered if the baby in my mother's womb was even his. He followed her to work, watching from across the street with binoculars. He paid a private investigator $2,000 to help spy on her. He took a pair of her dirty panties to a laboratory for analysis. He could never prove she had cheated on him, but he could not shake his suspicion. Why was she always putting on makeup to go to work? Why was she always coming home so late? Surely Mark Anthony had come.

How strange that these two men shared a name: Marco Antonio, Mark Anthony. I puzzle over the significance of this. Was it a joke of the cosmos? I fear my father and I were a glitch in my mother's fate, leading her astray.

I call Mark Anthony nearly twenty-five years later, finding his clinic's phone number on the Internet. A picture of him on Vitals.com shows a middle-aged chubby brunette with smiling brown eyes. When I mention whose daughter I am, Mark Anthony exclaims my mother's name. "Jeannette Del Valle . . . the first girl I ever proposed to," he says, sighing. He remembers the phone call. He confirms my mother rejected him. He never saw her again after she left New York. He confides, however, that the woman he married looks like my mother. "I love her," he says, and after he hangs up, I'm not sure whom he meant.

Back in 1987, Marco, unwilling to admit he had been recording Jeannette's calls, instead confronted her with the telephone bill. Who had she been speaking with in New York? She claimed she didn't speak to anyone besides her sister. Enraged, Marco disappeared for days, leaving Jeannette uncertain about the future of her unborn child. Panic gripped her. She loved this man, why was he acting jealous, why had he vanished? She visited Carolina in despair. *He's been recording your phone conversations,* Carolina said. *I'm not saying I think you've transgressed. I just want you to be aware.* Jeannette was shocked. Why would Marco tap her telephone line? Was there something wrong with him? Such a high level of paranoia struck her as sick—something a mentally ill person would do. She waited for Marco to return, hoping to allay his fears without betraying Carolina's trust. But she wasn't sure she wanted to be with him anymore. How could she trust a man who had tapped her telephone line? She wondered if his drug use had induced in him a level of psychosis. Days passed without a word. Jeannette felt the need to make a drastic change—anything to feel she had control. She decided to move to La Jolla. She paid a deposit on the first place she found. Then she called Carolina and confessed she was considering—though she deeply did not want this—an abortion. Through tears, she explained she could not raise a child alone in San Diego, while fulfilling her Service Corps obligations, which would not end until 1990. She still had to take the American Board of Internal Medicine's certification exam, a notoriously difficult process that would take years.

Carolina was horrified. She was a conservative Catholic, and vehemently opposed abortions. She also knew how difficult it was to raise children. She had struggled to feed six in Tijuana, Mexico, with the unreliable financial help of Don Jesus, who for years guzzled alcohol and abused his stepsons, Marco and Alejandro. Carolina's two oldest children were the product of her first love—a mystery forbidden from conversation. For years she had considered leaving Jesus and crossing into the United States with her children. But she felt bound by her vows. When she finally sought permanent residency, she sought it for the entire family. Now her six children were grown, with stakes in a successful business that she helped run. She knew that anything was possible for certain kinds of women—for women like herself, women like Jeannette. She urged Jeannette to wait. Then she called her first son and persuaded him to swallow his pride.

My father showed up as the moving truck pulled into Beacon Cove. He begged my mother to forgive him, to stay. He promised to change. I imagine my mother weighing her options. If she had turned him down, she might have lived happily ever after. She could have aborted me, moved to La Jolla, fallen in love with a wholesome gringo. But she loved Marco Antonio, in spite of everything. She relinquished her deposit on the La Jolla apartment. In September, the couple flew to Guadalajara, rented a car and drove to the rural pueblo of Unión de

Guadalupe. Distant cousins of Marco's greeted them with ceramic mugs filled with warm milk straight from a black cow. Every house along the perimeter of the church belonged to his cousins, aunts and uncles. After visiting them, the couple went to the church to set a date for the wedding. The priest shook his head. He needed their birth certificates. Jeannette had brought hers in place of a passport, which she lacked, but Marco didn't have his. *I'm sorry, but I can't marry you,* said the priest.

In the evening, one of Marco's cousins asked him why he wanted to marry such a skinny gringa anyway. *Está muy flaca,* he said. *There's so many fine mujeres here en el pueblo, with nice big tetas!* Marco laughed. Jeannette's heart sank. She had gone to the bedroom to lie down and fight an asthma attack. The men's voices penetrated the walls. Why hadn't Marco stood up for her? Worse, why hadn't he argued with the priest? Why hadn't he suggested another church? Marco was a different version of himself in Mexico: indifferent, indecent. She felt she had two options: collapse in sadness or turn her feelings to stone. She had too much pride to be crippled. If he didn't want to marry her, she didn't want to marry him, either. But although Marco seemed to have forgotten about the wedding, he insisted on visiting Playa Azul in the state of Michoacán, the rainforest of Uruapán, the coast of Colima. Jeannette tried to enjoy herself, purchasing souvenir shirts, a *molcajete* and other crafts, tasting the local food, horseback riding, posing for photographs and snapping some of Marco balancing on treetops with his machete.

As a child, looking at these pictures from their false honeymoon—my mother with her natural, curly hair in the rainforest, eating a mango, or my father with his brown skin, splashing his face in a waterfall—I believed I was staring into an idyllic period in my parents' relationship. I fantasized about visiting this verdant paradise with some Prince Charming of my own. But my parents have since sworn to me this trip was 100 percent miserable for them both. Today, looking at those pictures, I wonder if their memories of unhappiness are exaggerated a little. They seem so happy, in love. I know people pose for posterity. But the future can blacken the past. Is the lie in the photograph, or in tainted memory? I tell myself they experienced some moments of joy.

•

In October 1987, Marco became the second man to ask Jeannette to abandon medicine. *Even if I wanted to, I can't—I am indebted to the government,* she said simply. He was convinced she could abandon her duties because she was pregnant. He wrote the Service Corps on her behalf, soliciting a copy of her contract. It arrived. Marco tore it open. Scrutinized it. Sent another letter. In November, the Service Corps responded:

> Dear Dr. Del Valle,
>
> This is in response to your request for an estimate of your indebtedness if you breach your National Health Service Corps (NHSC) obligation. The total estimated debt as of January 1, 1988 will be $217,192.38 (principal $103,830.00 and interest $113,362.38).

My father tossed the letter onto the kitchen table. He didn't have that kind of money. He would just have to accept that Jeannette would keep working at the clinic, with its male surgeons: prestigious, in pristine lab coats, American. He threw himself into the Butcher Block. When my mother's belly bulged, Papi bought a bulky Panasonic camcorder to film my budding existence. He took that camera everywhere. The videos contain clues of lingering contentment. I seek them out.

On Saturday, January 16, 1988, my mother awoke with his camcorder in her face. The white light of a cloudy morning streamed in through the bedroom window.

"*No me molestes,*" my mother said in a playful tone, pulling the sheets over her face.

My father chuckled. "*¿Cómo que no me molestes?* Wake up."

"*¿Qué hora es?*"

"It's . . . ten o' clock. You gonna make coffee for me or what?"

My mother sighed and swung her legs over the bed. Her pregnant belly protruded beneath her white nightgown. A nebulizer lay in a corner of the room. Even the San Diego winter was rough on my mother's lungs.

"I'll make it for you now," she said, rubbing her eyes.

"You're gonna do it now only because I'm makin' a film," he said, teasingly. "I tol' you ten times already." He followed her into the kitchen, where she laughed, because she found that the coffee had already been made.

•

Carolina worked hard to make her *nuera* feel she had a family in San Diego. It was unfortunate that the Unión priest had not married the couple; she didn't understand why her son hadn't simply offered the man a bribe. But it didn't surprise her. Men were never adept at matters of love. She organized a surprise baby shower for Jeannette, inviting all the women she knew. They made a tower of presents, decorated the house with pink and blue balloons and confetti, and covered a table with *entradas* and a cake. They turned off the lights and crowded around the front door. "Here she comes!" someone hissed. The door opened. A female chorus shouted: "Surprise!"

My mother entered the house in a silk yellow shirt. "Oh, how lovely!" she said in Spanish, covering her face. My father strolled in, wearing a cowboy hat. (His sister, Aimee, was filming.) Carolina took Jeannette's hands in hers. She gestured at the women. "These are my friends," she said. Carolina seated Jeannette in a large wicker chair. She arranged everyone in a half circle in front of the chair. Then she knelt in front of Jeannette and handed her a present. My mother unwrapped it carefully, trying not to damage the paper. "Just rip it!" Carolina said impatiently, tearing it with her manicured hands. She handed her gift after gift after gift.

•

Carolina taught Jeannette how to cook Mexican food for my father. One night, they made *sopa de tortillas*. My mother, visibly pregnant, still wore her engagement ring. She watched Carolina slice vegetables with manicured hands. Carolina was saying in Spanish: "And then you're going to get married when the baby is born, and . . . with the dress and everything, and we'll make a movie . . ." She detailed the recipe: "You put tomatoes in the blender, with some garlic, a piece of onion, some oregano—but fresh." Carolina's maid, Celi, a girl in her early twenties with black curly hair, began to confide her marital woes. She said her husband had lost all motivation to make her happy. When Celi was dating the man, he took her places, bought her things. Now he did nothing. "We have to eat standing up," Celi said. "He hasn't even bought a table for the house." Carolina shook her head in disapproval. "*Marco's* not so stupid," she said, stealing nervous glances at my mother. "Quickly he bought Jeannette the machine to make tortillas, the griddle, right away he buys her things. In that, she can't tell him twice." Jeannette chuckled. She blew a kiss at Marco.

Carolina stirred tomato sauce in a pan, saying: "When it's boiling you put the tortillas in there, chopped onions, cheese, cilantro, and that's it!" My mother glanced at the camera and giggled. "Now I'll make it for you," she said. The filmmaker didn't respond. "I'm going to make it for you," she repeated with a wink. "Sunday. You'll see." My father turned the camera toward his reflection in the window against the nighttime landscape of San Diego. His body merged with the light particles and the darkness extending to the sea.

VHS VORTEX

I was born on March 31, 1988. They named me Jean Carolyn, combining Jeannette and Carolina. No one could explain my blue eyes, which later turned green. Papi laid me on a bed between two of my brown cousins. I looked conspicuously white. My uncles elbowed my father with snorting laughter: *¿Estás seguro que es tuya?* The paternity jokes made my mother tense with indignation, but Papi just rolled his eyes. He knew I was his. My left ear had a strange elfin protrusion at the tip, like his. I was a cream-colored creature, but I was his daughter. He knew it from the moment I was born, bloody and muculent from the womb, not making a sound. My eyes were wide open, and I was staring straight at him. More than two decades later, Papi marvels at how lucid I seemed. "Like an old soul," he says, chopping *nopales* for a fruit shake. "Like, *man,* you were already like, *wow*. From the moment you were born, you were alert."

My mother believed my unblinking expression was a sign of shock, a by-product of the epidural anesthetic she had been given without her consent, causing her to lose sensation in her legs. My heart rate sped up, and she lost control over the birth. She suffered postpartum depression for weeks. Papi took the reins while she recuperated.

Fatherhood gushed purpose through his veins like a drug. He fed me, bathed me and entertained me with a silly, high-pitched voice. He made it his mission to catch every milestone on film: my first bath, my first word, my first watermelon. He zoomed in on my strange, elfin ear. He used his tripod to film himself dunking me repeatedly in his mother's hot tub, delighted by my lack of fear. He filmed himself tossing me several feet over his head on the beach. He snapped pictures of me perched perilously on the ledge of a second-floor balcony. Manipulating my little body came easily to him. He was completely confident in himself. And so was I. I was certain, like he was certain, that he would never let me fall.

He filmed everything. He filmed me watching films of myself. He was enamored with the creature he helped create and wanted to immortalize even the most banal moments of my life. I suppose it's no surprise that I would do the same for him.

•

Words are tethers that bound Papi and me. He brought me into the world with language, coaxing me out of the darkness with description, as my mother did with the blood of her body, the milk of her breast, the sweat of her brow. Papi named things in nature: *piedra, hoja, cielo.* He corrected my pronunciation, annoyed by lazy consonants, blended vowels. By my first birthday, my vocabulary was trisyllabic: *camino, ramita, Papito.* He spoke to me in Spanish so it would be my first language. He explained the facts of the world and I asked questions, simple ones like *¿Por qué?,* and he answered if he knew, or said, *No sé, investigaremos.* I remember the excitement in his whispering voice, in the gasps that preceded his sentences, as if the sky and the trees were relaying secrets he was astonished to discover and share. The world was a maze of shapeless mysteries, and Papi gave each puzzle a name. He pointed at the horizon, summoning it into my awareness: *El sol se* *va al otro lado de la tierra.* He dug holes in the earth with his fingers, placing my palms in the dirt, and said it was the path to China. Papi took me to Sunset Cliffs and spoke to me of *el Océano Pacífico.* He placed things in my hands: curling *conchas de mar,* tickly *cobitos,* slimy *alga de mar.* He thought I was precocious, except for one conspicuous flaw that he designed in me: I could not distinguish fact from fiction. I thought all the characters in *Grimm's Fairy Tale Classics, Timeless Tales from Hallmark,* Disney movies and other films I watched were real. Papi constantly tortured me by claiming he had seen my favorite characters. *It's the Little Red Riding Hood!* he cried in a crowd. *¿Dónde?* I screamed. He claimed I had just missed her. My inability to separate stories and reality, fueled by my father, would persist until puberty.

•

If I try to recall the past through vision, I fail. Voices are easier to follow through the years. Perfumes and flavors, too. But the most reliable conveyor is touch. The past awakens under my palms. I pull the threads of dead days, their textures and temperatures, rewinding and rewinding until I can go no farther back.

I am clutching Papi's shirt. *Nube,* he says. He rolls down the airplane window and strokes a cloud as we pass it. As I write this memory, I know it's impossible. But I see it perfectly, anchored by my fists: my father's tan fingers are tilting in the cloud. Inspired, I plunge my own hand into it. My fingers curl in confusion. The cloud is insubstantial. I expected cream, marshmallows, cotton balls. It feels like nothing: a ghost. The intangible tendrils of cloud confound me so much that every brain cell pummeled by the experience is linked forever: my first long-term memory.

For years, I thought airplane windows during the 1980s could be opened. Now I know the cloud-touching experience must have been an illusion, a product of suggestion. Papi stroked the window, prompting my mind to dissolve the plexiglass with my eyes and my hands. How an illusion yielded an insight about a celestial object's texture I can't be sure. What I do know is this: in my first memory, Papi is making me hallucinate.

●

Six months after my birth, my mother purchased a two-bedroom condominium with carpet the color of dark wine. My parents bought a stereo sound system and listened, above all, to Fleetwood Mac: "If I live to see the seven wonders . . . I'll never live to match the beauty again."

My mother became a popular physician. She was affectionate and familiar with her patients, calling the old men *papi* and the old women *mami*. Mostly Mexicans, they were charmed by her Puerto Rican accent. My father managed the Butcher Block as customers flooded the shop. Meat orders arrived from as far away as Arizona. In front of the meat-packaging counter, he established a small grocery store with sodas, tortillas, Mexican chips and other snacks. It seemed to Jeannette that Marco Antonio had been healed by the fact of my existence. They felt a mutual sense of accomplishment.

With his camcorder, Papi blended images of my face with flowers, and of my mother's face with the sea. He captured his mother at the new *carnicería*, sitting proudly in her office chair. My father's filming was unusually expressive, featuring sunsets, cloud formations, bird flights. I study his attentive eye for the poetry of light and contours, his descriptive curiosity at its crux. What happened to this person? I dip my hands into the dark sea of the past, and all I grasp are questions.

¿Qué miras? he asked me one day when I was only a small child. He was dangling me over the edge of a coastal cliff, ignoring my mother's protests. The wind lashed my face with the taste of salt and the smell of *mariscos*. *Agua*, I answered. He praised me for my astuteness, and told me that inside that water—which stretched across the planet and was deeper than I could imagine—lived *calamares* (squid), *barcos hundidos* (sunken ships), *ballenas* (whales) *y más*. Slowly, the ocean—its vastness, its unfathomable depth and aliveness—came into my consciousness.

•

My sister was born on September 29, 1989. Papi brought me to the hospital, filming our acquaintance. I saw the bundled infant and poked her head. Michelle Ruby was different from me: dark-eyed, dark-haired, eyes shut tight against the light. Observing my parents' affection for her, I became jealous and repeated "buh-bye" louder and louder, a futile incantation. "She thinks you're a doll," he told my little sister as I stared suspiciously. "But you're not. You're a *living* doll." Papi spent hours jumping on the bed to make us bounce and giggle. Since the Guerrero enterprise was operating at full steam, our father took days off to dote on us.

•

I search my father's VHS tapes for his point of no return. I find only foreshadowing and forecasts. Futile prophecies. The day after Michelle was born, my father connected his camcorder to the TV. He placed the camcorder on his tripod and pointed it at my mother, who was breast-feeding the newborn on the couch. He sat beside her. My mother smiled at him with adoration he didn't seem to notice. She kissed the corner of his lips. He watched the live stream. "Okay, I'm going to bed now," he said in Spanish. Papi disappeared as if by magic, experimenting with the Pause button on his camcorder's remote control. He re-materialized beside her. "Oops, I forgot something." He grinned mischievously, without clarifying what he forgot. "Okay, now I'm *really* leaving." He snapped his fingers and disappeared again, leaving my smiling mother alone on the couch with the baby.

•

Papi filmed me in an empty fish tank. I placed my hands on the glass, diverse emotions flickering on my face: amusement, confusion, boredom, annoyance, fear, adoration. He zoomed in on my expressions. A few weeks later, he captured a snake and placed it in the tank. He purchased a mouse at a pet store and dropped it in. "It's eating it now," he said, filming. The snake masticated the mouse, slowly, until only its tail protruded. The snake flicked out its tongue, savoring its meal. Like many of my father's videos, this one was recorded over a previously taped educational wildlife program. At the end of the snake footage, scenes of the Sturt's Desert Pea from a nature show take over. "Their flowering will be brief," says a male narrator. "And in their urgent need to attract pollinators, they provide copious nectar."

•

My father took my mother to see a house for sale in a neighborhood of Southeast San Diego called Paradise Hills. It was a three-bedroom single-story house with white paint that peeled off in exclamation marks. One side of the backyard sank into the backyard of the neighbors, the elderly Lockhart couple. A hill of purple-flowering sea figs rose on the east toward a fence where old man Mr. Bob lived. Straight back, behind a chain-link fence: a view of protuberant hills. We moved in January 1990.

•

My most vivid memories are tactile: the feel of sea figs breaking between my fingers, and their sleek, damp centers; the sandpapery red bricks on the front wall of the house; my father's bony, slightly hairy knees through the holes of his torn jeans; my mother's soft, gurgling stomach against my cheek; the rough, wrinkled bark that I pulled off trees in strips. I follow my fingers through recollections and encounter the slimy flesh of tadpoles. My father purchased them; I dipped my hands into the water of their tank. He bought two iguanas, Iggy and Izzy, for me and Michelle. I ran my cheeks against their ribbed backs. I sprinkled salt on hard-boiled eggs and kissed their still-warm surfaces. Leaves fell from the oak trees in our backyard. I crumpled them in my hands. I stared straight at the sun, swallowing its light with my pupils, experiencing the pulse of its heat. I wanted to make out the orb's contours, see if it had craters like the moon. My sister and I spent much of our time outside. Rolly pollies inhabited the landscape. I thought they were ugly, and the feel of their fourteen legs on my skin was too intense for me to stand. Michelle poked them until they contracted into spheres. She picked them up and they unfurled, crawling up her wrists.

•

One afternoon, as my father helped his brothers chop meat at the Butcher Block, his half sister Aimee strode in through the front door. Aimee was an eye-catching woman, with dramatic curves, luxurious wavy hair and her father's strong jawline. Her presence in the *carnicería* was unusual. As the second-youngest sibling, a full child of Jesus and Carolina as well as a teenager when the Butcher Block bounty matured, Aimee had enjoyed luxuries Marco had not. She completed her education in the United States, funded by her parents. She spent her free time taking her fiancé to San Diego's best restaurants. She had no need to dirty her shoes on the blood-spattered floors of the *carnicería*.

Aimee summoned her parents from their office and declared, in front of them and the customers, that my father had made a mistake. The Butcher Block phone number was registered as a private household number. Aimee argued that this evidenced tremendous incompetence on her brother's part. He was ruining the family business. She had just attained a business degree from a community college.

Her attack was ruthless and confident; everyone, even the clients, seemed transfixed. As she spoke, Marco felt himself shriveling against his will. His vision blurred; he tried to summon indignation, anger, some other fighting emotion—anything to match her self-righteousness. None came. He fished for a casual response instead, laughter perhaps. But the normally instinctual act of breathing suddenly required all of his attention. An old chasm widened inside him. Don Jesus was watching his daughter as if she were preaching a revelation: his business would be better run by his own blood. Nobody defended Marco; he could not defend himself. And so he walked out.

•

Marco Antonio came home in an alarming state, pacing, hyperventilating. He stared at Jeannette with wide, unseeing eyes. She touched his arm, anchoring him in the room, voicing questions in the reassuring tone she used with patients. *¿Qué ha pasado? ¿Estás bien?* His eyes settled on hers and he explained, in a broken way, what had happened. He insisted, through tears, that he was not angry at his family, that it was *his* decision to leave the business. My mother was furious on his behalf. She encouraged Papi to start a business of his own to outshine the Butcher Block. He could be a professional photographer, he could be anything. He was competent, brilliant, strong. She drove him to a community college to enroll in photography classes.

He got straight A's. He was already a self-taught master when it came to the basics: shutter speed, aperture, framing. His pictures were bold and creative. After catching a garter snake, he asked me and my sister to hold it on the porch. He captured us with the snake. He dressed up our iguanas, Iggy and Izzy, in our Barbie dresses, and posed them in our toy furniture with Marlboro Reds between their lips. Our mother framed his work, placing it prominently on our walls.

But it was too late. The incident at the Butcher Block had changed him. He lost interest in playing with me and Michelle. When Jeannette bought a Macintosh Plus so he could edit digital photographs, he locked himself up in the guest bedroom with the computer. He became obsessed with his assignments. Michelle and I pressed our ears against the door, listening to mysterious clinking and clattering. When we knocked, he ignored us or yelled *¿Qué?* My sister and I tried to occupy ourselves without him. We played with Ken and Barbie in our toy house. Ken became sick and grumpy, Barbie brought him medicines in bed, and Ken was cured and happy again.

Our mother purchased a giant poster showcasing the alphabet and educational books identifying objects with English-language words so we could start transitioning into real Americans, unlike the half-feral outsiders we felt like in public spaces, despite our citizenship and birthright. Gringos were so poised, with their pursed language, each sentence curled up and closed like tied shoelaces, unlike the openmouthed *español que hablamamos en casa*. But I loved learning the language. It gave me an excuse to dwell inside an alphabet. Like textures and other tactile properties, text itself made a special impression on me. Decoding those twisting black contours satiated a thirst in my skull. I opened my father's dusty dictionary, determined to pronounce its secrets. I sounded out simple words like "bad" and "big." The worlds in books seemed more magical than the worlds in movies—hidden, invoked, specially mine. I fingered the cryptic curvature in my mother's medical tomes, my father's old novels, imagining I could feel the loops of letters like braille. I didn't understand most of the English-language words yet. But I was fascinated. Mami enrolled me in a Montessori school at age three, telling me the most important thing in life was school because if I took it seriously, I could be whoever I wanted to be. I wondered who Papi would become.

•

Eventually, Papi realized that even if he succeeded as a photographer, his income would never match my mother's. This obliterated his desire to pursue an artistic path. He switched to real estate. The subject bored him. Then a new idea rekindled his passion.

Let's move to Tijuana. We'll buy a farm. I'll work the land, while you take care of the girls. You could spend time with them, he said, adding: *Like a mother should.*

My mother laughed. *If you wanted a farm with a housewife, you should have married a Mexican campesina.*

They each tried to forget about their differences by becoming more deeply absorbed in the things they'd never share. My father had always used drugs recreationally, and he began to do so more often. He planted marijuana in the backyard. My mother took on extra patients. Papi started sleeping in the computer room. He disappeared all night and returned in the mornings, when my mother was getting ready to go to work. He criticized everything about our mother—the "cheap" ink-black Pontiac she had shipped over from Brooklyn, her bright-colored shoes, her brand-name dresses. He called her a "pill-pusher" and modern medicine "a joke." She lambasted his use of illegal substances and called him "schizophrenic."

After visiting relatives in Tijuana one day, while in line at the San Ysidro Port of Entry, my parents' return trip was interrupted when German shepherds attacked my mother's Pontiac and U.S. customs officials sent the couple to a secondary inspection. They searched her vehicle, but found no drugs. They threatened to cut open her seats. *You will not touch my car,* she said, trembling with indignation. *I am a doctor and a U.S. citizen. If you're going to search anyone, search him.* She glared at Marco with such contempt that the officials seemed embarrassed. They let them pass. But my mother made a decision: she would never again cross the border. Mexico had always made her nervous, with its citizens' disregard for traffic lights and lanes, for laws in general, the corruption of police who accepted Marco's bribes, the brazen *machismo* of Marco's cousins. She now associated Mexico with everything that she believed was wrong with Papi—the unpredictability, the danger, the air of being just about to unravel.

•

One afternoon, when Papi was in a good mood, he invited me and Michelle to use his Macintosh Plus. He opened the word processor and typed *Hi girls* on the white canvas. He guided our fingers over the keys, having us poke letters to spell our names. Papi said we could deposit our secrets into the screen. They would be safe in the magic box, he said, not like on a piece of paper or notebook that anyone could find— the Macintosh functioned like a brain; you could "Save" a private document and "X" out of it and it would vanish. Retrieving it entailed searching for a secret blue "folder" strategically buried in other folders. I couldn't believe my eyes. Papi conjured pictures of me and my sister on the screen. He dropped images of us into the pollen of flowers. He placed us on clouds. The contraption was like a television you could inhabit—a hybrid of moving pictures and an empty book, waiting for the input of a human imagination. We were amazed. Most of the time, Papi kept his door locked. His Macintosh Plus acquired a strange significance. I believed the contraption had stolen my father. I wanted to destroy it. I wanted to play with it. I wanted to climb inside it and find Papi's innermost self.

•

I began to exhibit worrisome signs of sympathetic dependency with Mami—crying when I looked at her tired eyes, calling the hospital or paging her when she was with patients, clinging to her legs when she returned. My anxiety added to hers. We had a strict bedtime of 8:00 p.m. because our mother had to get up early for work and was often on call through the night. She was regularly sleep-deprived. I internalized her nocturnal distress. One night, while Abuela Carolina was visiting, I noticed it was past our bedtime. I demanded that my grandmother depart at once. When my mother told me to calm down, I burst into tears. I declared that I *needed* to sleep, that I would *die* if I didn't sleep. Mami snapped; couldn't I see? I was constantly adding to her problems. It hit me then: I had to learn to keep my sympathy zipped inside my stomach. After sleeping with my mother for about three years, waking up each time her beeper tore her from dreams with a summons to the emergency room, I requested my own bed. I distracted myself from my unease by watching and re-watching my favorite film, *The Neverending Story.*

In *The Neverending Story,* based on a German fantasy novel, a little boy finds a mystical-looking book titled *The Neverending Story.* The book has a bronze ouroboros on the cover—rather than the classic symbol of a single snake devouring its tail, it has two snakes devouring each other's tails, entwined in the symbol for infinity. Within the pages of the book, a young warrior named Atreyu embarks on a quest to save his world, Fantasia, from a stormy mass of clouds called The Nothing. To protect himself, he wears the ouroboros talisman from the cover of the book. I coveted his necklace as I watched the film, and touched the golden crucifix I wore on a chain around my neck—a gift from my mother—pretending it was the ouroboros as I galloped through Fantasia with Atreyu. Slowly, Bastian—the boy in the movie who is reading the book about me and Atreyu—becomes aware that Fantasia is a real place. It's vanishing into The Nothing because humans outside its boundaries are losing faith in their hopes and dreams. Bastian uses his imagination to revive the dying world. The movie reassured me that what Papi had taught me was in fact a law of the universe: that book worlds, movie worlds, dream worlds and computer worlds were all vividly tucked inside the tangible world, and that all of them belonged to me. I could rescue my parents from their sadness by perusing the photo album of their "honeymoon," where they lived happily ever after in a forest of waterfalls.

•

We were raised by a steady flow of Mexican and Central American teenagers who worked as live-in *muchachas*—my mother fired roughly thirty for various alleged crimes: stealing, not cleaning, not cooking. She found herself doing much of the housework. At the San Ysidro Health Center, she observed a pattern: her less experienced colleagues were receiving bonuses, raises, promotions—even those who weren't bilingual and couldn't provide adequate care to the Hispanic community. Most of them were men. She worked later and later hours, determined to be recognized. In the evenings, she brought us toys or pets to compensate for her absence. We heard her pull into the driveway and ran outside squealing, greedy for more Barbies, hamsters, Beanie Babies and betta fish to forget our sorrow. If Mami failed to stop by Toys"R"Us or Petco, we wept. When she brought groceries, no one helped her carry them inside. She no longer referred to our father as Papi or Marco but as Vago and Inútil. She repeated a lamentation: *I never have a break. I come home from work to more work, like a slave.* But when my sister and I tried to help, she laughed and chastised us. I squirted dishwashing soap onto the kitchen sponge, and my mother bumped me away from the sink with her hip. *No quiero que sean esclavas como yo,* she would say. She wanted us to focus on learning so that we would become so successful we wouldn't need to cook or clean for any husband. She was supplanting her dreams for herself with dreams for me and Michelle.

•

Papi called my mother at the hospital to advise her to get checked for gonorrhea. The confirmation of his betrayal felt like cancer in her body. But she could not crawl into a corner to try to mend her wounds. She had to take care of me and my sister. She awoke every morning, ignoring her grief, working and working. Papi admitted he was using prostitutes. He found it hard to resist now that the relationship was so stressed. He wasn't doing anything *really* wrong, he reasoned, so long as he returned home. The problem, from his perspective, was that Jeannette was too stuck-up all of a sudden, always making him feel inferior. Papi again tried to distract himself with hard labor. Soil clinging to his sweat, Papi installed a perfect green lawn in front of our house. He placed his camcorder on the tripod and recorded himself toiling on his knees. In the backyard, he built wire mesh cages and a wooden shed for compost. He purchased hens, roosters and cockatiels to crowd his constructions. He fed branches into a wood-chipping machine and used a rotary tiller on the soil. He stacked wooden logs to create enclosures for strawberries, potatoes, *frijoles*. Using wire mesh, he made a towering trellis for tomatoes. He lined pots of cacti and other desert plants at the base of our sea fig hill. The backyard became a labyrinth of crops and cultivating machines. Back bent over the earth, sawing and sowing and shoveling, Papi was building my mother her very own Garden of Eden.

DÍAS DE LOS MUERTOS

Once Papi's *jardín* was ready, he retreated under his comforter. He did not let me or my sister join him for naps or cuddles. Something was dying inside of him, or perhaps had died upon his departure from the Butcher Block. Nature echoed him as if in sympathy. Flies reproduced in his compost pile and populated our house. With a swatter, I flattened their bodies, plucked off their wings and made piles of them. His garden began to deteriorate. His fruit shriveled into wrinkled black sacs. Flowers drooped on their stalks. Even the cacti turned a sickly brown. The worms came out to feast.

The rare times Papi emerged from his bedroom, he sat on our living room leather couch, burping, staring at the turned-off television. My sister and I picked the lint out of his belly button and the cheese out of his toenails. He smelled of cigarette smoke and sweaty armpits. I examined his hands' pinkie nails, an inch longer than the rest. *Why are your pinkie nails so long?* I asked. He thought for a few seconds. *To more easily pick the boogers out of my nose,* he said, Big Bad Wolf–style, then unleashed his cartoon chuckle: *Heh, heh, heh.* We cackled; it was contagious. It was years before I discovered that addicts use long pinkie nails as organic cocaine scoops.

We had accumulated numerous pets: the chapped-lipped iguanas, stuck-in-time tadpoles, a frog or two, maternal hens, violent roosters, a stray cat, fish, ducks, red-eyed rabbits, fat guinea pigs, hamsters and nearly a hundred cockatiels. Our creatures began to die in synchrony with Papi's slumber. Our cockatiels, which had emerged from a single incestuous pair, died of deformities or homicide. Carcasses littered their cage. Our hamsters crawled off tall surfaces. A chubby classmate of mine came over for a homework assignment, asked if she could hold our pet frog and squeezed it with such nervous excitement it exploded in her hands. Our chickens toppled into our neighbor's backyard, where their Rottweiler ate them. Mami rescued one at the last minute. She heard the horrified squawks, jumped into the Lockharts' backyard and pried the hen from the dog's jaws. In the bathtub, she washed it and sewed it back together. We ate its eggs.

Whenever a pet died, we put it in a Payless shoebox with flowers and snacks for its journey to Heaven. We made a cross of toothpicks for its grave. Our backyard became bloated with bodies. I asked Mami if I, too, was going to die. *Never,* she said. She smiled, but her eyes were sad. The incongruity of her expression stayed with me. I repeated my question often. She sighed: *We all die, mi amor. But when you die, well, you're going to go to Heaven. You're going to become an angel.* Her expression stayed suspicious: downcast eyes and stretched-out lips that didn't quite curve upward. Even our firsthand experience contradicted her words: our dead animals went *down* into the gross dirt, not *up* into the sky. I couldn't imagine this place called Heaven. Paintings at church depicted an amorphous landscape of clouds and light. Heaven seemed nowhere near as real or as solid as our backyard, which swallowed up our animals and made them nil.

A dark dread flowered inside my chest. It had sharp petals, like a spiky succulent. During the first years of my life, I spent more time with Papi than with Mami, who was busy seeing patients. My father took me outside, imparting his amazement with the natural world.

Now both parents were inaccessible. And everything was dying. The movies we were set in front of began to seem terrifying, their songs maniacally chipper, the animated characters demonic in their jerky movements. My sister and I started having nightmares and night terrors, detracting from our mother's already scarce sleep. Whenever I stood still, the succulent-thing grew, creating what felt like bottomless holes that displaced my body's center of gravity. I developed hypochondriacal tendencies, constantly asking my mother to take my temperature and blood pressure. Once, I became so feverish I hallucinated voices—I repeatedly screamed *Shut up!* to a silent room—but my mother refused to take me to the hospital, certain I would recuperate on my own.

I delved deeper into make-believe with my sister. I was no longer interested in playing with *muñecas* or watching TV. I needed to use my whole body to enact fictions. I had to move to prevent the pain of the spiky dread, which flourished on boredom and stillness. We marched like soldiers in the living room. We crawled along the hardwood floors, pretending we were scaling vertical surfaces to rescue our parents from the edge of an imagined precipice. I threw on my mother's lab coat and moved her stethoscope all over Michelle's chest, curing her with frantic rhymes and extravagant gestures. I plunged my hands into our tank of tadpoles, cupping them and kissing them, attempting to turn them into princes, or at least frogs; they had been tadpoles for what seemed like years, it was making me really anxious.

I found solace in vanity. I begged our *muchacha*, a Central American woman named Maria, to take me and my sister on walks. When we went out, strangers stopped us and said things like, *Oh my gosh! That is the prettiest little girl I've ever seen!* My mother's patients and coworkers made similar comments: *She's the loveliest thing, she looks like an angel!* Then they turned to my sister and said things like, *This one is adorable, too,* or *So cute.* For the first time since my father's deterioration, I felt a level of control over my environment. I was discovering that my blonde hair and light-colored irises granted me a seemingly immutable privilege: strangers were pleased by the sight of me, and wanted to please me in turn, with compliments and candy. I looked like the princesses and other lovable girl protagonists in popular culture: Cinderella, Rapunzel, Goldilocks, Sleeping Beauty, Barbie. My skin turned golden in the sun, like my father's, but it did not quite brown like my sister's; she was Prieta and I was Güera, and for some reason that gave me a social advantage. I spun in front of the mirror, staring at my wavy golden locks and green eyes, thanking God for the luck. Since multiple people had used superlatives to describe my beauty on separate occasions, I concluded it had to be true—*I was the most beautiful girl in the world*. The belief was a symptom of my inability to distinguish fact from fiction, both a sickness and a coping mechanism.

Papi was immune to the spell of the rest of the world. During the few times we interacted now, he insulted me. *You should be more like Ruby,* he said. He liked the fact that when my sister was hungry, she did not demand food, but rather snacked on dirt from our backyard; this *gusto* made her badass in his eyes. Once, as I went number two in the bathroom toilet, I noticed three daddy longlegs spiders in a corner by my feet. My screeches stirred Papi from his slumber. He stomped into the bathroom, scooped up the spiders and placed them on his head. I sobbed: one of the spiders crawled onto his lips. He looked horrifying: the whites of his eyes red, his irises black with pupils. He flicked his tongue out and ate the spider. *See? No big deal,* he said.

Once, as I ran from a green June beetle, Papi snatched it out of the air and planted it on my head. He held it there as I screamed. The insect became entangled in my hair. When Papi removed his hand, it roared like a chainsaw drilling through my skull. I sobbed hysterically. My father disappeared in quest of scissors. When he returned, he liberated the creature by chopping off a chunk of my tresses.

It became clear that Papi, who previously adored me, now felt only contempt for me: I was a girly girl, a crybaby, a bimbo.

Sometimes, the rare inspiration struck him, and he cooked elaborate *mariscos: caldo de pescado* or *ceviche de pulpo*. Once, he carved slingshots for us. Most of the time, Papi stayed behind his wooden door. His room became off-limits. If my sister or I bothered him, he threatened to whip us with his leather *cinturón*. We developed a terror of the hallway that led to his room. Beyond the threshold was a black hole.

•

My sister became dangerously ill. The housekeepers weren't feeding us properly. This posed no problem for me—I raided the kitchen cabinets whenever I pleased, and often ordered the women to make me *quesadillas*. But Michelle was not yet two. Attempting to acquire the minerals she was starved of, her body experienced intense cravings for dirt. She repeated one word again and again: *tierra*. Dirt. Nobody noticed she was sick, because Papi was locked inside his bedroom and Mami was busy with work all day.

In one of the last VHS tapes my father filmed, in 1991, Michelle implores the camera for dirt, brown curls sticking to her sweaty forehead. I prance around, smiling at my reflection in our jeep, running my hands through my hair. "*Tierra,*" Michelle begs. My father tells her she can't have any. "*Tierra!*" she sobs. The film cuts to Michelle contentedly devouring dirt from her palm. "Look at this little savage we found on the mountain," my father says affectionately.

My parents disagree about who first noticed the thick vein throbbing irregularly on my little sister's neck. Either way, when the vein's unusual size and rhythm were detected, my mother tried to take Michelle to the hospital; my father plucked her out of her arms. Papi said pill-pushers would pump my sister full of medicines more harmful than whatever she had. He believed her body would benefit from fighting it off—probably just a parasite. But Michelle got worse. When my mother finally took her to the children's hospital, the doctors told her Michelle was severely anemic. Her heart had swelled to nearly twice its normal size. Compensating for the lack of oxygen in her body, it had been pumping furiously for months. She required an immediate blood transfusion.

A social worker materialized, threatening to take away my mother's custody of my sister. Dr. Del Valle's explanations—about trusting the wrong nannies, about our father's unreliability, about working like a slave—sufficed to move the social worker, who let my mother take Michelle home. My mother fired the babysitter. She took three months of unpaid leave. She nursed Michelle back to health.

Papi seemed racked by guilt. He cried, paced back and forth, shut his door very quietly. He dove farther away from us, deeper into his abyss, to a place where real-life villains resided.

·

My mother organized extravagant fiestas on our birthdays, with Astro Jumps, mariachis, piñatas, balloons, ponies, a Disney princess or clown, a tiered cake and a tower of presents. She invited all of the Guerreros, and dozens of our paternal cousins crowded the backyard. Because my sister and I were jealous of each other, we had joint parties each year— one in March and one in September—double the presents. Papi chain-smoked in a solitary corner of the backyard.

My sister and I were opposites. She was a quiet brunette; I was a bubbly blonde. She had a low, hoarse voice; mine was high-pitched and squeaky. She was shy and affectionate, still sleeping with our mother for many years; I had become restless and independent. My sister wore cotton pants and T-shirts; I preferred frilly dresses. We were best friends.

Together, we entered the cage of the dying cockatiels. The blushing creatures slapped our faces with their wings. We begged our mother to domesticate one. What was the point of having so many birds if we couldn't touch them? She couldn't bear the thought of taking a newborn from its mother, so she purchased an incubator, stole some freshly laid eggs and warmed them. Out came hideous, pink little monsters covered with spines and purple bulges in place of eyes. Then the bulges cracked open and became eyes and their spines sprouted yellow feathers. My mother gave all of them away except for one. We fed it formula with a syringe, watching its see-through veiny stomach inflate like a balloon. I remember the feel of its tiny body in the palm of my hand, warm as a cupcake straight out of the oven.

The bird grew until it could sit atop our heads and fly around the room. My father arose from slumber to converse with the creature. He named it Piojito, meaning "louse," because it perched on our heads. Piojito joined us at the dinner table, a talkative little brother depositing feces in our hair. A few years later, he disappeared. Our *muchacha* said she had left the back door open while sweeping. We had never clipped Piojito's wings—he had flown away. My mother taped a hundred flyers around the city featuring Piojito's color photograph and offering a $100 reward for his return. Our phone rang. I answered our see-through Conair phone on the kitchen wall.

Hello? I said in my best American accent, twirling the yellow cord with my fingers.

I have your bird, a man said.

You do? I was ecstatic. I could actually hear a little bird squeaking. It was Piojito! *Yes. But listen carefully. If I don't get five hundred dollars by Thursday, I'm going to kill your bird,* he said. *Do you hear me? I need—wait, hold on a second.* I heard things being moved around, the cage jostling, Piojito screeching. Suddenly: a little boy's innocent voice. *Hello?* he said softly. *You know, I really don't think you're going to get your bird back.* I either fainted or hung up. My memory goes black there. We never saw Piojito again.

·

Amused by my perpetual inquiries about the afterlife, one of our *muchachas* told us, in detail, how *el Diablo* was going to torture us in *el Infierno* with fire and metal contraptions. *Are you sure we're going to Hell? Why can't we go to Heaven?* I asked anxiously. *Because,* she said. *You're evil girls.* Her prophecies induced nightmares and hallucinations for me and my sister. One night, we observed the Devil's eyes at the exact same time and place, emerald green, floating outside our bedroom window in the night. Michelle also saw two ghosts: the shadow of a man moving around her room, disappearing into the wardrobe, and a weeping woman in a white dress I can only assume was La Llorona, a legendary Mexican woman who drowned her children to spite her indifferent husband.

The storytelling *muchacha,* like so many others, was fired. One of her successors was a Nicaraguan girl with an appetite for mourning doves. My sister and I were playing outside one afternoon when she emerged from the house with an empty shoebox. She tiptoed up to a mourning dove perched on our chain-link fence. The *muchacha* brought the box down onto the dove, ramming it through metal spikes on the fence rim. The gored bird flapped its wings, trying to escape, then perished in a puddle of blood. Traumatized, Michelle and I refused to eat her "chicken soup."

The only *muchacha* we ever loved, a Mexican girl named Paola, took us to the movies with her boyfriend, bought us milk shakes and paid for a few shots of the four of us in a photo booth. She had a mole on her chin with long black hairs sprouting from it. She quit to go to community college; on her last day with us, she cut the hairs from her mole and put them in a glass vial, which she gave us as a parting gift.

•

I started kindergarten at a private Episcopalian school. In Montessori, I had been permitted to speak Spanish. In the car on the way to this new English-only institution, Mami taught me the phrase "I do not understand."

The teacher, a pale lady with auburn hair, made us perform what I perceived as stupid, purposeless tasks, such as cutting squares from paper. I took advantage and said, "I do not understand." The teacher demonstrated. "I do not understand," I lied again. I hated school. We had to sit for hours on stiff chairs, wasting our bodies, wasting our lives. I wanted to be at home, playing with my sister, creating worlds with our minds. But then the teachers taught us to read and write long sentences. I learned quickly, thanks to my practice at home. I traced each letter of the alphabet with my pencil in neat, clear curves and angles, randomly alternating between capital and lowercase letters, taking pleasure in playing with the shapes. Suddenly, school became a utopia of Scholastic book fairs. I came with cash crumpled in my pockets, buying books with animal protagonists: *The Rainbow Fish, Stellaluna, The True Story of the 3 Little Pigs!, Treasury of Fairy Tales.*

The stories were vivid escapes, better than moving pictures, as I had intuited when I first eyed the twisting symbols of bookshelf tomes. Literary worlds swelled beyond the channel of their conveyance, yielding full-body 3-D experiences rather than strictly visual-auditory ones, due to the high-voltage power of strings of text connecting with my brain. Writing became a godlike experience. When Mami bought me a blank book as a gift, I scribbled a story about a ladybug who falls in love with a worm. I felt I was conjuring a literal world with my markers. Drugged with power, I killed the worm I had engendered. I simply made him drop dead. I planned to bring him back to life as a butterfly— his coffin was in fact a chrysalis—so he could fly through the skies with his soul mate. Meanwhile, the heartbroken ladybug embarked on a search for "a beautiful land." I ran out of pages. My heart plummeted into my stomach. I hadn't yet brought back the ladybug's lover. I had killed him. I had actually killed him. The ladybug would be alone forever. I burst into tears. My mother offered to glue additional pages into my book, but they were the wrong color, I kept sobbing. I guess I found a way to cope: I invented a false memory. For years, I recalled that story as one in which I did, in fact, resurrect the worm. Fact-checking, I asked my mother for the book. As I flipped to the last page, I remembered the despair I felt upon realizing I had ruined everything. The worm would be dead forever.

•

Most of my roughly twenty classmates were Mexican-American. We all wore uniforms: white button-up shirts, navy blue sweaters, and plaid gray skirts (for the girls) or gray pants (for the boys). But I stood out as one of only two or three blondes. I made no effort to befriend anyone; I was interested only in my sister. I could be completely myself with Michelle, I could overflow with my own sloppy being, make weird faces and noises. With my classmates my body felt out of tune;

I had to constantly modify my gestures, my tone, even my emotions—it was taxing. When my sister started school, I was excited: finally we could play together at recess. To our dismay, as soon as the teachers noticed our friendship, they prohibited us from speaking to each other, saying we had to learn to socialize with *everyone*. My sister sat alone, despondent. I joined my classmates, feeling bound by the rules.

Every evening after work, my mother helped us with our homework, smelling of perfume, brown irises bright. Unlike my questions about death, my academic questions inspired her, especially the ones related to math and science, the subjects I found most difficult. I volunteered for the class spelling bee, and my mother went through the long packet of word lists with me again and again, until she was falling asleep at the kitchen table. I won first place. To ensure our integration, our teachers prohibited speaking Spanish. If you were caught, you had to write *I will not speak Spanish* a hundred times in detention. Within a couple of years, after mastering English, I would renounce my native language, associating it with delinquency. I was desperate to impress my teachers and give Mami pride and happiness. I rose to the top of my class. Until I moved to Mexico at age twenty-two, I would not be able to speak Spanish beyond a child's capacity.

•

The neighbor on the east side of our house, Jenny, was a grandmotherly English teacher with glasses and a cotton ball of yellow hair, who became our informal guardian. Jenny taught us English words we didn't know (menace, mischief, unruly), corrected our pronunciation and introduced us to American snacks: apple slices with peanut butter, Oreo cookies dipped in milk. We jumped from our elevated backyard into hers, tiptoeing so as not to wake her villainous, hen-devouring Rottweiler, Kiki. Jenny tried to make us love Kiki, turning the pages of a mostly wordless picture book called *Good Dog, Carl* about a friendly Rottweiler. We loved Carl but continued to fear Kiki. A massive yellow garden spider lived on a large web in Jenny's front yard, and when we expressed our disgust she told us the spider was good. She brought us the David Kirk children's books *Miss Spider's Tea Party* and *Miss Spider's New Car*, about a very polite spider. She always gave us books on our birthdays, signing them by drawing a little padlock and heart: *Lockhart*. I tore off the wrapping paper and pressed the pages against my face, ravenous for the smell of ink on metamorphosed trees. Michelle sketched pictures inspired by the images in the books—the dawn of her painting career. Whenever Jenny grew tired of us, she tried to make us sleep, tucking us into water beds we found so exciting we couldn't close our eyes.

●

The only signs of Papi's continued existence were his smells and occasional sounds: howling, yawning, snorting, phlegm-hacking. Sometimes, I heard his door open, his footsteps down his dark hallway, the tinkle of urine in the toilet. It caused a mixture of contradictory emotions: comfort that he was alive, fear that he would put some insect on my body, sadness that he no longer seemed to love me, confusion as to why.

One day, feeling brave, I wandered down the hallway to the bathroom as he urinated. I don't remember my exact intention, only that I had a question. I saw him standing over the toilet. *Papi*, I said. He jerked his head around. A volcanic eruption occurred in his eyes. He zipped up his pants. I ran away, panicked. He pursued me, roaring in Spanish, accusing me of spying on his nudity, of being a pervert. He unbuckled his leather *cinturón*, slithered it off. I cowered in a corner, crying. He raised his belt up in one hand. He was going to whip me. Suddenly his irises became a sickly yellow, like old chemicals in test tubes. An unbearable sadness undulated in his eyes, in his lips. He stopped himself and disappeared into his room.

I was six when Mami finally asked Papi to leave. Too many strange, frightening things were happening to us, and she believed he was to blame. Two of her cars, a Pontiac and its successor, a Toyota 4Runner, had been stolen from the driveway. One was found on a nearby horse trail, stripped of everything except a single, crumpled photograph of me and my little sister in frilly pink dresses. The photograph had been burned around the edges.

Strangers were following us. One evening at the mall, my mother started zigzagging me and my sister in pointless directions. Then she dragged us to the parking lot. She told us to get into the car—quickly. *Métanse al carro. Somebody has been following us since we arrived at the mall.* We jumped into her car. We sped through the streets, making unnecessary turns and U-turns. My sister and I looked over our shoulders. A dark male figure was driving the pursuing vehicle. I can't recall any of his features except that we could see his teeth—he was either grimacing or smiling at us. Either way, it felt sinister. My mother pulled into the driveway of a house on a busy street to imply that she lived there. Our stalker slowed, as if to memorize the address, then sped off. *You got him good, Mami!* we cried.

One morning at the pharmacy, my sister and I were picking out stickers for our sticker books while Mami purchased essentials in another aisle. Absorbed by a strip of sparkly unicorns, I didn't notice Michelle disappear from my side. When I looked up, a white-haired old lady was dragging my sister down the aisle toward the exit. Michelle was staring back at me with a startled look. I ran up to her and yanked her away from the stranger, who abruptly exited. *¿Qué hacías con esa vieja?* I asked. My sister said the lady had claimed she had toys in her car.

My mother concluded that my father—who had been unemployed for years—owed somebody drug or gambling money. She asked him to leave. She had tolerated his unhappy presence for years because she loved him; she believed he was a sick man, not a flawed one. She believed he would get better. But her patience had limits. She no longer felt we were safe. Papi moved into her condominium with the wine-colored carpet, which she had been renting out for additional income. She told him he could stay in it for free.

Our birthday fiestas deflated in size and grandiosity. My mother no longer felt comfortable inviting our Guerrero cousins to the house, and she had no family of her own in San Diego. *¿Dónde está Papi?* I asked repeatedly.

He's in the condominium, she replied.

¿Por qué?

Porque sí.

The tautology was confounding, but I could not find a way around my mother's circular logic. My *why* questions always exasperated her. *Why is the sky blue? Why does two plus two equal four? Why does everything die?* Because. Because. Because. She accepted the world the way it was, nonsensical, confusing. Her complacency with the world's mysteries was the most bewildering mystery of all.

The unknown tugged at me like the gravity in a black hole. Why was Papi gone? What had made him so sad? I needed explanations. My mother would not give them.

I have a vivid memory from what I believe was this time. The succulent in my heart was back, it was growing, pulsating, writhing— alive. I had to move, move, move, move, move, move, move. I paced in socks, hyperventilating, vision blurred by tears. The leaves kept lengthening, wriggling, chomping like fanged worms, the movement of my limbs wasn't restraining them, I couldn't breathe, it hurt so bad, I walked into the kitchen, grasped the wooden handle of a steak knife and pressed the tip to my heart. Death. I wanted it. I would send myself to Heaven, see if it was a real place. This world was ugly, anywhere was better than here. My mother watched me from the sink. I remember the watery sight of her through my weeping. She had no fear in her face. She knew what I didn't know: I wasn't going to hurt myself. I shouted something. I can't recall the words, only the scraping in my throat. She didn't flinch. She just held my gaze. The pain broke inside me like a wave. I cried from the relief.

She did what she could to comfort us. She revived our backyard garden. She cultivated tall shrubs of dahlias and zinnias, which she plucked for her patients, trimming off their leaves and flicking off the greenhoppers. Kneeling beside her, we scattered the papery seeds of strawberries, *frijoles* and various flowers with our fists. Green strings sprouted from the earth, erupting into pods and leaves, bursting into soft arrays of fragrant petals or edible, brightly colored fruit.

Seven oak trees ringed our backyard, casting shadows with their dark green leaves. Mami purchased buckets of paint, dipped her brush into their bright colors and rushed from tree to tree. She gave the trees toothy, full-lipped grins and sparkling eyeballs. Her pale skin gleamed with sweat; wisps of her curly golden hair stuck to her forehead. She was smiling at the trees as she gave them life, and thus seemed to be instructing them: *Like this, see?* When she finished, she fell to her knees beside her buckets of paints. We loved those living trees.

She took us to Home Depot to buy praying-mantis eggs and live ladybugs for our *jardín.* Somehow, the bucket of ladybugs came open in the car. A *mariquita* tickled my shoulder. I saw one on my sister's cheek. Then they were everywhere: crawling, flying, floating. The car filled with them, like winged droplets of blood. At first, we were frightened, and hurried to roll down the windows. But then Michelle started cackling. It was contagious. We rolled the windows back up, laughing like crazy in that tornado of ladybugs. My mother kept driving.

We forgot the praying-mantis eggs inside the house. They hatched, crawling up and down our walls for many days. We found the critters in our cupboards, in our clothes, in our comforters: countless guardians in Christian pose.

The insects brought our fracturing reality into focus. They crystallized chaos into something we could grasp. The insects portended not death or decay, but protection—an army against villains and garden pests. Papi had taught me how to dissolve the fabric of reality with my mind. From Mami and Michelle, I was learning the alchemy of interpretation. We could make our anguish luminous.

●

The separation reinvigorated Papi. He felt he had done something good for once: he had freed us of his presence. With a loan from my mother, he launched a Mexican drive-through restaurant called Saguaro's. He hired an artist for the logo: a humanoid saguaro cactus, smiling in a sombrero. The saguaro is the tallest cactus in the world, growing to over seventy feet high and living as long as a hundred and fifty years. In late spring, its long, spiky limbs sprout enormous, mobile white flowers with yellow tongues. The flowers unfurl for the moon and curl closed in the afternoon. Their nectar feeds bees, bats, doves. My father had always liked the saguaro: how it thrived in the most austere environments, providing sustenance to more sensitive life-forms.

The menu of Saguaro's was similar to that of Roberto's, with a *mariscos* flair: spicy shrimp burritos and halibut tacos as well as *carne asada* burritos, *chimichangas,* rolled *taquitos*. Papi was a perfectionist, firing employees for preparing something too hastily, too slowly. He did most of the work himself. Sometimes, he slept behind the counter. From 1994 to 1998, I have almost no memories of my father as he applied himself diligently to Saguaro's. I had grown accustomed to his absence prior to his departure, but his failure to visit convinced me and Michelle of his indifference. We begged our mother to take us to Saguaro's, desperate to show off in front of our father and win his love again. We sang, danced, expressed our most fascinating thoughts while sipping *horchatas* and chewing on *chimichangas*. He ignored us. A single tendency evidenced a shred of persisting affection: although my father did not pay child support, whenever we visited Saguaro's, we got food free of charge.

•

Our maternal grandparents moved into the house in Paradise Hills to help raise us. Michelle and I called them the Cocos. They brought coconuts from Puerto Rico and showed us pictures of a dog named Coco. Mami's mother, whom she called Mami, had fun cotton-ball hair, like our neighbor Jenny. Her body was a graceful parenthesis, thin, prone to hugging. My mother's father was thicker and shorter, with silver hair as soft as a rabbit's, and brown skin that smelled of Old

Spice. I had never lived with a man who wore cologne—my dad was always au naturel—and the novelty of my grandfather's fragrance in the house was delightful. He carried us on his shoulders, and we absorbed his deep, rumbling laughter. The Cocos loved us at first: we were cute. But quickly, they lost patience with us. My sister and I were ill-mannered, almost savage. That winter, they took us to a park and glared at us as we sat on a table. We had refused to use the bench attached to it, in spite of their orders. Michelle and I were chatting about Santa Claus. *Santa Claus isn't real,* my grandfather snapped. *That's just your mom, killing herself to please you brats.* I brought my eyebrows together and made the ugliest, angriest face I could make. I had suspected that Santa Claus wasn't real—the story seemed too silly to be actual, unlike the fairy tales I read and the movies I watched, which were all coherent and clearly true. Still, my grandfather's audacity struck me as cruel: *How dare this man take it upon himself to ruin the fantasy?* My sister burst into tears.

My inability to distinguish fact from fiction would persist until I was twelve, but everything religious made me dubious. Initially, I was pious, like Abuela Carolina and my mother desired. I relished the extravagance of my first Communion, my white lace dress and religious-themed presents, the papery feel of Jesus Christ's body on my tongue. But I felt my mother's faith wavering amid the chaos of her life. I begged her to take us to church. She was too busy or too tired. I watched a film about a girl who heard the voice of God. I was jealous of the protagonist and watched, mesmerized, as she freed Jesus Christ from a handheld crucifix, causing him to materialize before her in the flesh, life-size, healed. I looked up at the crucifix on our bedroom wall and walked over to it. I pulled it down and, in a strange reverie, ripped the nails from Christ's hands and feet. I stared at the freed son of God in my hand. He did not grow. The holes in his bloodstained limbs did not disappear. He stayed as he had been, crown of thorns drawing blood on his forehead, arms paralyzed in crucifixion. But now he looked obscene, suffering with his arms outspread for no reason. A horrifying conviction gripped me: I had blasphemed. I searched the ground for the nails I had tossed aside. I searched under the bed. I searched the corners of the room. I searched every inch of the floor. I searched until my mother found me on the ground in tears and told me, with bored eyes, to forget about it.

•

The Cocos moved back to Puerto Rico. They had concluded we were a lost cause, tainted by the DNA of *el Mexicano* who had ruined their daughter's life. There was no point in trying to civilize us. After they left, my mother told me I had to take care of myself and my sister. She taught me to heat frozen meals in the microwave, made me recite rules. Never open the door for anyone. Never leave the stove on. If someone calls the house and asks for Jeannette Del Valle, never, ever say, *Mami isn't here right now.* Always say: *Mami is in the bathroom; may I take a message?*

•

In the summer, when many of our classmates visited islands and amusement parks, my sister and I accompanied Mami on hospital rounds. We sat in doctors' lounges, devouring snacks, pressing buttons on the TV remote controls, interviewing handsome male doctors who passed through. *Do you know Dr. Del Valle?* I asked. *Dr. Del Valle, oh man, she is so beautiful!* they said, or, *I love your mother, she's such a great doctor and just a great human being.* I glanced at their fingers, only to be disappointed that they donned shiny rings of commitment. At home, we asked our mother: *When are you going to remarry?* She had told us she was divorced from our father.

Never, she said, chin up, tossing her hair. *I don't need a man.*

But we want a father like the ones on TV, we said.

She grinned. *I am your mother and your father.*

•

While shopping for groceries in 1996, my mother bought a Celine Dion music album, *Falling into You.* She inserted the CD into our stereo sound system. The living room filled with the sounds of the breeze and piano keys twirling inside it like bright yellow leaves. Celine Dion sang about a cold wind in the night. Her voice was strong and soft, like strips of velvet. My mother swayed and joined in: "There were days when the sun was so cruel . . ." Suddenly, the tone of the song changed, the voice swelled and became defiant: "I finished crying in the instant that you left . . . and I banished every memory you and I had ever made." My mother moved every limb, sang at the top of her lungs. Michelle and I felt buoyed by ecstasy as we watched her catharsis, we hugged her hips and danced with her. Then Dion's and my mother's voices swerved again, to a sudden tenderness, a softness so vulnerable it could break. They recalled the man's touch, they were starting to remember: "It's so hard to believe but it's all coming back to me . . ." The piano keys began to chase their voices, a panting tambourine came into the song, the pace picked up: "It's all coming back . . ." All of the instruments rushed together in a revelatory leap: "There were moments of gold! And there were flashes of light!" The windows were pulsating, the three of us were spinning. Michelle and I learned the chorus and sang with our mother, the three of us were screaming. Then the song was over. We stared at one another in silence, sweating, eyes glowing, waiting. The next song, "Because You Loved Me," started. Mami sang, looking at us: "You were my strength when I was weak . . . I lost my faith, you gave it back to me." We danced to those songs again and again, shouting the lyrics, falling to the floor, jumping up, watching our mother crying and laughing, crying and laughing, while crying and laughing with her.

·

Mami enrolled us in ballet classes, swimming classes, piano classes. She wanted to keep us busy so we would not have time to think about our father. I loved piano because sheet music reminded me of hiero-glyphs, or little birds reposing on telephone wires. With the smooth feel of cold keys under my fingers I was inspired to improvise, and my father, during a rare visit, heard me play a song I had composed. He said, *Wow, you wrote that?* I felt a glow so intense I thought I'd catch fire. I decided to play my nameless song at a Christmas recital where I was supposed to play "Rudolph the Red-Nosed Reindeer." The day of the recital, Mami seemed more stressed than usual, juggling patients, getting me dressed up, doing my hair. She sighed and scolded me repeatedly. I tried to forget my anxiety at my piano teacher's house. Strangers crowded her living room. My mother had invited a coworker. Papi, predictably, did not come. I swallowed and walked up to the bench. I placed my fingers on the cold, creviced keys, the feel of which filled me with sudden confidence. I played the song I had composed. It started as a simple, chipper melody: three high staccato notes repeating amid a descending line of keys. Then it erupted into rhythmic chords that rose and dipped, rose and dipped, until they changed their minds and rose and rose and rose, punctuated always by a low note at the left side of the piano, which made their rising sound miraculous. Suddenly, the rising chords ended in a sound of shattering light. The chipper melody returned, but this time, my fingers were soft and slow, not plucky, and the happy melody sounded sad—a smile with downcast eyes. The chords followed again, legato as well, until they reached a golden high note that echoed, and I finished the song with a double-pounding on one of the lowest keys, stepping on the sustain pedal. I felt tremors in my gut as the final sounds passed through me, and stood from the bench flushed with pride. I turned to the crowd. Everyone seemed distracted; they smiled and clapped without real emotion. Only the piano teacher noticed I had done something unique. She looked enraged. I fought the impulse to burst into tears. After the recital was over, when the guests were socializing, the teacher pulled me aside, hissing like a scarlet-colored snake. Spittle flew into my eyes. *You were supposed to play "Rudolph."* I was disturbed by the intensity of her reaction. I decided to quit piano and all of my hobbies; my sister followed suit. Life was not turning out as we had hoped. Creativity was a crime. Innocent creatures were mortal. Fathers left their daughters and broke their mothers' hearts.

·

After a heavy rain, the earth in our backyard was covered in countless *caracoles*—ugly, slimy snails. Lethargic, I asked my sister to help me beautify them with our scented Magic Markers. We decorated the shells of the snails with swirls and spots of colors. The coloring only highlighted their hideousness. Disgusted, I told my sister we had to kill the preposterous *caracoles*. The thick, tentaculoid roots of a tree bulged and converged aboveground, forming a pool where we often gave Barbies mud baths. We filled the pool with water from our hose and dropped in the coiled creatures. They made satisfactory plops in our swamp. We smiled. The surface rippled and was calm. It felt good to have killed the snails, served them right for being so disgusting. We sat there in satisfied silence, then the wind picked up. Guilt seized us. *Save them, Michelle!* I screeched, too repulsed to do it myself. *No, I'm scared,* she said. Darkness crept over the backyard, casting shadows everywhere. We ran back to the house.

The next morning, I shook my sister awake. *Go check on the snails,* I begged. *Only if you come,* she said. We entered the backyard holding hands. We took tentative steps until we reached the roots. The muddy soup had hardened. Two gruesome trails of bubbly, white slime led out of two holes in the dry earth. We were petrified. We imagined the incredible strength of the snails we had tortured. We felt certain these creatures would someday seek revenge.

•

Everything was vanishing. Even the succulent-thing in my heart had disappeared, replaced by a low-frequency pain and emptiness in my chest. Where did everything go? Nobody knew. The culprit was always: *No sé. No sé. No sé.* The unknown was the root of every kind of erasure: my father's departure, our pets' deaths, the disappearance of the indestructible snails. I remembered a faraway, happy time full of unfrightening mysteries, full of threads that could be pulled. I had nothing to pull now, no path toward understanding to pursue. I had a feeling Papi could answer my questions, or perhaps already had, in his excited whispers about the sky and the trees and *el Océano Pacífico.* But I couldn't remember the content of those whispers, and he was a stranger now, I couldn't ask him anything. *What happens when we die?* All evidence pointed to: nothing. A vanishing. A simple ceasing to exist. The concept of true nothingness began to form in my brain like a wart. It seemed a worse fate than Hell, but I couldn't imagine it. It was the unknown again. I needed to comprehend it so it would lose its sinister power. I entered the bedroom, closed the door and sat on the floor. I closed my eyes. Then I asked myself, over and over again: *What is nothingness? What is nothingness?* I pushed myself against the envisioned blackness, which I knew was not quite nothingness, and erased the empty space that took its place. At first, empty space replaced empty space. I could not go beyond. But after two or three minutes, something happened. It is impossible to describe or fathom in retrospect. The closest sketch I can make is as follows:

I felt the whole universe rush in through every pore of my body, causing me to swell and expand at the speed of light. I felt the heat of stars flooding my veins, moons bombing my eye sockets, the pink fog of nebulae exploding in my lungs and black holes blowing my heart to smithereens. And then, suddenly, I was infinite. I was everything and nothing at once. I was not only conversing with God, like the girl in that religious film—I *was* God. I was his black blood, his Milky Way fluids, his fiery guts and his omniscience. I was his voice, saying: *Everything is exactly as it is supposed to be.*

After a few seconds, the experience subsided. I returned to my flesh-coated girl-self. It was what some might call a spiritual experience, induced by the hypnotic quality of the repetition. I had perceived nothingness as the most fertile ground in the universe: the seed of life and creation. Death could never prevail; its sowing reaps forever.

•

Of course, I didn't understand the experience in those terms. All I knew was that it felt amazing. Quickly, I learned I could repeat it. Every time I asked myself *What is nothingness?* over and over again, my body's borders yielded and I experienced that internal eruption for an eternal instant. It became a guilty pleasure, a comforting ecstasy, a cure for all of my existential anxiety. Whenever I could, I locked myself in the bedroom and stimulated my mind with the question until the astronomical climax came. I told no one. I could not hope to explain it. I feared that what I was doing was wrong.

CURATIVE BOOKS

My reading tastes evolved in middle school. I selected romance novels from the Price Club book section because their covers featured beautiful women who looked like real-life princesses surrounded by darkness and fog. They often featured soft-core porn, but they didn't corrupt me; my mother translated the difficult English words for me—a man's *bulge* referred to his elbow, and *nipples* were a sort of beauty mark. I also read *Goosebumps*, whose ghoulish creatures I thought lurked in our garage.

It dawned on me that every story revolved around a conflict. No fairy tale or book was any good without toil and trouble. The absence of a father meant I was *interesting*. Every conflict in my life, I concluded, was a blessing. Suffering fertilized me like a storm nourishes flowers. It was better to be interesting than to be happy. *Please let me have a life of calamity, full of villains, pining, betrayals, damsels in distress, beasts, curses, near-death experiences and apocalypses,* I beseeched God, repeating my wish a hundred times every night. I was sure that if I prayed longer than anyone, He would hear my voice. But I punctuated each prayer with a supplication: *However, please, please let my mother pass her test and please help her live happily ever after.* For as long as I could re-member, my mother had been studying for the internal-medicine cer-tification exam, failing to pass each year despite hundreds of hours highlighting passages in tomes, downing coffee after coffee, never tak-ing time off. Every gift I gave my mother as a child had a de-stressing theme (a mug urging her to stress less, a self-help book on managing stress, a mouse pad with a quote about relaxation). No matter how much I prayed, she failed the exam by several points each year. Eventu-ally, I grew so frustrated with God that I ceased praying. That same year, my mother passed. But that would not happen until 2002.

•

Our iguanas, which had survived the die-off during our father's dete-rioration, vanished from the cage Papi had built for them. My sister and I were accustomed to loss and barely noticed. Our neighbor Jenny spotted one of the reptiles, enlarged to twice its original size, basking on a tree branch in her backyard. Jenny called our mother. She was busy with patients. My mother called Papi. Our father arrived with a plan. I couldn't remember the last time he had stepped into our house. I watched his every movement, transfixed. Papi pushed a wire through a long plastic tube and created a loop at one end with the wire. He slipped the noose around the iguana's neck, tightened it, and yanked the lassoed reptile from the tree. My sister and I squealed and ap-plauded, so proud of our father the superman. He left as quickly as he had come.

Sometime later, Papi brought over two long ropes and plastic black hoops. He tied the ropes to a tree branch and knotted the black plastic loops at their ends. *Use them,* he said, then departed. Michelle tiptoed and grabbed both strings with her hands. *No, not like that,* I said. I stuck my arms entirely through the plastic loops, up to my armpits, lifted my legs behind me, and kicked off. *They're for flying!* I cried, and pre-tended to soar, ignoring the strain of suspending my legs parallel to the earth. Michelle and I took turns, giggling with glee. The trees watched us with their large eyes. Their smiles seemed to stretch. Their twigs trembled, raining leaves down all around us. We flew. We flew for so long, with such abandon, that I ceased to feel the plastic loops under my arms—I felt I was literally soaring over the land. When my sister told me she wanted to stop, I ignored her; I pushed her higher and higher. Finally, I noticed the blood soaking through our shirts. We had rubbed our armpits raw. "Look at me," I said, grabbing my sobbing sister by the shoulders, my heart pounding. "We can't tell Mami."

I was afraid of myself, afraid of what the incident revealed. I hid the balled-up bloody shirts in a corner of our closet. My mother found them anyway. I walked into the bedroom as if on cue. She turned toward me. In her eyes, there was fear—fear of me.

•

My mother stopped taking us to Saguaro's. She drove us to a nearby McDonald's instead, arguing that North Park was too far away, that she was too busy to drive us to our father's restaurant. If Papi wanted to see us, she said, he would come to us.

Mami's name changed—she became Mommy. Our father remained Papi. The word "dad" or "daddy" still feels foreign on my tongue if I try to use it to address him. Papi was stuck in time. Our mother was evolving. She no longer wore the colorful, flower-print dresses that had characterized Mami's wardrobe. The primary color of Mommy's clothes was black. In 1998, Mommy decided it was time for us to leave Paradise Hills. She wanted us to live in a more prosperous neighborhood. She scrubbed the faces from our trees, gave away our remaining pets and made us pack up our toys. Michelle and I became despondent. Our Paradise Hills house was pregnant with secrets I had not deciphered. I tried to run my hands over every inch, to memorize it. I imagined I could feel the years through the fabric of space-time, as if it were a malleable substance like gauze. I put my cheeks to the floor and heard my mother's laughter. I pressed my bare toes on the blue leather couch and felt my father's hands in my hair. Leaving that house was heartbreaking.

We rented a one-bedroom apartment, where we stayed for six

months as Mommy sought the perfect house. In a Lisa Frank diary, I wrote: *Dear rainbow chaser, It's crowded and lonely here . . . The only thing I like about this apartment is the bath . . . as they always say, be happy with what you have. I have no friends at school, please help!*

My hair was darkening, my nose was lengthening, my teachers grew disenchanted and disenchanting. Our lessons incorporated rote memorization. When I asked *why* questions, my teachers treated me like I was stupid, like I was failing to understand something obvious, and they refused to clarify. My science classes were particularly depressing. *But* why *does the cell divide inside the womb?* I asked. The teacher sighed: *I've explained it a million times. Read the textbook.* Some became angry: *Are you testing me? Don't question my authority!* I learned to stop asking *why* questions—only *how* was acceptable. I had to get straight A's to please my mother—even A-minuses made my heart plunge. I was increasingly aware that my sister and I were a burden on our mother. An alternating cast of characters picked me and Michelle up from school: Mommy's patients, a nurse friend, the nurse friend's parents.

While browsing the shelves at the local library, I discovered a science fiction book series called Animorphs, about five children trying to rescue humanity from an invasion by a slug-like alien species called the Yeerks. The Yeerks crawl into human ears to take over their brains. The Animorphs battle them by "acquiring" the DNA of animals through touch, then morphing into them. They confront moral dilemmas. They sacrifice youthful pastimes for a greater cause. On the back cover of each book is a message: "We can't tell you who we are. Or where we live. It's too risky, we've got to be careful. . . . The thing you should know is that everyone is in really big trouble. Yeah. Even you." I became convinced that the Animorphs would come find me, to incorporate me into their meaningful group. I told them in thought-speak that I was *super willing and ready to help battle Yeerks*. I started dressing like the kids on the covers of the books and drinking Mountain Dew soda, their favorite, although I didn't like the taste. I scanned crowds for the faces of the Animorphs. I wore Animorphs paraphernalia-lia, including a necklace I never took off. In my Lisa Frank diary, I wrote that one of the characters had visited me: *I met Tobias with a hologram over him to make him look like air. He told me none of the Animorphs can show themselves to me . . . without a hologram.*

It was an efficient coping mechanism. I became bubbly again. I maintained my grades, even though I didn't like my teachers anymore. I saw them with new, pitying eyes: they were Controllers, victims of Yeerk mind control. I wondered if my father was a Controller—perhaps that was why he had become so indifferent to us. Someday, I thought, I would rescue him, and my parents would live happily ever after.

My sister, meanwhile, struggled in school. Blocks of text and strings of numbers were uninspiring to her visual and visceral intelligence. My mother asked me to tutor her, but I was too wrapped up in Animorphs. At our old house, Michelle had sketched the insects in our backyard: ants, butterflies, worms, beetles. In the cramped apartment, she lacked inspiration. She lost faith in her talent. She had no art teachers who could tell her if she was any good. She was having a recurring nightmare since our father left: She and I are the only passengers on a bus when the driver disappears. We take over the wheel, but we don't know how to drive. We nearly crash. Somehow, we maneuver the bus back to our Paradise Hills home. But the house is gone. A melting blackness has taken its place, boring through the backyard to an imperceptible beyond. The sight is terrifying and impossible. Michelle had a deep desire to draw this vision, to purge it from herself onto a canvas. But it was too complex; there was no point in trying.

My mother found a two-story McMansion with a swimming pool and a hill of trees behind a fence in a suburb called Eastlake, in the city of Chula Vista, where our Abuela Carolina lived. Mommy, with tears in her eyes, showed us the house. She didn't want to disappoint us. *It's for you,* she said. We ran into her arms.

She bought a blue-green iMac G3. As I explored the computer, a buried memory flickered and emerged: After my father's departure from our first house, I had scoured his computer for clues about him.

Most of the text files seemed school-related, real estate and photography notes that didn't interest me. I sought to find his thoughts. I searched folders, folders within folders. A single text file caught my attention. I can't recall the title or the content, only that when I opened it I saw a short string of sentences on a largely blank page. They were florid lines in English that seemed to have been taken from a novel or a philosophical text. I understood the individual words, but I didn't understand their combined meaning; it was too complex or too abstract. I asked my sister to read it, but she didn't understand, either. We felt we could not ask our mother. The words had something to do with evil. When I try to remember them today, the words smear in my memory. I think I see one word, but I can't be sure: "carnal." Perhaps "carnality."

My mother had taken Papi's computer to the condominium shortly after his departure. She had heard that the Internet was a portal to a dangerous universe of kidnappers and serial killers, and didn't want us playing with it. But as our teachers began to demand typed papers and online research, she gave in, ordering us never to speak to strangers on the contraption. I opened up the new iMac G3's Word program and typed. The words flowed easily; I soon found I could write more than a hundred a minute. As I typed, I felt relief from an interior pressure. The pace of typing matched the pace of my thoughts. I typed and typed until I had composed a 137-page novel about a humanoid alien with long eyelashes who saves the world. I flew over pink oceans in her body, gazed at her multicolored sky, felt her thrill at ending the apocalypse. My sister read my novels and claimed to love them, although in general she hated reading. This induced in me the delusion that I was a better writer than the professionals who authored her assigned books. I started devoting all of my free time to writing on the computer.

I discovered Google: a portal to a vast universe of answers to existential questions. I typed my queries about death and the meaning of life and, to my astonishment, received endless responses about ghosts and gods with different names. But the information was confusing and contradictory. I researched fairies and unicorns, desperate to learn where in the natural world I might glimpse them. As I searched in vain for coherent information, I began to wonder if fairy-tale creatures even existed. I found forums full of strangers who explored the same questions as me—*Where are all the mermaids? Is Heaven a real place?*—but their conclusions were convoluted and incomplete.

I watched the movie *Harriet the Spy*, about a girl who spies on people like a detective, narrating their actions in her notebook. The dividing line between truth and tales, I was starting to realize, had to do with where events originated: in a person's head versus outside a person's head. It felt like a distinction without a difference—the world outside my head was still in my head—but I was learning that it was important to grown-ups and that I had to start paying attention. I felt inspired to try journalism. I asked Google about the 1947 UFO crash in Roswell, New Mexico, having read the Melinda Metz series Roswell High, about alien teenagers, and watched the corresponding TV series. I copied and pasted quotes from people on forums who claimed they had seen alien bodies and encountered pieces of indestructible metal strewn around their homes.

As I created my first nonfiction narrative, Michelle asked me to play Barbies or pretend with her. I declined. I was no longer interested in make-believe. She decided to befriend her reflection. She spent hours talking to her imaginary friend. When I wasn't monopolizing the computer, she used it to converse with SmarterChild, a prim online robot.

One day, I found a vintage bikini in my mother's drawers. It was made of a delicate, towel-like fabric, with lime-green and tangerine stripes. I found it beautiful in its antiquity; the degrading cloth seemed to radiate my mother's past. I asked Mommy for permission to wear it in the pool. She agreed with reluctance; it was a gift from a cherished, now deceased aunt. She told me to be careful. I swam some laps. Afterward, I stripped to take a shower. I discovered with horror that the bottoms of the bikini were marred by a dark brown stain. It had leaked out of me. I tried to wash it out with hot water. It remained. I had ruined my mother's bikini. I brought it to her, full of shame. She frowned, then said with a sad smile: *You've started your period. It's not a bad thing.*

But it was a bad thing. It was the worst thing that could have happened to a girl convinced she was the most beautiful person in existence. Pus-filled pimples erupted on my face, my nose widened, my hair frizzed and turned the gray color of dirty rats. It was a case of an ugly duckling in reverse. Thick brown hairs sprouted on my legs. My mother forbade me from shaving them, even after all the other girls started doing so. Suddenly, the fact that I was a bookworm with straight A's made me freakish. I became Loser, Nerd, Dork, the target of spitballs and chewed gum. My poor sister gained weight and became the Whale. My mother decided to put braces on us, turning us into Metal Mouths. I mistakenly believed choosing bright colors for the rubber bands—neon green, mustard yellow—would offset some hideousness. I befriended the only other person as nerdy as me, Victoria, a pale-skinned fellow Animorphs fan who believed saying "Oh my God" was a sin and strove always to defend his name. Her hair was set afire by a popular boy serving as an acolyte during school chapel. Occasionally, we ate lunch with Christopher Wiener, a boy in my sister's grade who was relentlessly ridiculed because of his large head, his last name and the fact that his parents ran a profitable pornography chain.

A new social order emerged: the Mexicans were the popular and privileged majority; the gringos were the despised and oppressed minority. The Mexicans bullied the Americans into handing over their most precious commodities: the answers to tests, their homework assignments, their lunch. I was considered gringa because of my once-blonde hair and my academic anxiety. The Mexicans were the carefree children of successful immigrants who ordered that failing grades be changed, that detentions be revoked, that punishments be replaced with motivational tutoring. Many of my classmates carpooled from wealthy neighborhoods of Tijuana. One boy arrived in a black SUV, escorted to class by two bodyguards. In contrast, the gringos were the nervous offspring of middle-class parents who could not afford to live north of Chula Vista, yet were willing to sacrifice everything to give their children a private-school education. Some took the bus. It was an ironic reversal of the world outside the classroom.

Because the Mexicans had money, they were stylish and beautiful, with slicked-back hair shining with the best products, wrists and necklaces jingling with 24-karat gold. The gringos had tangled hair, mismatched socks and circles under their eyes. When the Mexicans learned of my Animorphs delusions, they tormented me. *Even if the Animorphs were real, why would they come for you, of all people? You're a freak. Estás bien fea.* They insulted me in Spanish, thinking I couldn't understand. The teachers encouraged this division across racial lines, allowing the Mexican girls to wear makeup—thick mascara, glittery lip gloss, sultry eye shadow—but ordering the white girls to wash off the slightest trace of powder. The teachers curved each test, and my top scores made me Enemy No. 1. Being unpopular was unbearable. I had long felt so superior. My fantasies were my only consolation. What if what my classmates said was true? What if the Animorphs were just characters in a story?

I hadn't asked myself about nothingness since leaving Paradise Hills. I had stopped the ritual because I lacked privacy in the apartment. In my new bedroom, I asked myself, *What is nothingness?* I chanted and chanted and chanted. Nothing happened. No matter how many times I repeated the question, I remained a prisoner of my mortal flesh. The hormonal changes that had made me hideous had obliterated my capacity to have climactic experiences through contemplation. It occurred to me that the whole thing might have been a hallucination, a trick of my young brain, like the memory of touching a cloud on a plane. Perhaps the world was this: just this.

I became convinced of it. Life is an accident. Any encounter with meaning is a delusion. I stared at my hands: frog-like, juice-filled appendages. I was a nasty creature, an insignificant malodorous animal with frizz that had spent its whole life under the illusion that it was a powerful princess. Papi had seen my triviality. He wanted nothing to do with me because of it. I was disgusting, worthless, doomed to die. For hours I stood paralyzed, afraid that if I moved I would crumble.

I looked up at my shelf of books. When my mind felt like it was spiraling out of control, I slid into the curves of printed letters, allowing the text to rein in my mind like ropes, anchoring me to the page, to a concrete—though fictional—reality. It didn't matter that the stories weren't true. They were sanctuaries from the senseless universe. I buried my head inside the pages, pushing the covers against the sides of my skull, containing the hurricane I felt roiling within. I decided that even if there was no purpose to life, I would create one for myself: to write a book, a medicine, a weapon like these.

FAT FLIES

Papi sold Saguaro's in 1998. His sister had launched a Mexican drive-through restaurant, Asada, and it was far more successful than his. Hers was right off the freeway in a shopping center their parents owned. Papi couldn't get over the feeling that he had failed—as a father, as a husband, as a mortal being running out of time. When he met my mother, he felt the whole world was accessible to him. He could throw knives, swim miles across the sea. He could do anything, be anyone. He had a hundred dreams. Now he had two daughters who were strangers to him, and he didn't want anything at all. He was filling his car at the gas station when he saw her—a scantily clad girl with chocolate-colored skin on the curb. *You need a ride?* he asked. *Sure,* she said. It was the second time he met a woman at a gas station, the second time the world would change his life at a gas station. She was a gypsy, a wanderer, without any interest in talking. They succumbed to their bodies, blotting out the knowledge of their brains. When he walked in on her burning a white rock in a pipe, she tried to hide it. He'd never seen it before, and when she spoke its name—crack—he was curious. It looked like a piece of calcite, something pure and promising from the guts of the earth. *Let me try it,* he said, and then he took a hit.

•

Papi spent six weeks at a Tijuana rehab, Clínica Nuevo Ser. When he was released in the summer of 1999, he asked our mother if he could take me and Michelle to Mexico. My mother would have refused, but she was studying for her internal-medicine certification exam. Perhaps, with a break from mothering, she would finally pass the test. She asked Abuela Carolina if Papi could be trusted. Abuela Carolina reassured her, arranging for our seventeen-year-old cousin, Jeannie, to join as our guardian. We would visit my uncle Alejandro, Jeannie's father, who now lived in Jalisco with his second wife.

Here was an opportunity to show my father that I was no longer the annoying girly girl I had once been. I was courageous and cunning like the heroines of my science fiction books, a warrior like the Animorphs. I had long pined for adventures in the jungle. I would show him that now I was a daughter worth loving.

A few days before we left, my stomach bloated, my face sprouted mountain ranges of pimples, my uterus gurgled and cramped. Warm liquid dripped out between my legs. My mother stuffed my suitcase with super-absorbency menstrual pads. *What if Papi sees them?* I asked. The prospect of my father discovering something so personal was mortifying. *Just don't let him,* Mommy said. My sister laughed and said I was disgusting for bleeding out of my vagina. *That's never gonna happen to me,* she said.

Prior to our departure, our mother pulled us aside and said, ominously: *Be careful. Your father is . . . not normal. Tell Jeannie if he does anything . . . strange. And remember: Mexico is a dangerous place. Be on your guard at all times.*

I don't remember the flight to Guadalajara, or the drive in the rental vehicle to Autlán. I recall arriving in a small, cold house where Alejandro, his wife, Rosie, and their three boys lived. My uncle and my father laughed about things I didn't understand, in a deep, sinister way, like my *tíos* often did when they were drunk at fiestas. My father had grown a thick black mustache, and his skin had a strange clammy texture. I saw *cucarachas* crawling on the floor. My aunt Rosie stepped on them, then wiped their guts with a paper towel. Papi's and Alejandro's voices lowered. They went outside to prowl the streets. I went to bed terrified. I woke up trembling and hyperventilating in the middle of the night, though I had never truly gone to sleep. I was falling in and out of nightmares—hallucinations, seemingly, because every time my mind tried to slip into the dark pit of unconsciousness I caught myself as if tripping, grasping and gasping in my sheets. I was soaked all over with sweat; my eyes dripped tears I could taste in my mouth and feel in my ears; my underwear was damp with blood. My cramps were torturous, my fear relentless. I loathed my stiff mattress, the stains on my lumpy pillow. I ran my hands over my head, grasping at my hair: frizzy. I touched my face: oily, pimply. I pushed against my stomach, trying to hurt the cramps away. I hated Mexico, hated my hatred, hated my fear, hated myself. Michelle lay snoring beside me.

I sobbed. My hyperventilating was uncontrollable. Papi threw open the door in the dark. *What's wrong?* he gasped, mouth agape. *What's wrong? What's wrong?* He looked terrified. He threw his arms around me. I could feel his heartbeat reverberate through my body, pounding even harder than mine. His abrupt presence had startled me, but his touch stretched through memories and stirred a sleeping trust. I couldn't remember the last time my father hugged me. It was so reassuring that my impulse to sob was obliterated, but instead I wept louder, harder, because I wanted him to stay. He rocked me. I tried to memorize the moment—the feel of his sweat-soaked shirt, his familiar odor of cigarette smoke and armpits. *I want to leave this place,* I said, sobbing. *Okay. We'll leave tomorrow. First thing, I promise. I promise.* He rocked me until I fell asleep.

•

In the morning, the family piled into two vehicles. We arrived at a tiny coastal town called Cuastecomates four hours later. Lush green mountains emitted a croaking toads' chorus. Cradled between them was a single rustic hotel, Bahía de Cuastecomates. Large boulders jutted from a royal blue sea. Storm clouds coalesced on the horizon. Every molecule in my body ached with fear. The town felt savage. But I told myself to be happy: this was a big improvement from Autlán. Papi asked for two interconnected rooms with "the best ocean view."

In our room, Michelle and I opened our sliding-glass balcony door. The sea breeze bathed our faces and transformed my frizzy hair into a tangled tumbleweed.

Wow, Papi, it's so cool! Michelle said.

I walked into the bathroom to change into my bathing suit, then froze. It dawned on me that I couldn't swim in a pool without creating clouds of blood. I emerged from the bathroom and threw my swimsuit into my suitcase.

Papi's eye quivered for an instant.

What is it? he asked.

I felt a wave of contempt for myself and said: *I just don't feel like swimming.*

In the room connected to ours, Jeannie had changed into her bikini. She sat cross-legged in bed, staring into a pocket mirror, smearing on plum lipstick. Jeannie was my only blonde cousin. We had once looked very similar. For her *quinceañera,* I had played the role of young Jeannie in a ceremony that represented her departure from childhood. Puberty had metamorphosed me into a gray-haired monster, while she had become a model, her image featured in swimsuit calendars and on Tijuana billboards. She pressed her eyelashes with a metal tool and applied a globby coat of black mascara.

Why are you doing that? I asked.

Why wouldn't I?

It's gonna wash off in the water.

It's waterproof.

Outside, Papi and I sat beneath a shady *palapa* watching others throw a plastic ball around in the pool. I ordered a virgin piña colada.

Papi ordered a Corona. He pulled out his Marlboros and offered me the pack. *Want a smoke?* he asked.

I gasped in horror.

Heh, heh, heh, he said. *It's a joke.* He lit a cigarette and took a drag. The bartender brought our drinks. I took a sip of my piña colada and gagged.

Papi, can you taste this? I think there's alcohol in it!

Papi took a sip. He made a sucking sound with his teeth. *Jóven,* he said. *Are you trying to intoxicate my ten-year-old daughter?*

Eleven, I corrected.

Discúlpeme, the man said, apologizing, and replaced it.

I stared at the pool, sipping contentedly. I wanted to talk to my father, but I had no idea what to say. My brain sought words where there were none; my thoughts swam in my throat, in my chest, in my stomach. I noticed a shirtless teenage boy in the water. He was brown and muscular, staring back at me with a solicitous smile. How could it be? I was a frizzy-haired eleven-year-old with bad posture and oily, pimply skin, wearing a Taco Bell Chihuahua shirt. He looked seventeen or eighteen—a gorgeous teenage god.

Jean, a voice said. I turned around: my cousin Jeannie was right behind me. Of course, the beautiful boy had been smiling at her, not me. Her golden hair shimmered despite the lack of sunlight, her clear skin glowed. *Why don't you come in?* she asked.

I have a stomachache.

Oh, I see, she said, with a long, dramatic wink that disturbed my heartbeat. I stole a glance at Papi to see if he had noticed her tactless expression. Jeannie grabbed my hand. *Come, I want to talk to you for a second.*

She dragged me away from my father. *Michelle told me why you won't go in the pool. But you know, you won't bleed if you go swimming. It's like magic. Water stops periods.*

I don't know if I believe that.

Cross my heart. Plus, my dad wants to take us for a ride on the banana boat. Come. Don't be a party pooper.

The banana boat was an enormous yellow flotation device towed by a Jet Ski. Papi, Alejandro, Jeannie, Michelle, Alejandro Jr. and I clung to its handlebars as it tore across the sea. It was thrilling at first, like racing on a mythic marine serpent. Saltwater sprayed our faces. The wind turned the fuzz on my head into a slick wet mane. Then the speedboat made a sharp turn and the world flipped upside down. Disoriented, sinking, we scrambled toward the surface, limbs bumping into one another's. My uncle kicked me in the face with the full force of his two hundred pounds. I gasped and sank, spinning in blackness. An all-powerful arm hauled me out of the sea. I coughed water out of my lungs as Papi lifted me above the surface. *Are you okay?* he asked, his eyes terrified. The waves rocked us. I couldn't speak. He held me up, kicking with all the strength of his legs, allowing me to breathe with my head clear of the sea. *Let's go back,* he said.

•

Michelle woke up in the middle of the night. She felt thunder in her body . . . as if her heart had reproduced while she slept. Multiple hearts resided there, simultaneous beats pounding. I was asleep. She noticed an orange light spilling from a gap under the bathroom door. She tiptoed over and knocked softly, so as not to wake me. *Papi,* she whispered. No answer. She tapped again. *Papi.* He opened the door with his mouth agape and his eyes wide with horror. A strange smell wafted out with him. *What's wrong?* he gasped. *What's wrong? What's wrong?* She brought his hand to her chest. *My heart is beating so fast. I don't why.* Behind him, his crack pipe sat with his toothbrush. The fumes of his crack had intoxicated Michelle.

•

The next evening, at the outdoor hotel restaurant, black insects the size of beetles buzzed around us. *Are those . . . flies?* I asked. Papi nodded. *Yes. And they bite.* I shivered. My stomach gurgled with hunger. I had ordered a chocolate milk shake what felt like an hour ago. Why was it taking so long? I looked over my shoulder toward the kitchen.

Our waiter was dipping his finger into a tall glass of chocolate milk shake. He brought his finger to his tongue, dipped it in again, and tasted once more. He walked over and placed the milk shake in front of me. I gawked in disgust. *Close your mouth,* Papi said, exhaling smoke from his Marlboro into my face. *Or the flies will lay eggs on your tongue.* The feel of his cigarette smoke in my lungs provoked in me an unbearable mixture of nostalgia, revulsion and a fear of getting cancer. I found myself lit aflame by an impulse to destroy the cigarette. I plucked it from his lips and threw it with all my strength. I imagined the cigarette reaching the ocean, to be carried away by the frothy green waves to the golden coast of California, where a seagull might pick it up and drop it at my mother's feet on her way to work, and my mother would pick it up with a frown and shake her head knowingly, understanding the pain I was in, and come rescue me, but instead the cigarette landed with an unsatisfactory plop on the pavement.

I could see the veins in Papi's eyes thickening and splitting like rivers of blood. Jeannie put her arm on his shoulder. *Cálmate, tío. She's just looking out for you—she doesn't want you to get cancer.* He took a deep breath and lit another cigarette.

Our food arrived. *I'm not hungry,* I said. Papi chewed noisily and gestured with his fork. *Don't eat, then. Starve. Your sister knows what's good for her.* Michelle was combing her noodles with a fork, disentangling them meticulously, as if determined to get them into a certain arrangement but not by any means conveying a desire to eat them. I was hungry but I didn't trust any of the food. My father's fish ogled me with its dead eyeball; Papi pierced it with his fork. I put my forehead on the table and closed my eyes and tried to imagine I was somewhere else . . . in the arms of the teenage boy from the pool, perhaps. Jeannie had said his name was David. They were friends now.

Hey Jean, guess what? Jeannie said. She slid a thin, folded piece of notebook paper across the table. I flattened its creases. It read in Spanish: *Dear Jeannie, I have never seen a more beautiful girl in my life. I had to leave the hotel, but when I turn eighteen, I will fly to America to find you. Wait for me. With eternal adoration, David.*

I looked up. *Why are you showing this to me?*

The cute boy in the pool, remember? He left it under my door last night. It's for you.

If it's for me, then why is it addressed to you? I asked.

It's not addressed to me, silly! He was calling you Jeannie to be lovey-dovey. He told me he was in love with you.

I hit an internal Pause button and deliberated. I knew what she was saying wasn't true. But I wanted it to be true. I realized it *could* be true. All I had to do was succumb to my desire, like when I was a child. When I pressed Play, the flies of Cuastecomates ceased to be hideous. They transformed into fairies, my sister was a friend, my cousin was my *muchacha*, and my father, who was lighting another cigarette, was a king. I drank deep sips of my delicious chocolate milk shake. But then the vision flickered and turned off. I could no longer supplant reality with my imagination.

•

We headed to the state of Colima, where Papi thought we would be more comfortable at an all-inclusive hotel at the port of Manzanillo. Gran Festivall was a luxurious water adventure park, with serpentine slides and variously shaped swimming pools. We rented a spacious three-bedroom apartment decorated in festive Mexican colors. The buffet served Mexican food as well as hot dogs and other American junk my sister and I relished. The place was perfect, but every day at sundown, the darkness of my father's country terrified me as it never failed to do. One night, as the adults drank beers in the living room, I sat paralyzed, listening to the ominous crickets screaming outside. I didn't feel safe. I asked: *How much longer do we have to be here?*

Ten days, Papi said. The prospect made me panic. My face became wet with misery. Michelle avoided eye contact as I wailed. Alejandro's wife, Rosie, fanned herself with a brochure. Alejandro laughed cartoonishly. Papi looked defeated.

We went back to the United States a week earlier than planned. I breathed a sigh of relief when I saw my mother: gentle, familiar, ever beautiful. I ran upstairs and threw myself on my queen-size bed. My dependable mother had washed the sheets while I was away. I inhaled the flowery smell of detergent. I had escaped my father. I no longer wanted his approval. He was a scary man—a stranger. The Papi I had known and loved had died in the house at Paradise Hills.

BRAIN IMPLANT

My father's breakdown coincided with the new millennium. When I consider the timing, it seems significant somehow: 1999 turning into 2000, the most momentous calendar crossing in a thousand years. My classmates and I believed the world would end at midnight. We had inherited the paranoid ethos of a culture bracing for "Y2K," a potential software disaster, which seemed to me to be code for "two thousand Yeerks." But like mystics who study the Tarot, pre-adolescents do not contemplate apocalypse literally; they see it as the end of a cycle. We were thrilled—the year 2000 would bring the Future.

•

Papi heard voices in the walls of the condominium. He made hole after hole after hole in the walls with a hammer. He shoved his fists into the holes, pulled off chunks of plaster, searching for hidden cameras, radio-wave receivers, microphones. He found only the wires of the electrical system. He switched off the power generator, put on a pair of rubber gloves, tore the wires from the walls. He snipped them with wire cutters, one after the other. Still the voices persisted. He fell to his knees and put his ear to the floor. He tore at the wine-colored carpet with his hands, skinning the floor, searching and searching and searching. Suddenly, he smelled a poisonous gas: some kind of nerve agent.

Papi called 9-1-1, saying someone who wanted to kill him had tres-passed onto his property. When the police showed up, they found no evidence of foul play except the damage the panting man acknowl-edged having done himself. The officers asked if he was a tenant, cal-culating that the aggrieved party was not him but the unlucky owner of the condominium. Papi told them the place belonged to his "wife," Dr. Del Valle.

My mother got a call from the police. *Would you like to press charges, ma'am?* an officer asked. She declined. She showed up to survey the damages. The condominium had been torn apart as if by a wild ani-mal. The floor was skinned bare of its carpet, walls punctured, electri-cal system obliterated. Cigarette ash carpeted everything. The smells of smoke were so pungent Jeannette could hardly breathe. Papi, trem-bling and terrified, gave her his hypothesis: someone had implanted a microchip in his brain. They were sending voices into his skull. He seemed so genuinely frightened, she wondered if it was true. She searched his head for a scar. She found none. *Estás usando drogas de nuevo,* she said. He shook his head and begged her to believe him. She offered to drive him to his mother's house. His eyes widened. *My mom's behind all this,* he said. Jeannette lost all doubt. Marco was suffering from drug-induced psychosis. Carolina would never harm her son. He was exhibiting classic symptoms of paranoid schizophrenia. She weighed her options. Marco could no longer stay in the condominium. It was hers, he had destroyed it, she needed to repair it, she was going to sell it. But he had nowhere to go. *You're welcome to stay with me and the girls at the house for a few days, Marco, while you get back on your feet. But I don't want you doing drugs. I'll call the police if you do. And no matter what, you can't go upstairs.*

•

I started writing in an online journal a year after Papi's breakdown. I wrote an average of a thousand words each evening, documenting banal details of my pubescent existence. It helped alleviate my anxiety about death. I believed recording my experiences would give me a kind of immortality. Unlike writing on paper, which could be ripped up and thrown away, writing into the Internet felt permanent. I could "X" out of my journal and power off the computer, only to find my thoughts again by typing a URL into a browser. I planned to clone my soul into the World Wide Web so that I would never die. But I rarely mentioned my father. Somehow I managed to type a few retrospective paragraphs about Papi's post-breakdown stay in our house without a single relevant word: *I feel like talking about the first time I ever met Stefano. . . . I opened the door and Stefano was all, "Hey, I'm the guy in the back of your house." . . . He asked if I wanted to go for a walk . . . and I was like, "Um, sure, let me just ask my dad." At the moment he was staying with us. Anyway I asked and he said okay. So I went . . . and we became friends!*

My blog also reveals the onset of self-mutilating tendencies—something I had forgotten. I started digging my nails into my palms and thighs until they bled. I twisted my joints until I felt I was tearing cartilage. The pain made me feel good. My exhaustive accounts of each day actively and unnaturally avoid the subject of my father—not as if I found the topic uninteresting, but as if I found it too awful to mention. There are two notable exceptions:

> *July 27, 2001: I can't tell anybody about my dad so I just have to swallow it up and deal with it myself. My mom's side of the family cares too much about pride and hides problems as if they were shameful, horrible things.*

> *January 19, 2002: I always hurt myself when I'm depressed. . . . Sure, I've got problems, but sometimes I think I might be overreacting . . . other times I think I'm just insane, like my dad. That I'm gonna end up like him.*

My mother had sworn me to secrecy about my father. I obeyed, and literally deleted him from my mind. I can't recall anything about his post-breakdown stay at our house except curled and crisscrossing configurations of elastic ropes around my bedroom doorknob. I recall contemplating them in confusion; I kept pulling them off only to find them there again.

·

My sister remembers everything. Papi wrapped himself in tinfoil and told us to do the same. He watched the backyard with binoculars, describing stalkers he said were hiding in the bushes. He said they wore camouflage paint on their faces and hats that looked like trees. He marched up and down the stairs with an air rifle, to intimidate them. He grabbed a helium tank from the garage and placed the hose under the door of his bedroom, where he heard someone whispering in the walls. He covered the gap under the door with towels, then let gas spill into the room, to suffocate the government agents inside.

On the third night, Papi crept upstairs. My mother, who had told him he could stay with us so long as he remained downstairs, heard his footsteps. She hadn't slept since his arrival. She got up and tiptoed to her door. Papi was staring into Michelle's room, his face contorted in terror. My mother stepped into the hallway. In the calmest, most reassuring voice she could manage, she said: *Marco. There's nobody there. Come, sleep beside me. I'll stay awake. Nobody is going to harm anyone under my roof.* Papi followed my mother into bed. For the first time in years, Marco Antonio lay at Jeannette's side. His breathing slowed. He slept. Jeannette stayed awake all night. When the sun rose, she called Abuela Carolina. *He's your son,* she said. *I can't help him anymore.* My grandmother arrived in her golden Lexus with her chin up, designer sunglasses shading her eyes. She took her first son to live with her at her house. My mother told me my father no longer existed. I had to stop talking about him. And then, in synchrony with our silence, Papi vanished.

Part II

HOUSE OF DARKNESS

My grandmother holds my father in Mexico City in 1957.

FERTILITY

Her neighbors call her *La Señora de los Mil Pájaros*. The Woman of the Thousand Birds. When I visit her these days, my grandmother leads me outside to gaze at her more than a hundred lovebirds, which emerged from a single pair, like our childhood cockatiels. They flit around in a large wire-mesh cage Papi built in her backyard. Their feathers carpet and color the cage floor: yellow, blue, pink, black, green. Their songs are audible through the suburbs.

Nearing eighty, Carolina looks fifty. Her skin is luminous and smooth. Her hair is muted scarlet. She wears clothes of vineyard colors. Her nails are always manicured. Strangers often breathe words like *bella* when they meet her. Her mouth is still like the mouth of Michelangelo's *Delphic Sibyl*, conveying mourning in repose.

Her lovebirds are homicidal, like our childhood cockatiels. When a tumor the size of a golf ball erupted on a blue bird, its relatives butchered it to death. My uncle Alejandro, a recovering crystal meth addict who lives in Carolina's guest bedroom, scooped up its corpse and brought it into the kitchen. Carolina placed a hand on her chest and shook her head with a somber expression. *Let's store it in the freezer,* she said. *I want to know what the tumor is made of. We can dissect it later.*

The deformed lovebird remains in the freezer as I write this. Nobody has had time to dissect it. My grandmother still works full-time. While eating cantaloupe at her house, I ask her if she isn't repulsed by the carcass's proximity to her food. She stares at me with confusion. *Why would I be?* She walks to a nearby cupboard and reaches inside. From between wineglasses, she pulls out the carcass of a lizard. She says: *Mira.* She cradles it in her palm. Its eyes are missing. Its reptilian skin peels away like paper, exposing its stringy skeleton. She inspects it with both hands, then places it beside her plate of fruit. *I have several dead creatures,* she says. *I collect them.*

I look inside the cupboard. Two other crispy lizards repose by a tiny round nest of plant fibers sheltering a dead hummingbird. Back at the table, Carolina grabs a slice of cantaloupe with the bare hand she just used to touch the carcass. She places the fruit on her tongue. I realize then: nothing can make my grandmother unclean.

•

In the early 1990s, Carolina told Jeannette about a rape and a kidnapping—secrets she had never told anyone. My mother, with half-formed whispers, told me without telling me: my father was the child of those events.

I knew I had to ask Abuela for those details. My father's origins could help me understand why he ran away for so many years. My American education had taught me this: Behavior can be traced to biology or experience. Nature or nurture. Surely, Carolina's memories held the key to my father's mystery. But the prospect of interfering with my grandmother's composure paralyzed me with fear. She seemed so polished and impenetrable, in spite of her warmth. I procrastinated. My phone rang one day when I was writing in Mexico.

The caller ID said: Abuelita. I answered the phone. *"Bueno?"*

"I hear you're writing a book about the family," my grandmother said in Spanish. "You know how your father gets when he's drunk—he talks too much. He says you're afraid to ask me questions because you think I'm a private person. I'm just calling to tell you I have no secrets anymore. I am no longer afraid of the truth."

•

My grandmother holds her chin up, hands crossed in her lap as she sits on a chenille couch in her house in San Diego. She wears a flower-print blouse that shows more skin than usual—beneath her neck, around her clavicle, her skin looks smooth as silk. Behind her, on a plush pillow, a black-and-white miniature Chihuahua, Panda, watches me suspiciously, baring needle-sharp teeth.

I turn on my recorder.

"What do you want to know?" she asks.

"Everything," I say.

"There is so much," she says, sighing.

She looks up at a multitiered glass shelf of family photos. She has eighteen grandchildren and fifteen great-grandchildren. Most speak only English. She can converse with only a few, including me.

"Tell me about your first crossing," I say.

When she begins, her voice is immersed in the shrill songs of her *mil pájaros,* which sound like an endless shattering of glass.

•

The barbed wire between two steel posts lay trampled on the earth. Her father, Antonio, pointed at the mangled border fence. He wore an elegant beige suit and tie. *Allá,* he said, golden eyes squinting against the sun. Beyond alfalfa silage and maize fields lay the town of San Ysidro.

Carolina, fourteen years old, lifted her white skirt and swung one leg, then another, into *los Estados Unidos.* She followed her father and brother down a dirt path to the bus station, passing buildings in neat rows of congruous colors. The roads were flat and smooth, the sidewalks clean. Even the clouds seemed to hang higher here.

In a Los Angeles factory called Mission Pak, Carolina arranged fruit into baskets, which she decorated with red ribbon. Her father had told her she could keep her earnings. Her hands felt the buzz of a new magic as they moved on the apples, oranges and pears—somewhere invisible, these gestures were creating cash. The power was exhilarating. It was a welcome change from her domestic chores, which had no payoff save her mother's pride.

The Valenzuelas' fairer skin meant they could blend in with Americans, so long as they kept their lips sealed. But one day, immigration officials stopped all of the laborers as they left the factory and asked to see documents. Dozens, including the Valenzuelas, were corralled into buses for deportation.

Back in Mexico, Carolina felt giddy. All her life, her father had been disappearing to *los Estados Unidos.* That country was his unyielding obsession and sickness; it was why he was always absent. For the first time, Carolina felt she understood her father. She had gotten a taste of *El Norte* herself.

·

Carolina was a devout, introverted girl with that paradoxical beauty of mixed blood. Through generations, Spanish *conquistadores* had passed on arched eyebrows, *cacahuate* skin and an Audrey Hepburn nose. From her indigenous *abuelas,* she had inherited thick black eyelashes, dramatic earthy curves and a sensuous mouth. I look at photographs from back then. She strikes me as the most beautiful girl—the kind men go insane about, the kind artists immortalize.

Antonio wanted to keep her far and hidden from the lascivious eyes of *Tijuaneros.* One of her classmates, Ramiro, had recently had the audacity to knock on the front door, requesting permission to court Carolina. Antonio had chased him down the street, wielding an empty bottle of whiskey. He pulled Carolina out of school. Women in Mexico had acquired the right to vote that decade, but many people still considered their education a waste of money.

Generally, Antonio was an agreeable drunk, showering his children with compliments, coins, candy. He hired mariachis to serenade his wife. (*Great, now he's drunk again, that man,* said Maria de Jesus each time "Jesusita en Chihuahua" wafted in through the walls.) But the predatory lust of young men for his daughter provoked Antonio's murderous side.

Almost every summer since the onset of puberty, Carolina's parents had sent her to a ranch in Unión de Guadalupe, her mother's birthplace. Her *tías* wrapped lengthy pieces of cloth around her chest, flattening her breasts, and took her to church every day to recite catechisms. Carolina clutched her rosary, praying to the sinless woman with the sorrowful smile, La Virgen de Guadalupe. She loved the quiet, idyllic life in *el campo*. The town was accessible only by mule, and she looked forward to the daylong rides up the Sierra del Tigre. When it rained, she wore a thick cape of *hule*. She loved the pattering sounds of the skies on the material, the *canciones* of the insects.

Nearly everyone in Unión de Guadalupe was related to Carolina. Her older cousins bathed her in cold water from a bucket, making her scream, then giggled and spoiled her afterward, braiding her hair and telling her stories. Once, as her uncle saddled a mule to take her back to the city, she ran into the wilderness and hid behind the large blue leaves of a maguey plant, desperate to remain in *el campo*.

Other times, her parents sent her to Tlaltenango de Sánchez Román, where her father grew up. She stayed with Abuelita Juanita, a clairvoyant *curandera* who wore long white dresses. In the living room of her adobe house, her grandmother sat in a chair surrounded by candles, eyes shut, communing with *espíritus*. The townspeople formed *filas* at her door to buy healing potions and converse with their loved ones. Juanita was known as La Adivina. Listening to the voices of spirits, she located lost livestock and buried money. During her free time, she played songs of the revolution on her guitar.

In Tijuana, Carolina's classmates ganged up on her. They clawed at her arms and tore out her hair. Carolina wept timidly. When Carolina's little sister, Irma, witnessed an attack, she lunged like a lioness, scratching and sinking her teeth into flesh. *Don't worry, hermana,* she said. *They're just jealous of you.* Carolina was confused. She had felt envious of only one person in her life—her sister. Irma was the obvious favorite of their father. Antonio thought Irma was plain, and was charmed by this. *My poor daughter! Nobody is going to love this ugly thing,* he said, scooping her up. Irma had the ideal life, in Carolina's eyes. Irma had a playmate: an upper-middle-class neighbor who shared her tricycle, *muñecas* and other toys. Meanwhile, Carolina cooked and cleaned all day. She was in charge of the handkerchiefs and socks, which her mother loathed to touch. Her father's handkerchiefs were covered in viscous, clotted mucus, often so stuck to the fabric that she had to use a stick to remove it. Carolina fought her gag reflex for her mother's sake, scrubbing against the stone washboard.

Unlike Irma, Carolina had no friends except the girl in the mirror. When she was alone, she spoke to her reflection. Of course, she knew the girl in the mirror wasn't really a friend. But she liked to pretend. She called her friend Pandora, a name she had heard somewhere and liked.

•

Carolina's mother was born in Unión de Guadalupe in 1911, when the roads outside were red with revolutionaries' blood. Maria de Jesus clung to images of La Virgen that her parents promised would protect her. When she was a teenager, Plutarco Elías Calles, a black-eyed, fanatically anti-Catholic man with arched eyebrows and a cropped mustache, became president. He threw priests into jail and cut off their heads. In 1926, Cristero rebels in Jalisco launched a violent uprising in defense of the Church. The army came to Unión de Guadalupe on the Sierra del Tigre, a strategic base against the rebels because of its altitude. Maria de Jesus and her sisters were smuggled out of town by mule, curled up in corn baskets. Their father, Cidonio Arroyo, rode back a few days later to feed the cattle. He was shot and killed—among tens of thousands of victims of the Cristero War. His murder fueled the flames of Maria de Jesus's faith. She regarded La Virgen as the ideal role model for her daughters. If immaculate conception had been an option, she would have recommended it without hesitation. She decided to keep her girls ignorant of sex and reproduction for as long as possible. When Carolina began bleeding between her legs, Maria de Jesus wiped her tears away and assured her she was not going to die. It was a symptom of becoming a woman, that's all.

·

My grandmother neither smiles nor frowns as she recalls the past. She maintains her poise, as if posing for a painting. But the words that spill from her mouth are salty with tears and sweat and blood. Her voice quivers. It's not difficult for me to imagine her as a little girl getting her first period. She seems so young even now. But Doña Carolina no longer bleeds. She is a woman at her crux, the matriarch of a six-tentacled Mexican-American tribe. Her pubescent self couldn't have imagined her power. I think of what happened when Doña Caro's favorite Chihuahua, Habibi, went missing in the 1990s. She deployed all of her resources to recover the female dog. Her employees, children, grandchildren, nieces and nephews stalked all of the potential kidnappers—neighbors, other employees, friends of employees, relatives of employees, relatives of neighbors, friends of friends. They found Habibi at the house of Carolina's neighbor's maid's daughter, one of the suspects. A much larger dog had mated with Habibi repeatedly; she was pregnant and traumatized. Doña Carolina wept upon recovering the creature. It squirmed in her arms, whining as it licked her face. My grandmother did not bother to call the police. She did not threaten the kidnappers. She merely wiped her tears, raised her chin and wished them luck in Hell. A few weeks later, Habibi gave birth to one lopsided puppy. Abuela called it Mía.

·

Carolina was not yet twelve when she encountered a skinny girl with a shocking mutation: a gargantuan spherical tumor on her stomach, contrasting with gawky limbs. The sight disturbed Carolina. She was even more confused when, months later, she saw the girl again, slim as Carolina herself, cradling a bundled infant. The experience clicked only when a classmate confided that babies don't really come from *la cigüeña,* but rather from human stomachs. Suddenly, the mutation made sense: the girl's stomach was big because of the baby inside, and returned to normal once the baby was born. How the baby had emerged or entered the stomach, however, remained a mystery.

After Carolina had been pulled out of school, she regularly crossed the border with her father to work in San Diego and Los Angeles. She sewed dresses in an American woman's basement and swept the floors of an upper-class family. Her father merely wanted to keep her tucked out of sight—in factories, in offices, in the houses of elderly people—so she would be safe from teenage boys. But she worked happily. She loved the thrill of earning money at her father's side. When the United States launched Operation Wetback in 1954, work opportunities vanished there. Antonio found her a job in Tijuana, first calculating sums with a pencil for an accountant, then tying knots on chorizo for two Spanish-Mexicans who paid Antonio a commission to sell their meat.

The entrepreneurs, Mateo and Mario Perez, were born of Spanish immigrants in Mexico City. Mateo lived with his wife and three children in Tijuana. Mario was a restless widower, having married a fifteen-year-old when he was twenty-two and watched her die less than two years later of tuberculosis. In 1955, at age thirty-seven, he had green eyes, dark brown hair and a brooding, mysterious aspect. When he looked at Carolina—and he looked at her often—he seemed to be sharing a secret with her. She felt a strange, nervous feeling in her stomach.

One afternoon in Carolina's seventeenth year, Beatriz, Mateo's wife, knocked on her door to invite her to a family gathering. Maria de Jesus decided to give her daughter a break from domestic servitude. She knew the Perez family and trusted them. At the party, Carolina was received warmly, offered a chair and a cup of Coca-Cola with liquor in it. Mario Perez stood in a corner of the room, his eyes fixed on Carolina. She found herself blushing. For the first time, she became tipsy.

Mr. Perez approached her. It was too loud inside to talk. He asked her to follow him. They walked into the backyard. He helped her into the back seat of a car parked under a tree. He leaned forward, turned on the radio and spun the volume dial clockwise all the way. Then he threw himself on Carolina. At first, she kissed him back. The alcohol made her feel uninhibited, free, capable of being swept away by any current. But then the lightness dissipated like a dream. His embrace became aggressive, greedy. It startled her awake. She realized he was undressing himself. He pulled something from his pants that was terrifying to her because she had never seen anything like it. She had seen her little brothers nude, but their private parts were flaccid, small, inoffensive. This limb was alien and protuberant. She tried pushing Mr. Perez away. He pinned her down. She begged him to stop, but nobody heard her.

•

When Mario finished, Carolina sobbed. Her private parts hurt. She felt obliterating shame. Her instincts told her this was precisely what her parents had always wanted to protect her from. Now it had happened, and she felt it was her fault. The experience had planted in her a seed of knowledge, which expanded like a nuclear explosion. She saw, suddenly, how the mysteries of life were interconnected: the woman with the mutation, the symptoms of being a woman, rivers of blood pouring down her mother's legs as Maria de Jesus wept about a lost *bebé*. So that was how babies ended up in stomachs. That was how they emerged. Any minute now, her stomach would start to swell.

Mario told her she had to keep their deed a secret. What they had done was illegal, he said, because she was a minor and they weren't married. Carolina believed she had not only betrayed God and her family but also broken the law. *I can't go back to my house,* she thought, weeping. *I can't look my mother in the face.*

She was drowning in panic, grasping for help. Inside, the women of the Perez family comforted her as she cried. Beatriz reached out and took Carolina's hand. *Come with us to Mexicali,* she said. *In two days, we're leaving—you can head south to Mexico City with Mario, and get married. Then everything will be okay.*

•

When Antonio discovered his daughter was missing, he took her picture to the police. *My girl has been kidnapped,* he said. *I want the perpetrator castrated and imprisoned.* In the 1950s, Mexican law defined rape as sexual relations with any woman younger than eighteen who is "chaste and honest." The penalty was between one month and three years in prison, as well as a fine. But there existed a loophole: if the man managed to marry the girl, the penalty would no longer apply. The crime of kidnapping, punishable by up to six years in prison, could also be nullified by marriage.

Carolina was desperate to marry Mario. She believed that if she married him, God would forgive her transgressions. The couple sped south to Mexico City. They arrived at the cramped house of Fredesvinda Perez, Mario's mother. She was a tiny old woman with a cane, gray hair in a tight bun. A young Spanish immigrant, Ildefonso, had seduced her while she mourned near-simultaneous deaths: her son's, her first husband's, her mother's. She gave him four children: Mateo, a girl named Blanca, Mario and Mario's twin sister, Gildarda. Animosity toward Spaniards lingered after the revolution; the *capitaleños* attacked her children as *gachupines* for their fair skin and hair, even after Mario dyed his blond hair black in shame. The couple had to pull them out of school. Ildefonso taught his children to read and write. Then he flew away to Spain and never returned.

Mario's mother gestured at her cluttered home and informed the couple she lacked space. Mario took Carolina from stranger's place to stranger's place. They slept in slums, on cardboard and bare mattresses. Mario told Carolina to stay indoors—out of sight—until she turned eighteen, to avoid arrest. He disappeared for days, driving a green-and-white taxi. When he was around, he slumbered. Carolina rarely had anything to eat but bread. Her birthday came and went. Mario seemed to have forgotten about marriage. One evening, he waxed poetic about his alleged true love—a cantina owner in Veracruz who knew how to make love, compared to whom Carolina was "insipid." Carolina could think of nothing but her hunger.

Her stomach began to protrude as if by magic. When the couple moved into the small studio of Mario's twin sister, Gildarda, Carolina watched, ravenous, as Gildarda peeled a single banana for her three sons. She threw the peel in the trash and cut the fruit in three. Gildarda's sons eyed them with anticipation. She served each boy a piece. Carolina fought a savage urge to lunge at the table and stuff their bananas in her mouth. She watched the boys gobble up their dinners. The next thing she knew, she was leaning over the trash can, stuffing the banana peel into her mouth and devouring it like an animal. More than fifty years later, my grandmother recalls this moment and weeps.

•

I place my hand on my grandmother's shoulder, trying to root her back in the present. It's hard to maintain my grip; her body quakes. "Abuelita," I say. "Perdóname, we can stop." My fears are unfolding; I am doing violence to Doña Carolina's composure with my questions. But when her eyes settle on mine, they look fiercely aglow. She says: "No, I have so much more to tell you."

•

Carolina wrote a letter to her favorite aunt in Unión de Guadalupe, informing her she was alive and in good health, about to get married, with a baby on the way. The police arrived days later. They told Mario he was under arrest for kidnapping a minor. Mario protested: *I didn't kidnap anyone! She came voluntarily! Plus, she's eighteen now!* Mario locked his eyes on Carolina. She opened her mouth and said yes, it was true, she had come of her free will and she was now an adult. The police rolled their eyes. Carolina was a chaste and honest girl and Mario had corrupted her, they declared. In vulgar terms, Mario insisted that Carolina had been plenty experienced when they met.

The police handcuffed them and took them to jail. Within hours, they were released. Gildarda either paid a bribe or convinced the police that Carolina was neither chaste nor honest when she met Mario. *You have to marry the poor girl,* Gildarda told her brother. *I'm not going to help you next time.* She accompanied the couple to the civil registry, serving as their witness as they became husband and wife. Decades later, Carolina would compare the experience to "getting a vaccine."

•

The couple moved in with a friend of Mario's, Samuel, who had a one-bedroom apartment behind a family *panadería,* or bakery. Samuel's teenage daughter, a tomboyish girl named Timo, gave Carolina her bed. They became friends, sharing pastries and secrets. Carolina felt something akin to hope. She told Timo about her three-bedroom house in Tijuana, which sounded like a mansion to the younger girl. Timo urged Carolina to write her parents for money to travel back home. *Let's go there together,* she said. *Let's leave this pigsty.* But Carolina was sure her family would want nothing to do with her if they knew what she had done. She refused to send them a letter.

Mario started smoking marijuana. The drug made him paranoid. He punched and kicked Carolina, calling her a *puta,* accusing her of sleeping with Timo's father. He took her to Villa de Guadalupe, the site of the legendary La Virgen apparition that inspired natives to convert to Catholicism after the Conquest. He rented a room in a house full of strangers. Rats hissed in the hallways, scampered on the ceiling. At night, terror kept Carolina awake. Mario told her an old male tenant was spying on her while she slept. One night, she heard the bedroom door creak open. She lay paralyzed beneath the covers. Was it a rabid rat? The other tenant come to force himself on her? A dark figure moved into the room. The light flicked on. It was Mario. He looked lost. She tried to yell at him, but suddenly water erupted between her legs. Contractions seized her, so painful she couldn't breathe. She was only seven months pregnant. Mario carried her into his cab and slammed his foot on the gas pedal. As he drove aimlessly, drugged, he noticed a dingy wooden sign hanging from an apartment building, advertising a midwife: *"Partera."* He parked his car and pounded on the door. A middle-aged woman with a tangled mess of black hair threw it open and invited them in. She gestured at a twin-size bed. Carolina cried as the *partera* pulled filthy-looking metal instruments from a dusty drawer, then inserted the tools between her legs. The *partera* shook her head. *There's nothing I can do,* she said. She advised Mario to take her to the hospital. As they wheeled Carolina into an elevator, she lost consciousness.

•

Carolina opened her eyes. Gildarda was there. *You had a baby boy,* she said, gesturing at an incubator on the other side of the room. *They had to use forceps to pull him out of you.* Carolina tried to sit up so she could see. But the effort made blood stream out of her body. It bloomed on the white sheets, expanding like monstrous rose petals. She heard a voice call the doctor. Again, her world went black.

•

If my father had been born on time, he would have been a Sagittarius— a fire sign like his mother, an Aries, like me. But he was born a Libra, an air sign: ethereal, shapeless, transitory as the wind. I wonder out loud how much his early arrival affected his fate. Clinical studies have shown premature births are correlated with a higher risk of depression, anxiety and psychosis. *"No sé,"* Abuela Carolina says. *"No sé, no sé, no sé,"* she repeats, like a mantra meant to banish unwanted thoughts. But it would be wrong to blame my father's future turmoil on a single early disruption. He was far too resilient.

•

Carolina survived the hemorrhaging. Nobody believed her son would live. She could hold him in her palms. In the 1950s, the chances for such a premature baby were very slim—especially in Mexico. The doctors pumped fluids and nutrients into his veins, just in case. He fattened and elongated. Against all expectations, he grew.

Carolina called him Marco Antonio. He had his grandfather's golden irises.

After a few days in neonatal intensive care, his right eye swelled shut. He had contracted an infection from Carolina's birth canal. The eye was sticky with pus; the infection was spreading to his brain. The doctor explained, grimly and reluctantly, that he would have to amputate the eye—or else the boy would die. But first he would try a powerful antibiotic injection, just in case. If his eye improved immediately, he wouldn't need to operate. Within hours, Marco Antonio's eye cleared. He grew and grew.

The doctors let Carolina take him home. They prescribed medicine for her sexually transmitted disease, instructing her not to breast-feed until she finished the antibiotic. When Mario learned of the STD, he beat Carolina, saying it was evidence she was a whore. He claimed he had no symptoms of any STD, so it couldn't have come from him.

Decades later, Carolina remains confused about how she contracted the disease, hypothesizing it was from the dirty tools the *partera* used on her. "I don't know how else it could have happened," she says. "It is so strange." Her eyes are wide as she mutters these words, her mouth slightly open; she seems haunted by the mystery, as if a more sinister hypothesis has occurred to her, perhaps punishment from God for her sins. I inform her that men can have certain STDs, such as chlamydia, without symptoms. Her eyes seem lost as I say the words; she doesn't seem to hear me. "Seriously," I say, adding that I know from research as well as experience. My voice passes over her like the wind. It's disturbing. I realize I'm seeing how the unknown can travel through decades, permeating a body and keeping it in its grip. In her office at the Butcher Block, Doña Carolina punches numbers into a calculator amid crisp stacks of $100 bills. She balances the books. Each of her middle-aged sons depends on her. She helps pay mortgages, health insurance, meals, drug rehabilitation. But immersed in

1956, she is a helpless little girl. A solitary man slashed her so violently, he left her enshrined in scars.

•

When Carolina tried to breast-feed her son, she discovered that her milk had dried up. She knew this did not bode well for her son: she would have to depend on Mario for milk formula. Gildarda helped with cash and gifts. One day, her sister-in-law brought an old crib. Her three boys came with her. They looked green and shriveled and made strange hacking sounds. Gildarda explained they had *tosferina,* whooping cough. Carolina thanked Gildarda for the crib. But she was afraid it carried *tosferina.* She pushed it into a corner. Within a few hours, Marco's face reddened and swelled anyway. She cradled him and watched, panicking, as he convulsed. He coughed and coughed and tried to suck in a single breath. His features turned blue, his mouth twisting into a large *O* for oxygen. She sprinted to a medical center, where a doctor handed her a diagnosis, a prescription slip and a bill for the consultation. *I have no money,* Carolina said. *I just need medicine. Please.* The doctor turned beet red. She fled. She walked around the city, clutching Marco Antonio to her chest, beseeching doctor after doctor. Finally, a kind pharmacist donated antibiotics.

Gildarda came over with advice: she should sew her son a very tight shirt out of thick fabric to keep his ribs from breaking. Carolina did this. The straitjacket-like shirt held him together as he coughed. It took weeks for the medicine to kill the infection, but once more her son survived. When Mario returned from the streets, he gave Carolina some good news: they could return to the *panadería,* where the tomboyish Timo lived.

The two girls plotted Carolina's escape. *Your baby will die if you stay here,* Timo said. *You must go home. Your parents will help you.* Carolina summoned the courage to write them. When Antonio read his daughter's words, he shared the return address with his first son, Goyo, who lived in Mexico City. He asked Goyo to visit her with a message.

When Goyo arrived at the *panadería,* Mario had been beating Carolina. Mario had wanted to make love and she had refused. The apartment was crowded with people, and if they had gone into the bedroom, everyone would have known what they were doing. Enraged, Mario tore at her hair and pummeled her with his fists. She fled to the bathroom and locked herself inside. Trembling and crying on the toilet, she heard an employee from the *panadería* say through the door that her half brother was outside. She splashed water on her face, fixed her hair, straightened her skirt and went to greet Goyo with a smile. She hadn't seen Goyo since she was a child. *Look at my son,* she said, holding up Marco Antonio. *Isn't he handsome?* Goyo praised the baby and informed Carolina that her parents wanted her back home.

This information lifted a crippling weight off her body. She realized she was free to leave Mario. She was not only free—she had a moral obligation to leave him, to save her son's life. Timo was right. Carolina started stealing money from Mario as he slept. She hid the money behind a curtain, and Timo added her own store of cash. The next time Mario beat her, Carolina fled to Goyo's with her baby. But in the morning, Carolina woke up to find dozens of bedbugs feeding on her son. She slapped and swatted the critters off. Red bites swelled all over his skin. Carolina returned to the *panadería*, but she feared she was running out of time. Her son seemed cursed to die in the capital.

Timo showed her the total sum of their money. It was enough for a single bus ticket to Guadalajara—where Carolina's aunt Lydia lived. From there, she could find a way to Tijuana. Early one morning when everyone else was asleep, the two girls said teary-eyed goodbyes. Carolina hopped on the bus, cradling her son. A second child was swelling her stomach. She cried as she sped away; her babies would grow up without a father. The few good memories of Mario flooded her brain, as they often do in moments of parting. Although Mario never changed a diaper or helped bathe Marco Antonio, he had often tried to teach his son what things were called. She remembered how Mario had cradled Marco Antonio in his arms, his face filled with wonder as he pointed out the moon and said its name: *Luna. Allí está la luna.*

MATERNITY

"Abuelita, you said Mario's eyes were green," I say. "Were they like mine?"

I had long puzzled over my eye color: seaweed green with yellow around the pupil. My grandmother searches my irises. I see a tremor in her mouth. She looks away.

"I don't know," she says. "It was so long ago. I can't recall."

"But they were green?" I ask.

My grandmother meets my gaze again. "Yes," she says, and takes a deep breath. "They were like yours."

•

Back in Tijuana, Carolina discovered that her father was sick. While Antonio was grooming horses for a wealthy family in northern San Diego County, his employers had noticed his chronic coughing, which stopped only when he took drags on his cigarettes or fainted. They persuaded him to stop working. Maria de Jesus took a job as a live-in nanny for the wealthy family's neighbors. Carolina's return was convenient. She adopted her mother's role, cooking and cleaning. Not then, nor ever, would her family press her for information about Mexico City. Carolina could tuck the details into a corner of her brain and never revisit them again. And that's exactly what she did, until half a century later when I asked her to tell me her story.

She bought meat daily; the family lacked a refrigerator. In a corner store on Calle O'Campo, she ordered steaks and chorizo at the *carnicería* counter. A pale young man with wavy black hair chopped the meat. He was burly, with a thick bull's head. Standing under the fluorescent lights, his face looked almost translucent, like a ghost. He smiled at Carolina and her baby. *What a cute boy,* he said, and introduced himself as Jesus. He made her uncomfortable. As Carolina browsed the store's vegetable section, Jesus followed her with his eyes. By now, she was aware of her looks, of the effect she had on men. She was careful not to encourage Jesus, responding in a flat, indifferent tone.

In December, her second son came into the world, healthy and on time. Carolina named him Alejandro. He looked just like his father, with the same blond tresses Mario had possessed as a child. But he was angelic, innocent, hers.

Carolina started making long, stylish dresses with an old sewing machine an aunt gave her. The neighborhood ladies brought piles of fabric and made custom orders. Carolina charged a dollar apiece and asked the women to spread the word. She was a strong girl with a solid capacity to forget, but still the world around her was a man's world. The number of dresses she could produce while preparing meals, sweeping floors, washing dishes, doing laundry, folding clothes, dusting surfaces, shopping for produce, bathing babies and changing diapers was negligible. Alejandro started regurgitating her breast milk. She had to ask her brothers for cash to buy formula. They were often out seducing women or sleeping in late. One morning, Carolina waited anxiously for Antonio Jr. to awaken. Noon came, and she grew impatient. She shook him awake. Red-faced with uncharacteristic fury, Antonio Jr. cursed at Carolina as he seized his wallet and hurled coins in her direction. They fell with plunks to the floor. *You're a parasite,* he spat. She picked the coins up off the floor, miserable and humiliated.

The December after Alejandro's birth, Carolina stopped by the *carnicería* to buy steaks. Jesus asked about her New Year's plans. She gave him the obligatory curt smile and told him, in a bored tone, that she was making dinner for her family. *What about after? I have a car. We can welcome the New Year together someplace scenic.* Carolina looked at him. Was he crazy? Not very smart? The last thing she wanted was more children. She learned to sew more quickly. Her toddlers waddled toward her, tugging at her skirts, longing for their mother's touch. But as soon as she finished sewing, she had to sprint into the kitchen to make dinner. She ignored the boys, growing tenser with each cry and poke. Sometimes, she lost her temper and yelled at them. She sent them across the street to collect coins tossed into the sky during baptisms at the church. She told them to use the coins to buy candy. She had to spoil them somehow.

•

Marco Antonio and Alejandro were near-opposites. Marco had brown hair, walnut-colored skin and the full lips of his mother. He was observant, sensitive, quick to tears. Alejandro was as pale as a Spaniard, his hair more bleached each day. He was carefree and mischievous. He never cried when he injured himself, and he injured himself often. Carolina let his wavy white locks grow long like a girl's.

One day, Carolina's brothers offered to take everyone to the cinema. Marco started sobbing for no apparent reason. Carolina was unwilling to forsake this once-in-a-lifetime opportunity. *Go ahead and cry,* she said. She followed her brothers out of the house with Alejandro in her arms, leaving her crying boy alone in the house.

When they returned, the front window was shattered. Marco had smashed it with a shoe in a claustrophobic panic. He sat on a wooden bench down the street, palms bloody, staring straight ahead, tears drying on his face. Marco stopped crying after that. He started sleepwalking. At night, as he dreamed, he often walked to that same bench—the one where his tears had stopped flowing. Carolina always knew where to find him if he went missing in the night. He remains a sleepwalker as I write this.

●

At work, Irma had met a Mexican man named Pablo. She urged Carolina to consider the butcher. *You should accept the* carnicero's *invitations,* she said. *That way, Papi will let me go out with Pablo.*

No sé, Irma, Carolina said.

Andale, it will be fun, Irma said. *You don't have to kiss him or anything.*

Jesus drove them to a drive-through restaurant. When Carolina mentioned her mother's work as a live-in nanny, he offered to pick her mother up on Fridays. Maria de Jesus had the weekends free, but didn't have a car to travel back to Mexico. Jesus obtained visas for himself and Carolina at the consulate, then drove them across the border with Carolina's two boys in the back seat. He let Carolina roll her window down. Wind in her hair, she turned to look at her sons. Marco Antonio and Alejandro slept peacefully, unaware they had made their first crossing into *los Estados Unidos.* Carolina felt exhilarated, the way she did when she was surrounded by nature in *el campo.* In spite of the asphalt here, this place was sprawling, and she could see the sky.

They arrived at a mansion in Rancho Santa Fe. A blonde German woman opened the door. *Mi casa es tu casa,* said Mrs. Roland-Holst, taking Carolina's hands in hers. The house was a labyrinth of cavernous rooms and halls. Outside, Maria de Jesus was playing with two angelic blonde girls amid rosebushes and chubby trees. They were fluent in Spanish, thanks to their nanny. Marco Antonio and Alejandro played with them.

Jesus drove Carolina there every Friday. He started taking her sightseeing on Sundays, his only day off. They went to La Presa, the city's main dam, and to the plazas to buy churros and ride a Ferris wheel. Carolina began to look forward to these outings. Jesus seemed to accept her as a friend. Perhaps he felt a kinship. His own mother had tried to raise him and his sister alone. In the early 1900s, Ramona Guzmán, a freckled eighteen-year-old redhead, had fallen in love with a married merchant named José Guerrero. Ramona bore him two children—Jesus and his little sister, Consuelo—but Mr. Guerrero refused to leave his wife. Heartbroken, Ramona migrated to Tijuana with her children to find work. She married a construction worker, Francisco Maldonado. He padlocked the windows and forced her to sleep naked, to keep her from slipping away to have nocturnal affairs. He beat his stepson without mercy or reason. Ramona bore him four biological children, hoping his new children would distract him. He used Jesus to provide for them. Francisco put Jesus in charge of a herd of goats. Jesus watched the herd behind the house, adjacent to a stretch of border without barriers. The goats crossed into the United States to devour wheat and vegetables, and sometimes Jesus played marbles— his only toy—to pass the time. One day, he looked up from his game to discover some gringos loading his goats onto a truck. He ran toward them, heart bucking in his chest. The men informed Jesus they were confiscating the goats for damage to U.S. property. Francisco nearly cracked Jesus's skull with a hammer. Streams of blood poured down the boy's face as Ramona begged Francisco not to kill him.

But Jesus did not resent his stepfather—he respected him. When he was twelve, he helped him build bungalows on the Rosarito coast. Francisco secured Jesus a job at a *carnicería* mopping floors, scrubbing toilets, preparing chorizo using a special recipe the owner taught him: California pepper, chili powder, cumin, onion and garlic powder. Jesus gave almost every cent to his parents, saving a small percentage for a shoe-shining business. He bought a brush, shoe polish and a footrest to earn extra pesos on weekends.

One day, at the age of seventeen, Jesus was sweeping the sidewalk in front of the *carnicería* when a drunk pedestrian shoved him. Jesus lost his temper and punched the man. The blow knocked him unconscious. The owner of the *carnicería* witnessed the impressive force of

Jesus's fist. He encouraged Jesus to enroll in the city's amateur boxing league. Jesus was reluctant; sports appeared to be a waste of time. But his boss insisted. Jesus agreed to try. He proved to be a natural fighter. His skull seemed tougher than steel. He won municipal championships, then accumulated trophies in states across the country, competing on weekends he could afford to travel. They called him *El Chivero*—the goat man.

Ramona was begging him to abandon his destructive hobby and start a family when Jesus met Carolina. From his last boxing matches in faraway states, Jesus sent Carolina postcards with short, straightforward messages: "All is going well for now, many hellos, tomorrow I start the championship."

•

Carolina was in the kitchen, as always, when a ceaseless honking perturbed her. She wiped her hands on her apron and threw open the front door, planning to tell the noisy driver to have respect. She froze. Across the street was the father of her children. He was slamming his fists on his *claxon*. She thought she was going to faint. She couldn't make her lungs expand to breathe. *Ven,* he hissed. Come. She found herself taking steps toward his green-and-white taxi, pulled by a monstrous magnetic force she feared she could not fight. She stopped and asked: *¿Qué quieres?*

I want to see my sons, he said. Carolina walked into the house with newfound strength. She scooped her sons into her arms, and asked her brother Jaime to follow.

Why did you bring that mocoso?

Oh, did I offend you? Goodbye then.

Carolina turned on her heel. She heard him scrambling out of his car. She clutched her boys against her hips. Jaime sprinted ahead. They ran through the front door, slammed it, locked it. She leaned against a wall as Mario pounded on the door. She was no longer a prisoner. She was free. She was free.

•

As Abuela Carolina recalls these moments, she refuses to use Mario's name, calling him *El Hombre Que No Voy A Nombrar*. The Man I Will Not Name.

●

When Carolina told her father about the incident, Antonio drove to the address of his old business partner, Mateo, Mario's brother. Days later, a divorce was finalized in civil court. A judge ordered Mario to pay Carolina the equivalent of about ten dollars a week in child support. When he came over to deliver the money, he parked on the opposite side of the street, forcing Carolina to cross to collect it. Once, he tried to drag her into his car. Carolina screamed and slapped, fighting back for the first time. She returned to the house disheveled and out of breath. Her father asked what had happened. The next week, Antonio marched outside to greet the taxi driver with a knife in his fist. He dragged Mario out of the cab, placed the edge of the knife against his gut and informed him he would be more than pleased to kill him if he returned. Carolina never saw him again.

●

One afternoon, Carolina's neighbor Margarita came over to help her cook. *Jesus is giving rides to some other girl*, she whispered. *I've seen him do it.* Carolina felt startling indignation. *He picks her up across from the* carnicería *after work sometimes. Let's go catch him.* They hid under a shady awning near the corner. *That's her!* Margarita said, pointing at a made-up brunette. Jesus pulled up next to the girl. She crawled into his vehicle. They kissed passionately. *How disgusting*, Carolina said. *Hurry, let's pass in front of his car so he sees me. Let's see what he does.*

Elbows interlocked, the girls passed quickly, but it was as if time had slowed. Jesus looked up. His eyes met Carolina's. His face contorted. He stumbled out of the car. Shouted her name. Carolina kept walking.

That night, music wafted in through the walls. Everyone looked at Antonio. But Antonio hadn't hired a *serenata*—he was sober. Irma went to the door. *It's for you, sister! It's the butcher!* Carolina stood up, mortified. Jesus was standing in front of the mariachi with a bouquet of flowers in his hands. *Carolina, that girl you saw me with means nothing to me. I was afraid to admit it before, but I love you. I want you to be my wife.* She shut the door in his face.

Jesus came back the next day to speak with Antonio. Jesus told him he was willing to provide for Carolina's two sons. He asked Antonio for his blessing. *He's a good man,* Antonio told Carolina. *He works hard and he takes you seriously. Why not marry him? You need help.*

Her father's words convinced her, once and for all, that she had been fooling herself. She couldn't provide for her children alone. She was a woman.

Jesus suggested the civil registry. The thought of once again marrying in such an informal way, outside of the church, made Carolina cringe, but she shook this feeling. *I'm not entitled to a ceremony,* she thought. *I don't deserve to wear a white dress.* The next morning, the couple went to the civil registry with Antonio as a witness. They signed a piece of paper dated December 6, 1960. Jesus was chopping meat at the *carnicería* again less than an hour later.

•

Carolina changed her sons' last names and told them to call Jesus "Papá." Marco was four and Alejandro was two. For years, they would believe Jesus was their biological father. She obtained a birth certificate for Marco that said he was born in Tijuana, legally erasing his past in Mexico City. Jesus found an apartment across from the *carnicería*, with a single bed and a sofa. *Where will the boys sleep?* Carolina asked. *On the sofa,* Jesus said. This was not the upgrade she had imagined for her sons. But she didn't want Jesus to think she was ungrateful. She kept her lips sealed. Quickly, the friendly mood of their relationship altered. Jesus forbade her from going out without him, even to her mother's. He was at ease only when she was in sight. She was ruled by fear of her dependence; he was ruled by fear of her beauty. Carolina had married him to devote more time to her sons. But she had to make lunch for Jesus and his three brothers separately every day. They took turns crossing the street in bloodstained aprons. Each wanted his food to be hot. Each wanted company as he ate. Carolina cooked first for one, then the other, then the other. One often cracked open books. His food would cool and he would request that she reheat it. She found herself with less free time than ever.

•

As she nears eighty, Abuela Carolina has a housekeeper, Julieta, who works part-time, cooking and cleaning. But in the evenings at around 7:30 p.m., after working all day in the Butcher Block, Carolina must serve Jesus his dinner. It is their custom. She pours the *frijoles* and *tinga de pollo* that Julieta has made onto a plate, heats it in the microwave, places it in front of her husband. She doesn't sit down until he has finished, in case he needs anything: more juice, another serving of beans, a slice of cake for dessert. He wants his *maíz* tortillas to be fresh, so she must walk over to the stove every so often to warm up another. She dines only when he is done. It doesn't matter how tired she is from counting money all day. *"Lo tengo que atender,"* she explains.

•

In 1961, at the age of twenty-three, Carolina became pregnant with Jesus's first child. Jesus sought to drown his insecurities in alcohol. At night, he went out to gamble and play cards. He returned reeking of tequila, stumbling over the furniture.

In November, Carolina's father walked across the border to see a doctor in San Diego. She and her mother went to visit him a day later, not realizing how sick he was. Antonio glared at them. He looked colorless, corpse-like, bloated as a frog. *Que ingratas,* he croaked. The two women tried to cheer him up, but he was inconsolable. He coughed up blood and pus. Carolina went back to Tijuana. The next day, Jesus answered the phone at the *carnicería.* He walked across the street to tell

Carolina her father was dead. She fell to the floor, remembering his last words to her. Her water broke as she mourned. Carolina's first child with Jesus was born two days later: Jesus Jr., or Chui.

One night, as she breast-fed Chui, she realized she had nothing to feed her older boys. Jesus had not come home after work. She poured coffee grounds into milk and fed them the mush. The next day, Jesus still hadn't returned. A storm raged outside. They were out of milk and everything else. Carolina closed Alejandro's small fists around a dollar she had saved from the sale of a dress. She told him to buy milk and bread. As Alejandro ran in the storm, the wind tore the bill from his hands. The darkness swallowed it whole.

Carolina started smoking cigarettes. She had quit making dresses when she married Jesus, determined to devote herself to domesticity. Now she made several. Carolina planned to spite her husband by looking more beautiful than ever. She would fuel his insecurities on purpose. She took driving classes. She obtained her driver's license.

Jesus became violent. *Don't you realize how lucky you are to have a husband?* he cried. He punched Carolina and threw furniture at her. Carolina defended herself by hurling dishes. Jesus directed his anger at Marco and Alejandro, too—whipping them with his leather *cinturón*. Most of the time, he acted as if those two boys didn't exist. Carolina relied on her mother, Maria de Jesus, for money to buy clothing and shoes for Marco and Alejandro. Marco began to suspect that Jesus was not his biological father, and asked his mother to tell him the truth. She refused.

At a family gathering, Jesus didn't like the flirtatious way Carolina said goodbye to a male cousin, referring to him as *papasito*. He charged at her like a bull. Marco Antonio stood up to block Jesus's path. His stepfather hurled him across the room with a single arm. Then he turned toward the crumpled boy. Carolina screamed, scrambling to defend her son. *Run,* she hissed. Marco stood in time to sprint past the drunken Chivero. Jesus stumbled outside, but the boy had disappeared in the darkness. Marco slept on a dirt road in the cold, curled up, hiding from his stepfather—as Jesus had, once upon a time.

Carolina bought anti-pregnancy ovules and inserted them inside herself two or three at a time. She dreaded having any more children with this volatile man. But when he caught her using contraceptives, he started taking her by force when she least expected it. She got pregnant again.

•

Marco Antonio led his brothers on mountain expeditions, searching for snakes and tarantulas to place in empty jars. He built things for his siblings—wagons, chests, slingshots. He lassoed a wild horse in the desert and brought it back home. Carolina watched her son galloping on the stallion. Marco was growing into such a curious, self-sufficient boy. He had lost his fearful nature. He was different from other children: pensive, inventive, intrepid, but also full of love. He regularly told his mother he appreciated her. She sat with him as he did homework, determined not to let his intelligence go to waste. *You must do well on your exams; you must not let me down,* she said. He nodded. *Cuentas conmigo, Mamá,* he said, his face totally serious, as if he understood the gravity of her command. She walked him to school, ignoring the frightening men who whistled at her.

•

Two days after the birth of the fourth child—another boy, Miguel Angel—Jesus launched his own *carnicería* in northern Tijuana. Jesus's mother, Ramona, insisted that Carolina participate. Carolina stayed up all night conducting inventory as her newborn screamed against her chest. Ramona informed Carolina the couple would move to a warehouse behind the new *carnicería*. Carolina awoke each morning to work at the shop, just as Jesus returned from drinking to sleep. His siblings took pesos from the cash register and beers from the refrigerators. When she told her husband, he accused her of attempting to sow discord. Ramona complained about her "bad attitude." Carolina's brother Joaquin came to visit in a fancy convertible he had purchased in San Diego. He had a green card and was working in *El Norte. Come with me to the old house. I'll help you.* She threw her scant belongings in her brother's vehicle and hopped in with her sons.

Jesus came and begged forgiveness. He bought a house in La Mesa, a new neighborhood on Tijuana's rural outskirts, far from the *carnicería*. It was a wooden shack with a single bedroom. It lacked water, electricity, even a toilet. Carolina felt she had won the lottery. It was miles from the matriarch Ramona and the chaos of urban life. And it was *hers*. For the first time, she had her own space in which to breathe. It reminded her, just a little, of Unión.

•

Carolina kept overdosing on contraceptives. She got pregnant a fifth time. Aimee, a girl, was a novelty. Carolina and Jesus kissed and cuddled her. She was the only child they both felt safe caressing. Jesus developed a remarkable capability: no matter how hungover or intoxicated, he woke up at sunrise to work. Jesus abandoned the family *carnicería* and launched his own in La Mesa, selling milk and canned goods in addition to meat. Jesus's hope swelled, and with it, his ambition.

He put Marco Antonio, age ten, in charge of the cash register. Jesus scrutinized racetrack records with a friend in the back of the store, marking up booklets with a pencil. The Agua Caliente resort was famous for its 5-10 betting option, with a prize of up to $100,000 for selecting the winning horses for the fifth through tenth races. Jesus always went for the 5-10, picking numbers on half-page slips that track employees checked by hand and stamped. One day, after the races, the two friends gaped at each other in the grandstand. They had guessed every winning horse in order. They were rich! All their problems were solved! Jesus couldn't wait to tell Carolina. Stumbling toward the register to claim their money, the two men checked their pockets for their winning slip. Which of the two friends had it, again? Where had he put it? Neither could find it. Neither ever did.

Marco Antonio watched as the merchandise at the *carnicería* dwindled. People arrived for beans; there were no beans. They wanted tortillas; the tortillas had run out. Clients stopped coming.

Carolina started plotting a move to the United States. She wanted to earn U.S. dollars in San Diego like her brothers, the way she did as a teenage girl. She flirted with the idea of taking her children away from Jesus. She was hearing stories about successful female breadwinners. In 1967, she took the bus across the border for a job tailoring men's suits. After a few days, she was able to hire a nanny with the money she earned. When the tailoring factory closed, she washed clothes at a laundry facility.

Jesus continued to take his anger out on his stepsons. In the summer, Carolina bought Marco Antonio and Alejandro plane tickets to Unión de Guadalupe. She felt they would be safe there while she worked. Marco Antonio wrote her a letter in July 1968, in Spanish:

> My beloved mother,
> I am here at aunt Lydia's house. I am well. Every day I wake up at 6 in the morning and we go to church. . . . We came to Unión on a very long road. . . . Alejandro sometimes pees [the bed] but he almost hasn't anymore recently. . . . I don't have anything more to write to you.
>> Marco Antonio who adores you.

My grandmother keeps his letters in a royal blue chest in her closet. She shows them to me. They are perfectly preserved amid pictures and postcards. Marco informed her about his adventures in *el campo*, of salamanders in streams and creamy milk straight from cows' udders. On torn fragments of paper, he included two- to three-sentence messages for his half siblings, promising bags of candy if they behaved well with *nuestra mamá*. His handwriting is neat, with clear curves, randomly alternating between capital and lowercase letters, expressing joy in tracing the shapes of the alphabet. His handwriting was identical to my childhood script.

"He was so sweet back then," my grandmother says. "He changed as a teenager."

"Why do you think he changed?"

"I don't know," she says. "He's always been serious. How can I say . . . he was different. He had brilliant ideas. I think he's traumatized because . . . because he lived a false life. Because I lied to him about what kind of a family he was from. Maybe that's why. I made a mistake."

"Is that what he tells you?"

My grandmother's lip trembles. She tells me that when she tried to hug my father a few days ago, he shrugged her off angrily and asked why she bothered to touch him now that it was too late. *"No sé. No sé. No sé,"* she says, her eyes filling with tears. "I feel a solitude that is so . . ." She stops, because she can't continue. We return to the couch, and she begins again with the old story.

•

Autumn came, and Carolina sent for Marco and Alejandro. She had saved enough money to install running water in the house. When a perfect stream first gushed from the kitchen faucet into her hands, she was so happy that she let out a shrieking laugh. She washed the dishes in ecstasy. Inspired by Carolina, Jesus started working at a *carnicería* in Los Angeles, then another in San Diego. He added a room to the house. For the first time, the Guerreros began to experience luxuries.

In 1969, Carolina went to the consulate to apply for a green card. She asked the Roland-Holst family for a recommendation letter, which she included in her application. Carolina was granted legal status months after the United States became the first country to send men to the moon. The lunar landing had proved that *el sueño americano* had no earthly limits. She requested permanent residency for her children, taking advantage of the Immigration and Nationality Act, which allowed family reunification. Carolina and her children stood in a neverending line in the hot sun outside the U.S. consulate in Tijuana. She had dressed them in the nicest clothes they had. Marco Antonio had a gaping hole in his sock and complained that the sidewalk's heat was seeping through his shoe and burning his foot. Alejandro lost consciousness. His skull hit the concrete with a crack. Carolina cried out and kneeled beside him. Alejandro woke up, dusting himself off, insisting he was fine. Inside the consulate, a woman at the desk shook her head. If they wanted visas, the man of the house needed to be present.

A few days later, Carolina found out she was pregnant again. She would now need to migrate not five children but six. *Please, God, let me have this last child and no more,* she prayed. Her sixth child was a boy they named Joaquin.

•

Abuelita celebrates her birthdays with mariachis. Listening to the trumpets and guitars, she claps her hands and sways. A beautiful smile illuminates her face. I filmed her once, backlit by the sunset in an ocean-view Tijuana condominium she purchased, surrounded by men singing in charro outfits. She is radiant in a beige suit, wearing a pearl necklace. She has a list of songs she asks them to play: "Cielito Lindo," "Guadalajara, Guadalajara," et cetera. But her favorite is "La Ley del Monte" by Vicente Fernandez. The Law of the Mountain. In the song, a man describes carving a woman's name on a maguey blade, interlaced with his own. When the woman falls out of love, she cuts off the maguey blade. The man is not disconcerted by her action. He knows something she doesn't: the maguey plants in their desert are enchanted. "I don't know if you'll believe the strange things my eyes see," Fernandez sings in Spanish. "Perhaps you'll be amazed—the new limbs that bloom on the maguey carry the carvings of our names."

•

The teeth of Carolina's children tell a cross-border tale. All of my father's molars are missing. Marco was losing teeth as a teenager. Carolina couldn't afford toothpaste back then, let alone fillings or root canals. Friends merely tore out his troublesome teeth. Alejandro and Chui are missing about half of their molars. The three youngest siblings, raised largely in the United States, have mostly healthy teeth.

The family migrated in 1973. They escaped Mexico just as its economy suffered the blow of a global oil crisis. Carolina had decided not to leave Jesus after all. She felt her efforts to migrate alone had been thwarted by God because He did not want her to break her vows twice. She prayed Jesus would stop drinking. The Guerreros moved into subsidized housing in southern San Diego—everyone except Marco, who at the age of seventeen dreamed of becoming a surgeon in Mexico. In the United States, the family's apartment had a boiler. Her children enjoyed the opulence of warm showers for the first time in their lives.

Marco's medical school dreams failed to materialize for reasons he preferred not to discuss with his mother. He followed his family across the border, moved in with them and began working in the shipyards. One night, he awoke sweating and sobbing. He had had a terrible dream. He was certain, somehow, that this dream had been more than just a dream. He had seen into the future. But it was all blackness, melting blackness. It was so horrible it was inconceivable. Carolina found him in bed, shaking and weeping. He tried to put words to what he had seen: *All I know is that it was the future, and that it was the worst thing, it was so traumatizing,* he told her. Carolina believed in premonitions; her grandmother had peered into parallel worlds. She took her first son to a *curandera* in Tijuana. Carolina didn't much trust that woman; she had read Carolina her fortune and said: *I see you surrounded by piles and piles of one-hundred-dollar bills. Money, money, everywhere!* Carolina had walked out laughing. Clearly, the woman was deranged. But she didn't know of anyone else. Perhaps she could give her son a cleansing?

The woman took one look at Marco Antonio and shuddered. *He has the veil of death over his soul. I have to tear it down, but it is going to be very, very difficult.* Marco Antonio refused. Her fee seemed absurdly high; he was convinced she was a con artist. He was determined to transcend the darkness on his own. He started meditating. He read

Eastern philosophy books. He kept stacks of notebooks, writing thoughts and queries. He told his siblings he was shutting himself up in his room to drift to another dimension. He warned them not to disturb him and bring him back into his body. He disappeared for weeks on solo camping trips, taking a homemade survival kit into the mountains.

In 1980, Carolina spotted a small filet-mignon supply shop for sale in downtown Chula Vista. She suggested that Jesus take a look. He purchased it, following Don Roberto's advice. The meat came from local slaughterhouses in halved, juicy carcasses hanging from metal hooks. In red aprons, Jesus, Alejandro, Chui and Miguel chopped the bloody meat by hand. Marco Antonio was busy at the shipyard from 7:00 a.m. to 3:30 p.m., but came in the evenings and on weekends to help. Jesus prepared chorizo with the recipe he had learned as a boy. The wealth of the Robledos and the Guerreros exploded in tandem. Carolina, in charge of payroll and accounting, purchased her own car. She found herself surrounded by piles and piles of $100 bills.

It was more money than she knew what to do with. In 1980, Carolina obtained a license from the California Social Services Department to operate a foster family for abused children. But the orders at the Butcher Block mounted so quickly that she had to start assisting with deliveries—dozens in a day, sometimes as far away as Escondido. Carolina picked up Aimee and Joaquin from school, then drove her meat-loaded car to restaurants. She was forced to give up foster care. Don Jesus continued drinking prodigiously, grasping the flask of liquor in his pocket with bloodstained hands. He was polite and attentive with customers, but it was not unusual to find him passed out on the floor after hours. One evening, Miguel—or perhaps it was Chui—kicked him as he lay drooling. *Eres una desgracia,* one of them said with disgust. That's all it took: the contempt of one of his biological sons. Jesus quit drinking cold turkey.

Marco Antonio counseled Jesus to invest in German slicing machines, which could slice in twenty seconds what hands sliced in five minutes. His brothers found it humanly impossible to finish chopping in time for the afternoon deliveries. They were taking methamphet-amines to work faster in the near-freezing temperatures of the plant. When the USDA shut down the Butcher Block, Jesus asked Marco Antonio for help building the new one. My father agreed.

The business had grown so lucrative that when Carolina drove by a home-construction site with ocean views, she stopped and asked to see the blueprints. She made an appointment to return with her husband. *The houses look so beautiful,* she told Jesus. *But I'm sure we can't afford them. They're $250,000.*

The gringo real estate agent sighed when he saw the Mexican couple, who could hardly speak English. *We don't have more terrains,* he told them, enunciating each word as if speaking to children. *Just this one, and it's the most expensive one: $300,000.*

Jesus, in his broken English, asked the man why that house cost more money than the others. *Because of the oh-shen veeh-you!* the man cried. *It's too ex-pen-sive for you, the best oh-shen veeh-you!*

Jesus turned to Carolina. *If you like it, we'll buy it.* She brought her hands to her face. He turned toward the real estate agent and informed him that he could make a down payment of $100,000—he had that in the bank.

●

Abuela Carolina's lovebirds go silent in the evening. My grandmother stops talking, and we stare at each other for a while.

"How difficult it all was," I say, finally. "But you achieved so much."

She sighs slowly. *"Ay mija,"* she says. "I don't know if it was worth it."

Carolina pauses, then continues: "It was so much working, working and working, day after day. And at the end of life you ask yourself, why? For what? What was the value of everything I did, if I did not experience my children, if I could not enjoy them?"

Her children have not lived the happy, healthy lives she wanted for them. In the late 1980s and early 1990s, as the Butcher Block became a multimillion-dollar enterprise, allowing her to buy properties on both sides of the border, she thought for sure the American dream was real, that *los Estados Unidos* had made all of her sacrifices worthwhile. But most of her children struggled with vices. All divorced or remained single; each still relies on her and her husband to some extent. Doña Carolina dreams of retiring, of traveling to *el campo* and walking amid maguey plants, inhaling the smells of wet *tierra,* forgetting her troubles. But Jesus has no plans to retire—he needs to move, move, move, constantly, to avoid thoughts, to chop and package meat until he drops dead. And he needs Carolina. No one could fill her role. Jesus doesn't trust anyone else with the Butcher Block finances.

"I'm roped up, I'm really chained," she says. "If I say I'm not going to work one day, the next day I have to stay double time."

My father tells her she has oceans of blood on her hands because of the Butcher Block. Countless slaughtered pigs and cows. My grandmother wants to be rid of the business as soon as possible. She has begged Jesus to sell it. Jesus refuses.

"Why don't you just retire?" I ask. "Who cares if they need you? Let them deal with it. You should be enjoying the fruits of your labor. Taking vacations."

Tears well up in her eyes and she begins to cry. She shakes her head. "Let's go outside," she says. We walk into her backyard to watch the sun dipping into the ocean. The backyard is a mess. Two years ago, Papi offered to renovate Abuela's backyard: installing drip irrigation, a new fence, a garden and a drain in the cage of her *mil pájaros* to make it easier to clean. He knows how much she loves *el campo* and wanted to create a little piece of it in her San Diego home. Abuela could have hired a team of renovators, but she was touched by her son's offer and agreed. He tore her backyard to shreds, digging deep holes, pulling down an old fence, creating mountains of soil. Her backyard became cluttered with tilling machines and piles of fertilizer. Papi did and undid and redid everything, unhappy with anything that was less than perfect. He succumbed to depression after depression. "That's how he is: he progresses, then he slips backward—*no sé por qué*," she says. "At least the fence ended up so beautiful, so lovely." Solar-powered lights adorn the vinyl posts. The fence is made of tempered glass, providing a view of the Pacific Ocean, resisting the force of strengthening winter gusts.

•

I receive a text message from my mother: "Carolina is going to be admitted to the Sharp hospital for chest pain I let you know more details as soon as I have them." I call my grandmother. She is in the emergency room. She hasn't told anyone where she is except her daughter, Aimee, and my mother. She doesn't want to give Jesus a heart attack. I speed to the hospital. Abuelita lies in a dark room, not a strand of scarlet hair out of place. Her nails are French-manicured. Her makeup is perfect. But her lids hang low on her eyes. She smiles and grimaces when she sees me. I don't let myself frown or express concern; she is almost shaking with fear.

"*Dios me dijo que me quiere,*" she says, her voice a little girl's.

"God does love you," I say. "You're going to be just fine, Abuelita."

Suddenly, she says: "Have I ever told you about my accident?"

"What accident?"

"The one on the bicycle. When I was fifteen," she says. "I think I forgot to tell you when you were interviewing me."

"Tell me now," I say.

Carolina was fifteen, riding a bicycle a neighbor had lent her. The wheel jolted against an object on the street. She found blood in her underwear when she came home. She wasn't menstruating.

I know why she is telling me this. "You didn't bleed when Mario took your virginity, did you?"

She shakes her head.

"I didn't bleed the first time, either," I say. "It's normal." I search her eyes and am relieved to find relief. I tell her about my first time, wondering what kind of secrets the world is whispering—about mirrors and mortality, about the womb that makes the bodies coursing with blood that cycles and cycles.

·

A catheterization clears up her clogged artery. My father persuades her to become a vegan with him; he has decided it's the healthiest diet. Doña Carolina, co-owner of the Butcher Block, stops eating meat, against the protestations of some of her other children. Marco brings her powders and potions, prescribes minerals and vitamins. He makes green smoothies and cooks delicious healthy meals. Her knees, which previously hurt all the time, stop bothering her. The pain in her stomach vanishes. She becomes more beautiful still. "Your father would have been a great doctor," she says, her skin aglow. *"No sé por qué no lo hizo. No sé. No sé."*

Part III

Hola, Jeannette
espero estes bien.
Yo tambien.
Saludame a todos.
Te aprecia, Marco

Jeannete

AIRMAIL

BANGKOK

THAILAND

เด็กชาวเขา
YOUNG HILLTRIBE, NORTHERN THAILAND.

ภาพ : จตุพร ... / Photography : Jatuporn ...

TC 689

HOUSE OF RAZORS

My father informs us he is fine while in Thailand.

WICCA

Mommy took me and my sister to the torn-up condominium in 2000. I was eleven. Electric wires spilled from the walls. The sticky, mutilated floor smooched our shoes. The wine-colored carpet of my early childhood was still in place on the stairs, marred by hard black cigarette burns. I touched it. A sense of well-being flowered in me, a tactile echo of the past. I removed my shoes and socks and walked upstairs, trying to summon dead days with my feet. A layer of ash covered everything. Cigarette stubs floated on the dark yellow water of the toilet. My mother called me from the kitchen—she didn't want us wandering here alone. She advised me to put my shoes back on.

Papi was missing, possibly dead. I had no clue why Papi had damaged the condominium like this. I had learned not to ask questions about him. He was a forbidden subject. The kitchen was filthy with grease and stacks of dirty plates. My sister and I helped our mother wash silverware, scrub counters, flush toilets, fill trash bags. We placed our father's things in boxes: notebooks, silverware, electronic gadgets, clothing. Papi's brothers picked them up. My mother hired a company to re-install the carpet and repair the walls. Abuelita Carolina paid for a new electrical system. When the work was done, my mother sold the condominium.

That year, I marred my straight-A record with a B in history. I was in sixth grade.

I had finally accepted that stories in books were distinct from reality. But reality was dreadful, so I decided to manipulate the fabric of the universe itself. Magic. I looked up spells online and purchased books like *True Magick: A Beginner's Guide*. I aimed to master the witchcraft of my childhood fairy tales. I knew better than to believe in goblins and mermaids and fairies, but my research had taught me that witches did in fact exist—Wicca was a religion, just like Catholicism.

My first act of magic was innocent: a strength spell. When I couldn't open a jar of pickles, I simply invoked the power of the earth, the wind, et cetera, and voilà, opening the jar would require a mere flick of my wrist. I was eager to show off this power, and whenever somebody had trouble taking the lid off anything—a gallon of Gatorade, a jar of Jif—I would rush to the rescue and say, casually: *It's a magic spell I know.*

Then I used witchcraft to improve my grades. I repeated a magic rhyme at the start of each test: *Earth, wind, fire and sea / As I say so mote it be / On this test I take today / I shall receive no less than A.*

It worked. My ambitions grew. I had learned no boy would ever like frizzy-haired, pimply me of his own volition. I decided to bewitch a brunette named Matt, one of the few boys who did not make gagging sounds when chancing upon my face. Once, he told me I was "not repulsive," which nearly made me faint with glee. He had full, heart-shaped lips, a retroussé nose and small, tan hands I longed to touch.

I lacked a silver goblet as required by the spell, but I figured one of my mother's wineglasses would do. I filled it with water and set it on my bedroom floor. I lit three red votive candles. I closed my eyes, visualized Matt's beautiful face and read a chant from one of my magic books thrice. Then I blew out the candles and took my "goblet" outside, to be charged overnight by the waxing moon. The next morning, I drank the magic water.

Matt kept his usual distance in class. But in the evening, he called to ask about homework. I answered his questions, then clutched the cordless and closed my eyes, bracing for the inevitable *buh-bye*. Instead, he said: "So . . . what's up?"

A dam came crashing down; my history poured out of my mouth. I told him I feared my father was dead. I had recurring nightmares of his corpse in a Mexican alleyway. I recalled a time when my father lived with us and everything was great. Matt told me he understood; whenever his parents were sick, he got sad. If one of them were missing, he would be devastated. He told me to call him any time I needed to vent. *I can't*, I explained. *My father is a big secret in my family.*

Matt remained distant toward me in class, but started calling me regularly. One weekend, he asked me to accompany him and his friends to the movies under a questionable pretense: *Eric's mom says we can only go to the movies if we bring a girl.*

I was ecstatic. My spell had worked. I was gaining control over the world.

•

I cast no spells to find my father. Abuela Carolina hadn't heard from him in months, and was considering filing a missing-person report. But Mommy had told me to forget about Papi. With an ache in my chest, I avoided numerous magic rhymes for locating "lost objects." On a subconscious level, I probably feared that if I used them, I would discover that my spells were a fiction like the Animorphs or fairy tales.

•

I started reading a Ruth White book, *Belle Prater's Boy*, about a girl named Gypsy whose aunt vanishes without a trace. Desperate to unravel the mystery, Gypsy interviews her cross-eyed cousin, Woodrow.

Woodrow tells her about a Jalal al-Din Rumi poem his mother read and reread: *The breeze at dawn has secrets to tell you. Don't go back to sleep. You must ask for what you really want. Don't go back to sleep. People are going back and forth across the doorsill where the two worlds touch. The door is round and open. Don't go back to sleep.* A crevasse opened in my chest. It didn't hurt. It radiated a warm, buoying light. I thought: *Papi crossed the doorsill where the two worlds touch.*

•

Mommy convinced her parents to leave Puerto Rico and move in with us. Abuelo Coco had diabetes, and Dr. Del Valle wanted to supervise his health care. She razed the pomegranate trees in our backyard for a second master bedroom. The roof of the addition rose higher than our living room sun window, decreasing the amount of light that could enter our house. *Please behave yourselves,* our mother begged me and Michelle. But this was impossible. The Cocos had concluded my sister and I were intolerable when we were cute little girls. Now we were ugly, hormonal, metamorphosing pubescents. If we drank milk in the afternoons, the Cocos called us *viciosas* (full of vices). If we watched any television show besides *Caso Cerrado,* a Spanish-language version of *Jerry Springer* that they loved, we were *malditas* (wicked). If we giggled, we were *mal-educadas* (poorly educated). If I spoke to Matt on the phone, I was a *guarra* (loose woman).

One day, I came home from school to discover that my spell books were gone. Of course I thought Abuela Coco was to blame. But my mother informed me it was she who had stolen them. *Why would you do this to me?* I sobbed. *Because you're inviting Satan into the house,* she said. *Witchcraft is against God.*

I was horrified. I thought that because Wicca allowed for both a god and a goddess, it was a mere expansion of our Catholic faith. My mother corrected me: if I kept dabbling in witchcraft, Lucifer himself would come. I renounced Wicca just to be safe. But I believed that if anyone had brought Satan into the house, it was the Cocos. In the span

of a few weeks, they were sapping my mother of her essential sweet-
ness. It drained from her eyes, from her smile.

A vast cultural chasm precluded pleasant cohabitation with the
Cocos. Michelle and I never made our beds, never washed the dishes,
rarely even put our plates in the sink. My mother had never asked us to
do anything besides succeed in school. I was a top student. I spent my
free time reading and writing. I considered myself the ideal daughter.
The Cocos' accusations made me feel I was the victim of a grave injustice. Perhaps it made sense for them to attack Michelle—she had B's
and some C's on her report cards. But why *me*? In the face of their
complaints, I talked back to the Cocos with self-righteous rage and
conviction. The deteriorated state of my Spanish made it impossible to
express the purity of my intentions with the eloquence I perceived in
my preadolescent imagination. The more I defended myself, the more
the Cocos attacked, which made me still more indignant, to the point
where I was slobbering as I screamed. *That's her father's blood in her,* the
Cocos told my mother. *Not yours, Jeannette. Not yours.*

•

I awoke in the middle of the night, gasping. I had perceived the secret
of life in my sleep: it was the reason why humans exist, the reason why
suffering occurs, the reason why death should not be feared. I stumbled to my desk, grasping for a pen and paper. I could feel the dream
evaporating from my memory. I had to write it down. I had to write it
down before losing it completely. I shoved aside books in quest of a
writing utensil. I couldn't see in the dark. By the time my pen touched
paper, all I could remember was: *Something About Mirrors.* I scribbled
those words and underlined them. I turned on the light and looked in
the mirror. I told myself never to forget.

•

Michelle and I received a letter in the mail. On blue-lined notebook
paper, a person purporting to be our father told us he was okay, not to

worry about him. It was full of misspellings and incorrect conjugations and awful grammar. It was nearly illegible. I informed my sister there was no way the author could be our father. Papi spoke excellent English. He was a reader of literature. His handwriting was always very neat. I told her my hypothesis: the person who had written the letter was our father's murderer. He was trying to make sure we didn't hire a search party. The letter served as confirmation of our father's death. Papi would never return.

•

One of my first real friends, Elizabeth, introduced me to a new fantasy book series: Terry Goodkind's The Sword of Truth, about a young man, the Seeker of Truth, who must save the world by asking the right questions. A boundary that separates a country of humans, Westland, from a country of magic creatures, the Midlands, is breaking. Magic creatures are spilling into the human country. They're fleeing an evil warlock, Darken Rahl, who's massacring them all in his quest to rule the world. The last surviving Confessor, a long-haired woman who extracts truth from people with a mere touch, escapes the Midlands. A handsome woods guide rescues her from three assassins. It turns out the man is the Seeker of Truth, spoken of in prophecies. Together they decide to fight Darken Rahl.

Elizabeth made me feel better about my long, ugly hair, telling me it meant I was like a Confessor. In the Midlands, only Confessors have long hair—a sign of rank. In school, I was bullied relentlessly for my hair, a waist-long, rat-colored cloak, which my mother forbade me from cutting or coloring because she did not want me to "sexualize" myself. I spent all my free time inside the Sword of Truth fantasy series. It made more sense to me than life. I mined the pages for wisdom I felt starved of at home and in school. Each of the books explored the wizard's rules of life. The Wizard's First Rule is: "People are stupid. They believe things mainly because they either want them to be true or fear them to be true." I thought this held the key to the Cocos. I never fathomed it could apply to me.

●

A decade later, seeking to fill in my memory blanks, I wrote Elizabeth, asking if she remembered what—if anything—I had told her about my father when we were kids. We hadn't spoken in years, but Elizabeth responded with surprising detail:

> I remember always assuming that [your father] had either passed away or that your mom had divorced him; either way, I detected that he was not someone you talked about in your family and that there was some sort of negativity surrounding him. The only mention of your dad I remember was once we were in some part of your house and I saw a picture of you and your sister in something like little flower pots (or were you dressed up like flowers?). I asked about it, and you said your dad took the picture. I still remember that because I was really surprised at you mentioning your dad, since I knew absolutely nothing about him. You said somewhat wistfully that he was really good at photography when he was around "back then." It seemed like you missed him, but I somehow felt like I shouldn't ask more about him.

One of my favorite wizard's rules from The Sword of Truth is: "To ignore the truth is to betray thyself."

●

My sister was spiraling into a deep depression. She dressed like a goth (thick black eyeliner, black-and-gray plaid skirts and chains), attended screamo concerts, read Satanism books. The bullying she endured was relentless. Her grades provided no solace. She fantasized about going to public high school, where the more diverse student body might accept her. She ceased studying, sabotaging her chances of getting into the Bishop's School, the private high school in La Jolla my mother wanted us to attend. "As a child, I always felt abandoned," she wrote in an essay I found decades later in my mother's garage. "I sat in my backyard until the sun went down, I sat there until my eyes felt like they were bleeding, I just drew and drew and drew. . . . Raising myself was tough." She gave up drawing, convinced she was no good. She surrounded herself with older punk rockers, dropouts and drug addicts who felt a similar emptiness. She started smoking cigarettes.

My mother clung to me, with my top grades, my obsessive adherence to the rules. *You have to be valedictorian,* she whispered. When I brought back A-minuses, she nearly cried in disappointment. My breathing became shallow from the tension in my diaphragm, which made it hard to expand my lungs. I needed all A-pluses and A's to make up for that B in sixth grade—I couldn't afford to let Mommy down. If I failed to secure the valedictorian title, I feared she would conclude that giving birth to me and my sister had ruined her life. Each time my teachers handed back tests, I became pallid, my hands quivered, my coronary movements felt like angry animals. My physical reaction was so apparent and so predictable that my classmates began to mock me: *Jean is going to cry, isn't she? Jean is going to have a heart attack; look at how she's shaking.* They knew I was going to be the valedictorian or salutatorian—it was between me and my crush, Matt, who, as the effect of my love spell faded, had fallen in love with a pretty classmate. One day, as I compared our report cards at the end of class, Matt told me to hurry—my hands were trembling and I was having a hard time calculating and contrasting our number of A-pluses versus regular A's versus A-minuses—and finally, he tore his report card from my hands and vanished. I burst into tears. A beautiful Mexican girl who rarely spoke to me stayed behind. *Don't cry!* she said, and hugged me. I sobbed in her arms, grateful for her unexpected kindness. I hadn't been touched comfortingly in what felt like centuries. I said: *But Matt's going to beat me at valedictorian and my mom is going to yell at me.* She patted my head. *Ay, it doesn't matter; you'll still get billions of awards,* she promised. I cried harder.

I wrote a poem that night: "I probably can't even win / Every B is like a horrid sin / I can't take a breath / Sometimes I'd prefer death."

•

Every day after school, I typed for two to three hours in my online journal, recording every innocuous detail of the day. I wrote almost nothing about my father, obeying my mother's commands. I vented about the Cocos. After dinner, I locked myself up with my Sword of Truth books. Mommy began insulting my writing and reading, saying I was doing so obsessively, like a "sick person." When Michelle returned from partying at dawn, Mommy directed her anger toward me. *Why aren't you guiding her, the way a big sister should?* She had no control over Michelle. So she turned against me. I twisted my knees and my elbows and fingers, trying to distract myself from her voice with pain. I dug my nails into my wrists until they were covered in red, bumpy scratches. I longed for my mother to notice the harm I was causing myself. But she persisted. She thought I was, like her, unbreakable.

•

Papi rematerialized. The news that he was still alive came from Abuela Carolina. I felt a ticking in my head, a static in my chest. I had grown accustomed to the idea of my father as dead. If he was dead, he wasn't willfully ignoring us. This belief had become a sinister source of comfort. Now I was scared again. What did his resurrection mean? Was he the same scary man we had traveled with to Mexico? Or the magical father from long ago, who had taught me about the horizon and the sea?

Our mother took us to see him. He was staying at Abuela Carolina's house, in one of her guest bedrooms, after traveling through Mexico and Europe. Michelle and I knocked tentatively at his bedroom door. Our hearts thumped. Sweat gathered on my sternum. The door opened, revealing a disheveled figure in the dark. *What?* he asked. A pungent wave of cigarettes and armpit odor emerged with him. It provoked in me a familiar mix of longing and despair. Michelle stepped forward to hug him. I stood paralyzed, unsure of myself. He patted Michelle on the head, his back straight and stiff. He retreated before I could touch him.

My mother told us he was Schizophrenic. I capitalize the word because of the disproportionate significance it took on for me. The word solved everything. Suddenly, I had an explanation for why my father was always absent. It wasn't because he didn't love me. It was the involuntary consequence of a chemical imbalance in his brain.

I became obsessed with Schizophrenia. But it was also terrifying. The disease, Google said, was genetic. Did this mean I was destined to become Schizophrenic as a grown-up? The word "schizophrenia" derives from the Latin *schizo:* to split, to divide, to cleave. The Abuelos Cocos constantly said I was "behaving badly" because of my Mexican blood. Meanwhile, my classmates called me gringa. My Americanness came from my mother, who spoke English with a Puerto Rican accent and criticized my gringa habits. I felt cleaved to pieces. I did not know what I was.

·

In the summer of 2001, at around 3:00 a.m., I awoke to spinning red lights. I looked through my window and saw an ambulance in the driveway. I walked downstairs, trembling. *Abuelo Coco had a drop in blood sugar,* my mother said. *Go pray.* He had suffered a stroke. He didn't recognize us when we visited him in the hospital the next day. He threw up and choked on his vomit. Abuela Coco pried his mouth open with her fingers. Abuelo Coco got better, but then he got worse. In August, his toe turned black. Surgeons cut it off, but then the blackness infected his foot. They cut off his foot. The blackness invaded his legs.

·

In eighth grade, when Matt and I were comparing report cards, he said: *Remember when you had your hair short in sixth grade? It looked nice. You should cut it again.*

I begged my mother, for perhaps the hundredth time, to let me cut my hair. My friend Elizabeth was no longer around to make me feel good about it. Her parents had sent her to an all-girls boarding school on the other side of the country. *Give me one good reason and I swear I'll never ask you again,* I implored.

Because I like it, my mother said.

Oh, that's a great reason. Because you like it, I have to be miserable.

She was in the kitchen preparing a salad with Abuela Coco. My intemperate tone provoked my grandmother. She lunged at me with the knife she was using to chop lettuce. *Irrespetuosa!* Abuela Coco hissed.

I retreated from the knife. *Oh my god, you're insane!*

My mother wiped her hands on a kitchen rag, rolling her eyes. *No, Jean, you are,* she said. *If you want to cut your hair, go live with your father. While you're under my roof, you have to follow my rules.*

I felt a wave of anger surging from the floor through my head. I screeched: *Bitches!* Abuelo Coco stood from his wheelchair, stumbled toward me, and slapped me on the mouth. I was shocked into silence. His slap was soft, almost a tap, but the unexpected nature of the action, the effort it took, sent a clear message: I was a bad, worthless girl . . . in spite of all my studying. *Tienes que respetar a tu madre,* he said in his deep voice, his eyes crinkled and watery, containing in them all the pain in the world. I burst into tears. If sanity was the Cocos, I decided, then sanity made no sense. For the first time I could remember, I felt allied with my father.

•

I have found one of the crossroads: it is here that Papi's absence reached maturation in me, and began to bear fruit in my body. How common is this crop. Eighty percent of single-parent homes are empty of the father. The disadvantage for the son is obvious: he lacks a role model. For the daughter, the damage is harder to define. It is refractory: The daughter sees her single mother slaving away, weighed down by love and duties. She is the girl's model, her future: toiling and tired and trapped. The absent father's magnetism lies, in part, in the contrast he represents. He is not tied down by anything. He has a freedom and a power she covets. Slowly the girl becomes aware of the borders of her female body. She begins to erase them. She conjures the absent father in herself.

•

My mother learned she had once more failed to pass her internal-medicine board certification exam, despite our prayers. I realized the God of Catholicism was a fiction—like the Animorphs and like the Confessors in The Sword of Truth. I had no need to fear the wrath of Lucifer. I informed my mother I was a Wiccan. When she protested, I argued it was my constitutional right to practice the religion of my choosing. I needed to arm myself against the Cocos. I opened my jew-elry box and retrieved my old Animorphs necklace, a silver square pen-dant with an emblazoned A. Using water and candles, I repeated the following spell thrice: *I cast a spell upon this item thrice, to protect me through my daily life. Earth, wind, fire and sea—as I say so mote it be.*

I slipped it over my head. Immediately, I felt the buoyancy of a pro-tective orb. I curled up with my latest Sword of Truth book and mate-rialized inside the Midlands, where the Seeker of Truth was hacking away at cackling evil creatures. Abuela Coco's screeching brought me back to the suburbs. *Ya está la comida!* I touched my necklace with a smile, knowing I was safe. But as I walked downstairs, I tripped. Pain shot up my knees and elbows as I crashed against the marble floor. Purple bruises bloomed like monstrous roses on my joints. I had never fallen down the stairs before. It was a curse from the spirits, a warning: the supernatural was not my realm. I took off my necklace and wept. Not even witchcraft could save me.

•

Papi invited Michelle and me on an excursion to Tijuana. We were sure Abuela Carolina had talked him into it. Every time we visited him, he greeted us with vexation—if at all. We ate lunch at a seaside Mexican restaurant filled with free-flying birds in nervous silence. On the beach, a man with a sombrero held a group of skinny horses. Our father asked, in an unexpectedly chipper voice: *Do you girls want to go horseback riding?* I had wanted to ride horses since I was a little girl, a symptom of my fairy-tale diet. We climbed onto three horses. Michelle was scared, so the *caballero* assigned her his most tranquil steed. A group of drunken teenage tourists scrambled onto the remaining horses. We followed the *caballero* along the shore. Suddenly, my father broke his horse into a gallop with a holler that sounded like *Hya!* As if afraid of being left behind, all of the horses bolted after his, except my sister's, which dragged its feet. I lost my stirrups. People screamed. An intoxicated tourist toppled off his mount. At first, I was terrified. I bounced violently in the saddle. But as my horse's stride lengthened, it became loping and smooth. I understood, suddenly, that all I had to do not to fall was not be afraid—I had to move with the horse rather than against it; I had to incorporate its power into my body. The wind lashed my face with particles of the sea as I pursued my father. My horse's hooves splashed in the waves. I felt like the young warrior, Atreyu, galloping through Fantasia in *The Neverending Story.* We were racing through the Swamp of Sadness, too buoyed by adrenaline to sink. Papi pulled on his horse's reins and spun it around. He saw me coming. As my horse slowed bumpily, I thought, with horror, that I was going to fall right in front of my father. I moved as best as I could with the horse as it halted. I stayed in the saddle. Papi said: *You're a natural.*

•

A few days later, I awoke in the middle of the night. My bed was shaking. I was unsure if it was an earthquake or demons. In my journal, I described it this way: *I was really scared and then I like, FELT, not heard, but FELT this voice that wasn't really a voice saying but not really saying . . .* "It will pass" in a reassuring way. I felt a wave of calm and fell back to sleep. In the morning, I walked downstairs. Abuelo Coco was watching the television from his wheelchair. I saw a plane flying into the World Trade Center in New York City. It was September 11, 2001. The apocalypse had come. Real-world villains weren't Yeerks or black-magic wizards. They were terrorists.

•

At night, Abuela Coco snuck out of her room into the backyard and tapped on the sliding-glass door of the living room to scare me and my sister while we watched television. It was pitch-black outside, so we couldn't see her out there. We scampered out of the room, limbs everywhere, bloodcurdling screams. The tapping started happening regularly. We told our mother about our psychopath stalker, but she just rolled her eyes. She said we were imagining things, we were "being Schizophrenics," like our father.

•

On September 20, I was in bed reading The Sword of Truth, envisioning myself as the Confessor galloping bareback into war. My mother threw open my door. Her lips were taut and pale; her eyes seemed too wide for their sockets. It was a new expression that was becoming familiar to me, but it made her unrecognizable as the soft, sweet mother of Paradise Hills. She sniffed. *You've been smoking in here, haven't you?* I gawked. She might as well have accused me of orchestrating the 9/11 attacks. *Mom, can't you see I'm reading?* She shook her head. She said, with disgust: *It's the marijuana, isn't it!* She stared right through me. *Look at this mess. You can't even clean your own room. You need to see a psychiatrist. You're Schizophrenic, just like your father.*

•

A few years later, in high school, I wrote a paper on self-fulfilling prophecies. One of the founders of sociology, Robert K. Merton, coined the term. A photograph shows a white-haired man with a friendly face and prominent forehead. In his 1948 article "The Self-Fulfilling Prophecy," he boils it down to this: "The self-fulfilling prophecy is, in the beginning, a *false* definition of the situation evoking a new behavior which makes the originally false conception come *true*.

The specious validity of the self-fulfilling prophecy perpetuates a reign of error. For the prophet will cite the actual course of events as proof that he was right from the very beginning."

How strange and sinister, the power of fear—the way it's rooted in love.

SELF-FULFILLING PROPHECY

Mommy was turning into Mom. She was harder than her previous incarnations. She had taken off my father's engagement ring a decade ago, but her fingers were covered in metal: her Service Corps ring, medical school ring, university ring, high school ring. I no longer craved her touch. I felt displaced by her body. When she looked at me, her eyes demanded so much that they seemed to vacuum up my strength. I could feel her in my breath, in my sweat. Her anxiety was in my chest, her disappointment in my teeth. We knew each other's phases and imperfections as if from the inside. My father, in contrast, was a mystery. A question mark. I pondered Papi like the riddles in The Sword of Truth. I was eager to unravel him. I thought of him as enlightened, rejecting the world because the world made no sense. I hoped he would come to my middle school graduation.

I got into the Bishop's School in La Jolla, the neighborhood where my mother had wanted to live when she first came to San Diego. The tuition was astronomical, and she would have to drive me forty minutes north and south every day. But nothing mattered more to her than my academic success.

At my middle school awards ceremony, Mom watched from the pews of the chapel as the principal-priest—a former actor who looked like a lean, handsome Santa Claus—introduced the valedictorian and salutatorian honors. He went on for what seemed like thirty minutes, with a booming voice and theatrical gestures, about how *close* the competition had been this year, how our class was the biggest eighth-grade class in the school's history, how because of that there would be *three* winners instead of *two*. I tried not to throw up. The priest claimed he had done a bit of research and discovered a third-place award for rare cases like this one: a triusian. Immediately, I knew he had made the word up. I was sure I would be the recipient of his fiction.

"And the triusian is . . ."

My mouth dropped open when I heard the name. *Matt?* Matt looked around with a confused expression, shrugged, then walked up to accept the award. The priest cleared his throat to announce the next award. "And the salutatorian is . . ." I closed my eyes and tried to still my pounding heart. "Jean Guerrero!"

I walked up, my legs shaking with nerves and relief. *At least I'm not the triusian,* I told myself. *At least I can commiserate with Matt.* I shook the principal-priest's hand and took my medallion. The final announcement came as I walked back to my seat, avoiding my mother's gaze. The valedictorian was one of the Mexican boys who tormented me, one of the meanest bullies, whose father was an important person in Tijuana, later assassinated by members of a drug cartel. The middle school coordinator had repeatedly told us he was in the running for valedictorian, but I hadn't believed her—I had seen a C and multiple B's on his report cards.

I was relieved to discover, after the ceremony, that my mother was not mad at me. *It's not your fault this school is full of* corruptos, she said, lip raised in repugnance. Other parents and classmates came up to me and said they knew I was the *real* valedictorian. I shrugged off the whole thing. So long as my mother wasn't disappointed, I didn't care. For all I knew, the Mexican boy really was the best-performing student. Perhaps I had imagined the bad grades on his report cards because of my bitterness about his bullying (he called me "ugly" more than any-body else, stabbed me with sticks and kicked soccer balls at my head for refusing to let him copy my answers on tests). While writing this, I didn't think it was fair to include this scene without asking for the boy's version of events. I found him on Facebook and wrote him a friendly greeting. He responded with a friendly greeting. When I explained why I was writing, the boy (now a man, of course) stopped respond-ing. I followed up several times, to no avail. To this day, I don't know what to believe. Was I blind to the intelligence of another child who toiled in silence? In the grand scheme of things, it was a silly middle school contest. It served me well to lose. I learned that nothing—no matter how badly you want it—is owed to you.

•

During the graduation ceremony, in my salutatorian speech, I thanked my mother and endeavored to inspire my classmates with platitudes. My voice shook. My braces were visible with each word. Stiff curls cascaded down my back. When I watch the video of the ceremony today, I feel a motherly sympathy for the girl I was in that long white dress: voice so breakable, hands quivering with a need to please. Papi didn't show up until after the ceremony, when the school videogra-pher had stopped recording and everyone was filing out of the pews. I recall seeing him enter the chapel with my Gucci-clad Abuela Caro-lina. He looked gaunt, in a simple black suit and his own camera around his neck. Suddenly, I could see no one but him. I gasped. *Papi, you're here.*

•

That summer, I persuaded my mother to let me start horseback-riding lessons in the hunter/jumper style. Mom agreed to pay for them if Papi agreed to be my chauffeur. I hopped into his passenger's seat, delighted by the situation. I sighed and slumped, trying to act fed up with the world—I wanted him to view me as a kindred spirit. But right away, I noticed his fiery eyes discerning the flaws in my performance.

Like Mom, he saw right through me. Unlike her, he wanted nothing to do with me. My hopes deflated. I should have known: he was driving me to the barn because Abuela Carolina had ordered it. He declined to watch me ride.

I rode every day except Mondays, when the ranch was closed. Papi drove me to and from my lessons, mostly in silence. When I started at Bishop's, he picked me up from La Jolla and dropped me off at the barn. I learned to jump and started competing in county shows. Mom noticed how much I loved riding and, after discussing it with my paternal grandmother, asked what I preferred on my fifteenth birthday: a *quinceañera* or a horse. Abuela Carolina agreed to pay for either. My mother would pay for board and feed. For my fifteenth birthday, I received Aspen, a bay mare with a white star on her forehead and a milk mustache marking. She was a Thoroughbred and quarter horse mix, with round dappled haunches that shone red in the sunlight.

I asked Papi if he wanted to see my horse. *No thanks,* he said. I was a teenager who guzzled Pepsi, listened to pop music and taped magazine pictures of male celebrities to her wall: vapid and typical, not at all the brilliant daughter he had envisioned when I was a curious toddler. Worst of all, I was the most spoiled person he had ever known. One day, when I was bragging about all of the first-place ribbons I was winning, he erupted: *Yeah, yeah, you spoiled brat.* Then he launched into a red-faced monologue describing all the ways in which I was shallow, spoiled and selfish. I was the most privileged individual in the history of our bloodlines, and had done nothing to deserve it. His vitriol sent me into a catatonic state of confusion.

Not everyone has Schizophrenic fathers, I wanted to say. *Not everyone has mothers who use those fathers as a weapon against them.*

But I remained silent. The months passed. The tensions of the unsaid accumulated. He offered to give me driving lessons in an empty parking lot. Every movement I made provided an excuse to attack me: I was stupid, distracted, lazy. A sudden rage awakened in my body as I wondered what gave him the right to criticize me. I shouted: *You're a nobody!*

Only a few days later, Papi was gone again.

This time, he told his siblings where he was going: Southeast Asia. He sent a couple of postcards from Northern Thailand—one for my mother and one for his parents, both to my grandmother's house. The one addressed to my mother pictured two grinning Thai children. In Spanish, Papi wrote: "Hi, Jeannette. I hope you're well. I am well. Say hi to everyone. He who appreciates you, Marco." I didn't see Papi's postcards until I was in my late twenties, looking through old documents in a dusty chest at my grandmother's house. Abuela Carolina either never delivered them to my mother or she told her about them and my mother declined to take them. My sister and I would remain ignorant of his whereabouts for two years. Again, we wondered if he was dead. I wanted to ask my father for forgiveness, but I had no way to reach him.

•

I obtained my driver's license. My mother bought a minivan and gave me the keys to her BMW. I started driving myself to Imperial Beach, just a mile north of the U.S.-Mexico border. I threw myself into the cold waves, buoyed by the vastness, by the act of surrendering myself to the turbulent water. I purchased a bodyboard and rode the waves. At my new school, things had changed: I used to feel like the smartest girl in class, but at Bishop's, *everyone* was smart. I started getting B's on my report cards. At Bishop's, all of the students seemed not only brilliant but rich. They lived in mansions in northern San Diego County, with spray tans and Chanel perfumes. I was one of only two people who commuted from Chula Vista. In middle school I had been called a gringa. At Bishop's, I was essentially an immigrant. I looked forward each day to the barn, the one place I felt I could excel. I dreamed of an equine career, a life dedicated to taming beasts.

•

My mother's father was dying. Both of Abuelo Coco's legs were amputated. He was in the hospital more often than at home. Reduced to a mere torso, he begged his daughter to let him die. But she refused. She purchased a hospital bed, monitor, IV, catheter and more to nurse him at home, where he could be more comfortable.

Meanwhile, her list of grievances grew: she complained about the B's on my report cards, about my sister's increasing delinquency, about my costly riding lessons, about the danger of my hobbies. Whenever I had a bad fall at the barn, resulting in a concussion or a limp, she threatened to stop paying for my lessons. Whenever I went bodyboarding, she told me I was going to drown. I started interrupting her monologues with high-pitched, maniacal giggles or singing at the top of my lungs, trying to shock her into silence. I no longer let my mother hug or kiss me. If she tried, I recoiled in disgust, feeling smothered. She wasn't happy about this, and assaulted me with her hands. *You came out of my body,* she said, her eyes wild with rage. *Do you understand what this means?*

·

Abuelo Coco stopped eating. Abuela Coco tried to feed him. He kept his lips sealed. Weeks went by, and it became clear he was going to die. Mom wanted him to feel loved in his last days. She asked us to kiss him good night. But the sight of his legless body made me want to bolt. When I tried calling to mind his positive attributes, I could think only of the rabbit-softness of his curly silver hair and the pleasant Old Spice scent that lingered in his wake. I knew he was a cherished human being—that my mother felt she owed almost everything to him. But in recent years, I had known only his disdain.

As he died, I declined to go near him. My mother's eyes filled with tears. *Abuelo is going to die tonight,* she whispered. *Please go say goodbye.*

Her sadness was suffocating, pressing against me like a horse's haunches. I couldn't bear it. I forced myself to go downstairs, steeling myself against the sight of him. As always, Abuelo Coco seemed not to notice my presence. He radiated erasure. *Buenas noches, Abuelito,* I said.

The next evening, my mother entered my room again. *Tonight is the night, Jean,* she said, weeping. *Please go tell him you love him.*

I refused. For days I pretended he didn't exist. His body clung to life despite his mind's determination to depart. Michelle did not feel the repulsion I did. Every day, she entered his room. She rested her head on his stomach and held his hands in hers. This moved my mother to tears. My sister was troublesome, perhaps, but at essence she was good. I was the coldhearted enemy, the wolf in sheep's clothing.

This time, he's going to die, my mother cried one evening. *Go say goodbye, I beg you.*

I took a deep breath. *You always say it's his last night. I'll go down today, but that's it, Mom, I swear.* I entered his room. His proximity to the afterlife felt contagious. His irises were glazed and pale. His mouth hung open. I was afraid to breathe the air in his room. *Kiss him,* my mother said sharply. *Kiss him good night.*

If his ears were working, I realized, he could hear her. My mother stomped her foot. *Kiss him! Kiss your grandfather, dammit! You're going to lose him forever, you egotist, you Schizophrenic!* Something cracked inside me. I threw open the door of the house and walked outside, my vision blurred by tears. An intricate spider's web stretched from the eaves of our McMansion to my mother's BMW. It looked nightmarish and impossible. I walked on, aimless, digging my nails into my palms, making them bleed.

·

The same day Abuelo Coco died, my mother called every relative in Puerto Rico to notify them. "Papi *murió*," she said, over and over again, staring into the distance with blurry bloodred eyes, golden ringlets sticking to her wet face. I felt so sorry for my mother, so unbearably sorry, that my sympathy, in that instant, snapped. I felt I would die if I kept suffering for her. At his funeral, I fought an incessant urge to laugh. The urge became irrepressible, and I exited the church.

My mother had always prohibited me from cutting my hair, shaving my legs or plucking my eyebrows. I shaved my legs. I chopped my hair off. I bleached it blonde. I accompanied my sister to a screamo concert, drank beer, smoked a cigarette. I asked her for makeup advice. She taught me to apply thick liner to make my eyes look bigger. She plucked my furry eyebrows, giving them a perfect arch. Suddenly, I was pretty again. I knew I wasn't the most beautiful this time, but I had power.

I met a boy named David, a Guatemalan-Mexican Crip gangster who boasted he had killed a Blood on orders, stomping his skull into the sidewalk. He was the first boy who ever told me I was beautiful, and I fell instantly. I loved his dark skin, his seductive lips, his danger. He was sensual, experienced. I gave myself to him to destroy.

When he took my virginity, he asked if we could have anal sex, too. I declined. He penetrated me anyway. I screamed in pain. He stopped after two thrusts. But the damage had been done. The next day, horseback riding was excruciating.

I felt like I was on top of the world.

I had discovered a secret: a person can live fully, explosively, become resonant with the Big Bang itself. All it took was surrendering empathy—for others, yes, but also for the self. Give up love and gain the utmost intensity of every other feeling: ecstasy, fearlessness, devastation. Now I felt I understood my father. The freedom of it was intoxicating.

•

David dumped me, then begged me to take him back. He did this repeatedly before he decided he didn't want me at all. I drove to David's house. I fell to my knees, clutched his blue Chargers jersey and declared I would die without him.

Damn, girl, he said. *Chill. Let's talk, aight? Smoke some weed.* I followed him into his room. He sat on the edge of his bed and rolled a joint. I threw myself on him. He recoiled. *I said talk, not fuck. Jeez. You actin' crazy.*

Crazy? You're calling me crazy?

Alright alright, let me rewind.

You know my worst fear is to become like my father!

I was watching myself from a faraway, amused place as I spoke. For weeks, I had felt I was no longer in my body. I was observing myself observing myself observing myself. It went on to a distracting degree. Everything struck me as both stupidly distant and hallucinatorily vivid. I was split between body and mind. My corporal half could writhe with any emotion, while my cerebral half observed with cynicism.

Well, Jean, I hate to break it to you: you are kinda like him.

His words shattered me, deliciously, and I drove back to my house in a teary delirium. My mother was drinking a glass of ice water in the kitchen. She stared at me with what I perceived as contempt. I grabbed a Tylenol bottle from the medicine cabinet. I stomped upstairs and locked myself in the bathroom, blaring the Emiliana Torrini song "To Be Free" on repeat at full volume. I stripped. First, I would slit my wrists. Then I would swallow a hundred Tylenol pills.

I sat in the bathtub and scratched at my left wrist with my Venus razor. It was hard to cut the skin. I pulled at the blades with my nails, blunting them. Still it was difficult to do deep damage. I rubbed the blade against my skin furiously, zigzagging, circling, carving mountains and canyons of meat. A thick stream of blood made satisfying swirls of gore in the tub. The concreteness of the pain anchored me. I leaned my head against the tile. I decided to postpone my suicide. The damage I had done relieved and relaxed me. I was suddenly sober enough to do an inventory of all of my banal and vain reasons not to die. I still had my horse. Riding was a reason to live. I was no longer getting straight A's, but I was still making honor roll. My English teacher, Mr. Brown, was praising my nonfiction writing. I was writing investigative articles for his class, about Southeast San Diego gangs and the county's allegedly haunted places, as well as essays about my father. I had finally broken my silence.

When my mother entered my room later, I was stanching the blood flow of my wrist with a red towel. In the darkness, she held up the razor I had used to butcher myself. *You should be careful about using rusty razors,* she said. My mother was perceiving my dried blood as iron oxide. I remembered the Wizard's First Rule.

•

I took the trolley south to the border, entered Mexico on foot. I walked through the rotating metal gates at the San Ysidro Port of Entry in a miniskirt and tube top. The U.S. side was quiet, clean, deserted. On the Mexican side of the border, the streets were littered with trash and a mob of male *taxistas* surrounded me, their yellow cabs congregated at the crossing. *Taxi! Taxi, señorita! Discount for the pretty lady!* They competed angrily, with flirtation, flattery, discounts. I hopped into the nearest vehicle. *¿Dónde está la fiesta?* I asked. I now spoke Spanish with an American accent, not quite opening my mouth enough on the vowels. He drove me straight to Calle Revolución. Tijuana had a fictional quality to it: flies drank from the eyes of donkeys painted as zebras; cloudy-eyed amputees consulted crumpled Tarot cards; the houses were all colors of the rainbow. The streets crumbled and curved into dramatic spirals. Every stimulus of nocturnal Mexico threatened to blot me out—the blasting mariachi, the consciousness-eliminating tequila, the sweaty bodies of drunk men in crowded clubs.

It felt liberating to dangle over the abyss in my father's country. I crossed again and again, crashing house parties, crawling into random cars, accepting drinks from older men. I was sixteen and Mexico's drinking age was eighteen, but nobody requested my identification. I woke up puking in strangers' toilets. When my mother found my trolley ticket stubs, she was horrified—she had heard of rising homicides and kidnappings in Mexico. But she couldn't stop me from going there. I was looking for my father. If I couldn't find him, I would become him.

In San Diego, I got so many speeding tickets in my mother's BMW that she made me use her minivan instead. I left a used condom in the back. When I realized my mistake, I had already returned the keys. I asked her for them with alcohol on my breath. She marched straight to the van. I stumbled after her. She threw open the doors and I lunged at the back seat, grasping in the dark. My hand found it as hers did. I pulled. She pulled harder. The condom snapped out of my hand, splashing semen into the air. My mother's face glistened. She wiped her face with her wrist. I felt anesthetized, as if in a dream.

I knew it! she roared, thunder itself. *I knew it! You're a whore, a filthy puta!* Her limbs were lightning. She tore at my clothes. She stripped me half naked on the driveway. She was trying to claw me back into her world. But I was untouchable now. All the things she said were true.

•

My mother bought us plane tickets to Puerto Rico. She had never taken a vacation before, and wanted to reconnect with us. I ignored her for most of the trip. One rainy night as I walked on the beach, I met a tall olive-skinned boy with seaweed-green eyes, like mine. He was also on vacation—coincidentally, from San Diego. Jason was a juvenile delinquent. He had assaulted a classmate with a machete. We became a couple back home. I knew, by then, how to hold on to men like him. I repeatedly dumped Jason, then returned to him. I refused to have sex with him. Once, Jason stormed outside, stole a neighbor's Ferrari and got thrown back into juvenile hall. From juvie, he wrote romantic letters filled with spelling errors. My mother opened them and threw them in the trash. But I knew where to search. Jason called me collect. *I'm gonna escape from here one day, and we can run away to Mexico,* he said.

•

One evening, in the middle of a fight with my mother, I said: *It's all your fault! You turned me into this!* Suddenly, she looked like a little girl as she begged, eyes red and wet: *No, no, no . . . please, it can't be true. I'm sorry . . . God, I'm so sorry.* For a moment, I saw the woman from Paradise Hills, the one who had drawn faces on trees, who had laughed at the ladybugs, who had taught me the alchemy of interpretation—and I wanted so badly to be in her arms. But I was not like her anymore.

•

My mother brought me the latest issue of a magazine called *Equestrian Vacations*. She asked me to choose a trip. She wanted to reward me for consistently making honor roll. I signed up for an intensive two-week equine-training program in Ireland at the world-renowned Clonshire Equestrian Centre: boot camp for young riders. We woke up at dawn, groomed and saddled our horses, then rode into the countryside, where we jumped over brick walls and haystacks. I rode Zeus, a bay stallion I had noticed in a corner stall. *Nobody rides Zeus; he's crazy,* someone said, so I saddled him up. Zeus had thick hooves and nimble legs that could fly over jumps of any height and land without a sound. He had to be first in line, or else he bucked and reared. After morning lessons, everyone fought over scraps of cold lunch, then rode again until nightfall. In the rain, we galloped down muddy hills. Once, I made a mistake preparing Zeus for a descending line of jumps on a hill. I led the charge with seven or eight riders behind. He screeched to a halt. I fell into the slippery earth. I looked up and saw muddy hooves dripping black water against the backdrop of a purple sky. The sight was exhilarating.

•

My mother feared an equine career would kill me. In four years, I had experienced several concussions inducing short-term amnesia and cracked a vertebra in my spine, which had paralyzed me from the waist down for a month. She argued for a literary path. But aspiring to author books felt too fanciful. I wanted to do something practical, be in the world, experiencing life, not locked up in my room imagining things like when I was a child. Mr. Brown convinced me to apply to a few journalism schools, in addition to the equine-studies universities that interested me. With four other students, I had helped him turn the school's trashy quarterly into a glossy literary magazine that people throughout Bishop's read. Mr. Brown gave me a copy of Mary Karr's famous memoir, *The Liars' Club,* about growing up with a binge-drinking father and an eccentric mother in eastern Texas. *You aren't doomed because of your father,* he said. *You can turn bad things into good things.*

•

One night, near the end of senior year, I awoke to Jason's voice. He was downstairs in the living room with my mother, beside a fat Samoan with blank eyes, telling her he had just been admitted to Harvard. *I had to come tell Jean right away. I'm turning my life around, thanks to her—she's an inspiration.*

My mother tousled his hair, then patted the Samoan's shoulder.

I'll go make you boys some tea, she said.

She vanished into the kitchen. Jason gestured at the Samoan, who unzipped his jacket and revealed a bottle of Jack Daniel's, a plastic bag full of white powder and a plastic bag full of pills. *I escaped from juvie, babe,* Jason said. *For you. I brought some pills. We can put one in your mom's drink. She'll pass out and won't notice a thing!*

I recoiled. *Jason, you're nuts, get out of my house.*

Jason spread his arms wide. *Are you serious, babe? I just, like, escaped from juvie for you, and this is how you greet me?*

I dismissed his lamentations with a hand gesture.

I'll visit you tomorrow after class. Where are you staying?

•

The house was nestled between boulder-studded mountains on a Kumeyaay Indian reservation about forty minutes east of my school. I arrived at sunset. Jason emerged from the house with cloudy eyes, in a white wifebeater like the ones my father used to wear. He cast a long, reaching shadow. He seemed alien, even ugly. I immediately regretted coming, but I couldn't think of an excuse to leave. I followed him inside, where shaved-headed, tattooed men sat on a mutilated leather couch, sharing a bong. One stuck a needle in his arm.

My mother was once again letting me use her BMW. Jason wanted to take the car on a drive. I refused. He tore the keys from my hands. I dove into the passenger's seat. He sped through the reservation at 110, 120, 140 miles an hour. I yelled at him to stop. He kept speeding, flew over a flimsy bridge, into the mountains. I was sure he was going to crash. It was dark when he hit the brakes back in front of the house. *Can we make love yet, babe?* he asked, out of breath with exhilaration.

I'm not ready yet, I said, trying to hide my absolute lack of desire to ever have sex with him by planting a kiss on his lips.

He wrapped his arms around me, encouraged. *But we've been together three months.*

I shrugged him off. *Um, that's not true. We broke up a million times, remember?*

Come on, babe, he said, grabbing my hand and pressing it against his crotch. I pulled away. I suspected Jason had sexually transmitted diseases.

He sighed. *Fine, let's go into the back seat and cuddle, at least.*

He crawled into the back. I followed, wondering how soon I could leave without making him angry. Jason unzipped his pants and pulled out his penis, which struck me as grotesque in its elephantine size. I realized, then, that if Jason wanted to, he could rape me; he could call his friends and have them rape me, too; they could kill me and bury my body in the mountains.

Jason, I told you, I'm not ready.

Jason grabbed my face and kissed me aggressively. I retreated. *What's your problem?* he asked. He grabbed my arm and yanked me closer. He stuck his tongue down my throat, twisted his body, pinned mine down. *Jason, I said no.* I didn't want to scream. I didn't want to piss him off. I was afraid to lure his friends. I lay there saying *no* and *no* as nicely as possible. He pushed my underwear aside as I tried to dissuade him in polite whispers. He pushed himself into me. He thrust: once, twice. When he saw tears on my face, he froze. *Okay, okay.*

He pulled out, sat up and zipped up his pants. *Fine, babe, fine.* He smoothed his hair, looking stressed. *You know I'm willing to wait as long as it takes. I love you, babe.*

I stared out the window at the black shapes in the dark valley, wondering if I now had an STD. Crickets chirped from invisible horizons.

You're not going to go and tell anyone I, like, raped you, are you, babe?

FAIRY-TALE NEURONS

I decided to pursue journalism. Both writing and riding gave me a sense of control. But while in riding that sense was limited to the horse, in narrative nonfiction it was all-encompassing. Narrative nonfiction felt like a superpower. I could lasso the whole wild world into paragraphs, cage it up in language. When I got into the Annenberg School for Communication and Journalism at the University of Southern California, I decided to continue riding only as a hobby, borrowing horses on the USC equestrian team. We sold Aspen. My mother bought me a blue Toyota Yaris for my new life in Los Angeles. Papi came back from the dead for my high school graduation. I was thrilled to see him again. I didn't care that he had criticized me with such loathing before vanishing; once more, I felt I had deserved his disdain. But now I was different. I believed I had truly become like him: fearless, detached, antisocial. He brought me a brown dress with threaded floral patterns and his copy of Ken Follett's *The Pillars of the Earth*—the first presents I recall receiving from him. I read the novel through my graduation ceremony, ignoring angry glances from administrators.

On my first Tuesday in a general-education class, Foundations of

Western Art, I scanned the hall for a place to sit and saw a tall boy with his nose inside a print issue of the *New York Times*. I plopped down beside him, wearing the brown dress from my father. He was pale and freckled all over, with moss-green eyes. *You're reading an actual newspaper? That's cute,* I said, with amusement. He blushed.

Alex aspired to become a writer of political speeches, ideally for the president of the United States. He was a Democrat from Texas, with a slightly nasal voice that charmed me. He used gorgeous words I had never before heard in conversation. He seemed to contemplate everything I said, probing me with catalytic questions. He quoted works like Ralph Waldo Emerson's *Self-Reliance*. He gave me his copy of Virgil's *Aeneid:* "The descent into the Underworld is easy. Night and day the gates of shadowy Death stand open wide, but to retrace your steps, to climb back to the upper air—there the struggle, there the labor lies." When he looked at me, I felt he was swimming inside my head. He sought my thoughts and motivations, and helped me clarify them. We lived one floor apart in the same dormitory. He invited me on evening walks. We ate lunch together after every art history class.

One day, after examining nude Greek statues at the Getty, we were driving home on the Pacific Highway when Alex took my hand in his. I pulled away. My appetite was for dangerous men with dark circles under their eyes. He knew that. Alex was wholesome and white. I said, *I'm sorry, Alex. I just don't think of you that way.*

He informed me that if we couldn't be romantic, we couldn't be friends, either. His feelings had become too powerful to ignore. *We've reached an impasse,* he said. Alex was my favorite person. He was funny and brilliant and, in his own way, handsome. I just couldn't imagine anything sexual with him. In my mind, he was akin to an extraterrestrial or a different species. I explained this. He asked: *Who said anything about sex? I'm a virgin, and plan to be until marriage.* I laughed. He didn't. It wasn't a joke.

We ate lunch on opposite sides of the cafeteria. I watched him with his friends. I sat alone. I hadn't had a real friend since middle school. Listening to the vapid conversations of my classmates filled me with contempt. I had just read Fyodor Dostoyevsky's *Notes from the Underground*. I fancied myself a female version of the antisocial narrator— hateful of others due to mental superiority: "To be acutely conscious is a disease, a real, honest-to-goodness disease. . . . One is not to blame in being a scoundrel." Alex was the only person I liked. After suffering his absence for a week, I took a deep breath, walked upstairs and pounded on his door. He emerged, disheveled and perplexed. *Okay,* I said. *I'll be your girlfriend.* I kissed him. An attraction flared up inside me the instant I touched him. My eyes opened to his attractiveness: to his broad chest, the subtle reddish tinge in his hair, his strong hands, his wheat-colored eyelashes.

A week after I took his virginity, I cheated on him during an intoxicated weekend excursion in Mexico. I confessed the sin I had committed. I had few ethical codes back then, but transparency was one. *I don't know why I did it. The guy was disgusting,* I said, sobbing with confusing guilt. *Maybe it's because I'm dying to feel something, anything, I'm so numb all the time.* Alex listened calmly. When I finished, he put a hand on my shoulder and stared deep into my eyes with a sad smile. He couldn't stay with me, he said, but he forgave me. I stared at him in awe and confusion. A few weeks later, he agreed to take me back. I had to promise never to cheat on him again. I swore I would not, but in my online journal, I wrote: *Did I mean it? I never know if I'm going to do something until I do it.*

I decided to minor in neuroscience after an introductory general-education course hooked me. I thought I could understand my father (and myself) by scrutinizing dendrites and action potentials. I suspected I had narcissistic personality disorder; its main symptoms were a lack of empathy and an inflated sense of self-importance. But instead of seeking to remedy my illness, I relished it. Flipping through Tolstoy's *Anna Karenina* on Alex's bed, I expressed admiration for its immoral characters as Alex tried to reason with me from his desk. I told him virtue and vulnerability were weaknesses tied to ignorance. He argued they were necessary for human connection. I became angry and left the room. Although I could talk to Alex for hours, I detested his wholesomeness, his heartfelt defense of humanity. Once, he called me, panicking; a stranger had robbed him at knifepoint on the street. I told him to grow some testicles. I thought it was good for him to suffer. In my view, he had led a sheltered life and needed to toughen up. Somehow, I was blind to my own privilege as a private-school-attending American who had at one point owned a horse.

I told Alex I had a genetic predisposition toward insanity and could not control my thoughts or actions. An ambient song whined from my laptop. I was curled up in my bed, barefoot, having neither washed nor shaved any part of my body in days. *If you love me, you'll just have to accept I'm a sick person*, I said. *It's not my fault I'm Schizophrenic.*

Alex blinked. *Have you ever heard of "earning your dialogue"?*

I raised an eyebrow, showing a modicum of interest.

You can't talk like you're in a movie all the time just 'cause you feel like it, he said. He stepped toward my laptop and closed it. My music stopped. *It's this soundtrack that puts you in a constant mood. You know what I think? I think you wish you were crazy.*

I felt naked in the sudden silence. With feigned indignation, I said: *You think I want to end up in a mental institution?*

If you were "like your father," he said, making air quotes with his fingers, eyes locked on mine, *you'd have an excuse for never growing up.*

And yet, if ever I showed up outside his door, drunk and sobbing about Schizophrenia, he would pick me up, place me on his bed and play the song "Bang Bang" by Dispatch on his guitar, singing: "She woke me up with a bang bang, looking over cross-eyed, had a big hunch that the world was a big lie." Alex knew how to abandon his pride while maintaining his integrity—something I was clueless about. *You are the most beautiful girl I have ever seen,* he would say, and I would respond that his freckles were like the stars. He had three aligned freckles on the back of his left hand, like Orion's belt.

I dumped him and took him back with callous caprice. Alex allowed himself to be broken again and again. He wanted to save me from myself. But eventually he realized he could not. I had let the wound of my father's absence displace me. The emptiness stretched more than a hundred miles—from Los Angeles to an old house in Paradise Hills, where a backyard was bloated with bodies. I could no longer tell what I dreaded from what I desired.

At the start of sophomore year, I met a former heroin addict with cockroach tattoos on his arms. I cheated on Alex a second time. Alex came over to break up with me in person. I lived on the fifteenth floor of the school's newest dorm, with a view of the downtown skyscrapers, the Hollywood sign and snowcapped mountains beyond—the perfect setting for a tragedy. *Someday, Jean, you are going to be the girl of my dreams,* he said. *But I can't sit around waiting for you to become her.* A new immunity shone in his eyes. He backed away, barricaded. I realized I had lost my grip. I had to do something. I stumbled to my Yaris in a blur of tears and sped to a nearby liquor store and bought a six-pack of Smirnoff Ice with a fake ID. Then I drove to the ocean. On the boardwalk in Santa Monica, I smashed a bottle and picked up a jagged-edged shard. I ran to the water and sat near the shore, carving three crooked lines on my wrist. Blood seeped out in satisfying black lines. The sea grasped and gasped soothingly. I sent Alex a text message: *I just butchered my wrist at the Santa Monica pier. Come save me.* I sprawled out on the sand. The moon was a corpse's face, swollen and yellow. I waited. Alex did not come. I wrapped my sweater around my wrist and returned to my Yaris, shivering. I had a neuroscience exam the next morning and needed to sleep.

•

Back on campus, I disinfected my wrist, wrapped it in gauze, set my alarm clock, curled up in bed and fell asleep. I awoke to an all-male crowd of LAPD officers, EMTs and campus security around 1:00 a.m. *We got a report you were trying to kill yourself,* one said. *Police are looking for you in Santa Monica.* How amusing, I thought. An army of men come to my rescue, yet none were my Prince Charming. *Nope,* I said, removing my gauze to show them my horizontal cuts. *Across the road, not down the street,* I said. They stared at one another in confusion. *I mean, the ambulance is already outside,* someone whispered. Another cleared his throat and said: *You're going to have to come with us.*

As they belted me into a wheelchair, I felt a giddy sense of climax. I had long feared becoming my father. Now I was a mental-illness patient. And Alex had made it happen. At the hospital, the perverse thrill gave way to real anxiety. I needed to be well rested for my neuroscience exam; the minutes were ticking by; the nocturnal anxiety of my childhood gripped me. I required at least eight hours of sleep a night, an obsessive-compulsive inheritance from my mother when she was sleepless and on call. I begged the nurses to let me go. They refused. California law allows the involuntary detainment of anyone deemed a danger to him- or herself. A skinny male nurse said with a giggle: *You should have thought about your test before trying to kill yourself, little girl.* I trembled with loathing. These ignorant strangers were *violating* me. They were doing with my body something I did not consent to. It was institutionalized torture. It made me sick with rage. I despised the world's authority systems, its arbitrary and irrational laws. A woman on a cot beside me had blood seeping out of her stomach. She wept: *I've been waiting for hours and nobody is helping me!* Around four in the morning, I called my mother. She answered with a groggy voice. *I just cut myself a little, Mom, because I'm stressed, but they're acting like it's a big deal. I'm going to fail my test because of them.* She called the front office and demanded that they release me. They refused. My mother told me to walk out of the hospital. I asked to go to the bathroom and was unbelted from the wheelchair. I made my way toward the emergency exit. Opened it. Walked out. Climbed a chain-link fence. And ran into the night of South Central Los Angeles.

●

I ended up half dragged, half carried back into the hospital. My mother sped a hundred and forty miles from San Diego. She stormed in, shouting: *Where is my daughter?* In her protective fury, she looked not like Mom or Mommy or Mami, but like all three women melded into one.

I felt a surge of love for her. In her rich dimensionality, she looked like a work of art. She took me to breakfast and wrote me a doctor's note. With sad eyes, she asked to see my wrist. I showed her the mess of cuts on my skin. It was the first time she saw my self-mutilations. *Why did you do that to yourself?* she asked. I shrugged, promising I wouldn't do it again. She required nothing else from me—no apologies, no supplications. Just like that, I never cut myself again. We took each other back.

·

In the fall of 2007, the underground raves of the nineties were making a comeback as massive, mainstream events. They were designed like fairy tales, which intrigued me. With names like Electric Daisy Carnival and Monster Massive, the raves were real-life immersions in landscapes like those that had excited my imagination as a little girl: fire-breathing trees and fields of glowing flowers.

I decided to enter their worlds when a fellow journalism student, Tim, invited me to take Ecstasy with him and his friends at Nocturnal Wonderland, four stages of DJs in a downtown Los Angeles parking lot. According to my neuroscience textbook, the drug burned holes in brains. Tim assured me he had done MDMA several times without adverse effects. Curious, I gulped down two blue pills stamped with the Apple computer logo.

At the rave, fairies and goblins on stilts wandered amid thousands of half-naked bodies. Electric lights of every color fluttered everywhere—luminous butterflies. Everyone shared massages, cigarettes, water bottles, glow sticks. My pupils grew to the size of dimes. *The moon is ripe for plucking,* I observed. It hung low and large, a glowing grapefruit beside million-eyed skyscrapers. Tim and I took turns pretending to pinch it between our fingers. We brought it back to our lips.

Each stimulus, from the smell of Vicks VapoRub to spinning lasers, acquired tactile dimensions, massaging my molecules down to their mitochondria. The bass of the electronic music—Carl Cox was spinning a remix of Splittr's "All Alone"—caused every inch of me to vibrate. I had the sensation of breaking open. The whole universe rushed in through every pore of my body, causing me to swell and expand at the speed of light. I felt smothered by space-time itself. For the first time since I was a child, I was feeling it again: the flowering outward into a borderless space. In contrast to my solitary childhood *What is nothingness?* ritual, I was surrounded by people: tens of thousands of beautiful, dancing humans. I was not only the Milky Way fluids of space, but also the crowd: their sweating limbs, their swirling irises, their warm breath. I was their arteries pumping galaxies, organs encompassing centuries, eyelids curtaining light-years. I realized, suddenly, that every person on the planet embodied the infinite universe. *Everything is one thing. Everyone is one thing.* I felt explosive love for Tim, for his friends, for everyone. I wanted to throw my arms around every person at the carnival and kiss them.

I remembered the blank dream of my childhood, the mysterious one about mirrors: *Every mind is the universe staring back at itself. Hold a mind before material reality and you have a God, a self-aware universe.* Unlike my childhood experience, which lasted seconds, this one lasted hours—through sunrise. I rode the free Ferris wheel and rotating swings, awed by the blooming bodies below, the arterial energies connecting us. Perhaps it was all meaningless—a breathtaking hallucination, nothing more. But one consequence was real: I was able to make friends in the months and years that followed. My social anxiety largely disappeared that night. A few months later, I wrote a letter of apology to Alex: *It was you who was right all along.*

•

When I got home from the rave around seven in the morning, I had no desire to sleep. I had never felt so lucid. I went straight to my neuroscience textbook and flipped to the picture of the hole-filled brain, allegedly due to Ecstasy consumption. There was no way the drug I had consumed could do that. I did a Google search of the study and nearly fell from my chair at the top result: a 2003 *New York Times* article entitled "Research on Ecstasy Is Clouded by Errors." My 2007 neuroscience textbook was citing a since debunked 2002 study that used brain scans of monkeys given methamphetamine—a wholly different drug—to prove that MDMA burns holes in brains. The study was formally retracted a year after its publication, with the scientist, George A. Ricaurte, citing a drug sample labeling error. I started a Word document, compiling my astonished questions. *Why was my textbook citing a debunked study? Why was MDMA defined as a Schedule I drug, implying a proven high potential for abuse and no accepted medical use, whereas methamphetamine—a drug that had disintegrated my uncles' teeth—was a Schedule II drug, implying a lower potential for abuse?*

I had recently watched the documentary *Zeitgeist*, which blames the U.S. government for the 9/11 attacks. It had made me paranoid. I imagined there was a conspiracy to keep people from taking Ecstasy. If MDMA consumption was widespread, I felt, there would be no incentives for war. Everyone would love one another. The military-industrial complex would crumble.

I spent six months in the campus library, researching and composing a twenty-page essay titled "Empathy Manifesto." What if certain drugs didn't cloud perception, but rather expanded it, as Aldous Huxley suggests in *The Doors of Perception*? Huxley describes taking mescaline and regaining "the perceptual innocence of childhood, when the sensum was not immediately and automatically subordinated to the concept." Studies suggest that infants are synesthetes, smelling what they see, hearing what they touch and so on. Their brain cells, far more numerous than in adults, are interlinked and multipurpose until they're pruned and compartmentalized by experience. Huxley says that as humans age, language petrifies their perceptual capacities. Words have an obvious benefit: they allow the sharing of information over time and across cultures. But they also create mental concepts that strip and subsume stimuli. Language slims the spectrum of the individual mind, literally chaining thoughts to the preconceived. I heard my mother's voice: *You're Schizophrenic, just like your father.*

Certain drugs can unlock these chains of categorization, Huxley argues. Ecstasy works by stimulating two neurotransmitters in the brain: serotonin and dopamine. In *The Neuroscience of Religious Experience*, the neuroscientist Patrick McNamara says dopamine and serotonin are central to psychosis and religious experiences. Together, they trigger what some scientists describe as "apophenia": the perception of meaningful patterns in random data. "When this circuit is stimulated in the right way, you get religious ecstasy. When the circuit is over-activated, you get various forms of religiously tinged aberrations," McNamara writes. Ecstasy, I concluded, stimulated the circuit the right way, provoking a perception of the meaningful interconnectedness of all things. I was not a slave of my genetics. I was not the prisoner of a prophecy. All the power in the world lay in my hands— and the hands of others.

On the night before I turned twenty, I launched a digital magazine, *Spectacles,* with essays, fiction and artwork from various students. The centerpiece was my "Empathy Manifesto," which encouraged everyone to take Ecstasy. I likened the drug to the forbidden fruit of the Garden of Eden: *Open your pupils. Take a bite of the fruit.* The home page featured an illustration of a bespectacled boy plucking an Ecstasy pill from a tree branch. My friends helped spread the word about the website by scrawling the link on blackboards: "Got Apathy? Put on your Spectacles." Students wrote me messages to thank me for introducing them to the wonders of MDMA. At parties, strangers stopped and asked: "Aren't you the Ecstasy girl?"

I considered Ecstasy a spiritual catalyst, and used it only four or five times that following year. But some of my friends used it monthly or weekly, and not everyone responded the same way. The ones who used it most frequently experienced memory loss. Others had bad comedowns. I realized unique brains could respond distinctly to the same substance. Then MDA flooded the market. It was indistinguishable from MDMA in Marquis reagent chemical tests and cheaper to make. It was poisonous. One night, after taking what I thought was an MDMA pill, I became impatient and took two more. I ended up hallucinating in bed for days, muscles feeling pulverized, lips swollen and bloody from chewing on them. I decided I no longer wanted to put my brain at risk. I quit taking Ecstasy. I removed my manifesto from the Internet.

•

My neurochemical experiments had renewed my childhood faith in planes outside the perceivable. I decided to focus on natural paths toward them. I started meditating. I launched a weekly column in the *Daily Trojan,* Scientastical, seeking connections between spirituality and science. I studied everything from parallel universes to the spooky way time slows down for fast-moving entities. My bookshelves filled with paperbacks on neuroscience and quantum physics. These relatively nascent sciences made no effort to downplay the hugeness of their enigmas. I learned that qualia—the subjective experiences of properties such as color and textures—possess an ethereal existence that has so far eluded microscopes and brain scans. I investigated the seemingly supernatural role of perception in quantum experiments: photons act as waves until the gaze of a scientist petrifies them into particles.

For years I had thought that if the world could be explained by mathematical equations and periodic tables, it could be reduced to those things as well. But *how* and *why* questions are different. I was starting to rediscover the beauty of the latter question, the thrill inherent in the world's mystery. I was learning that minds and materials interact in ways that scientists are only beginning to understand, and that what had always scared me about the world was in fact not the unknown but the idea that the unknown was nothing, that mystery was an illusion, that the world was this, just this. It was not. Science was teaching me that. Although we can describe how light waves interact with the brain to yield color, we can't justify or measure the result— we have no clue where qualia reside in the brain, if they reside there at all. Nobody has ever encountered them in the physical world.

•

A question occurred to me: what if my father was not Schizophrenic? I was studying the *Diagnostic and Statistical Manual of Mental Disorders,* the bible of psychologists. Its history revealed that some diagnoses were arbitrary, sometimes even as fictitious as the hallucinations they purported authority over: Homosexuality had once been deemed a mental illness. So had "pre-menstrual dysphoric disorder."

In her book *Agnes's Jacket,* the psychologist Gail A. Hornstein calls for paying close attention to the stories of people who appear to be mentally ill. She writes: "Madness is more code than chemistry. If we want to understand it, we need translators—native speakers, not just brain scans." The title of her book refers to a jacket a German seamstress made in a mental institution. Agnes stitched into the fabric endless symbols, most of which seem indecipherable except for one phrase: *I plunge headlong into disaster.* Hornstein believes there is meaning in all of the jacket's symbols, which look like writing in a dream, edges blurring and curling. She argues that the U.S. psychiatric community is blind to the insights in stories like the jacket's because they are dismissed rather than deciphered.

For the first time in years, I longed to ask Papi about his experiences. What if my father's symptoms were in fact not nonsense but insights into the true nature of reality? The cognitive scientist Donald Hoffman demonstrated that, contrary to popular belief, even the most sober perceptions are not accurate representations of the world. In a research paper called "Natural Selection and Veridical Perceptions," he and his colleagues observe that veridical perceptions can be driven to extinction "by non-veridical [survival] strategies that are tuned to utility rather than objective reality." In a TED Talk, Hoffman explained: "How can not perceiving reality as it is be useful? Well, fortunately, we have a very helpful metaphor: the desktop interface on your computer. Consider that blue icon for a TED Talk. . . . Now, the icon is blue and rectangular and in the lower-right corner of the desktop. Does that mean the text file itself in the computer is blue, rectangular, and in the lower-right-hand corner of the computer? Of course not. Anyone who thought that misinterprets the purpose of the interface. It's not there to show you the reality of the computer. In fact, it's there to hide that reality. You don't want to know about the diodes and resistors and all the megabytes of software. If you had to deal with that, you could never write your text file or edit your photo." I began to wonder if my father's "hallucinations" and "delusions" were in fact veridical perceptions of the diodes and resistors of reality. Maybe Papi saw more of the world than most.

•

I drove to San Diego to celebrate my twentieth birthday and my grandmother's seventy-first birthday at her house. My aunt Aimee had ordered catering from a Mexican taco company. Papi was there, drinking a beer by himself. As the mariachi band played, he dragged a chair beside mine and said: *I like your hair like that.* I had dyed it brown. *Thanks,* I said, surprised. My father hadn't complimented me since I was a child playing a song on the piano. I still remembered the elation I had felt when he emitted his *wow.*

He leaned in and said: *I have something to tell you.*

The CIA had experimented on him between 1999 and 2003 using electromagnetic and radio-wave technology, he said. The goal was to test the remote technology's power in manipulating enemy psyches. They had chosen him, he said, because as a crack addict with a green card he had no credibility. They knew if he spoke up, everyone would dismiss him as insane. Moreover, eradicating his addiction would prove the technology's efficacy as a war weapon—what greater evidence of radically altered behavior than that? My father traveled to Mexico, Belgium, the Netherlands, Thailand, Cambodia, Malaysia, Vietnam and the Philippines to escape their experiments. He was pursued by men in suits and black SUVs with American license plates, by taunting voices, by "painful electric shocks" that felt like icebergs erupting in his organs. In the end, he lost the battle: he was forced to quit smoking crack.

I stared at my father in mute shock, not wanting to break the spell that was causing him to trust me. Finally, I said, tentatively: *What you're describing sound like hallucinations. How do you know you weren't hallucinating because of the crack?*

He rolled his eyes. *I'm sure. I'm sure. I'm sure.*

But how are you 100 percent sure? Crack cocaine can induce psychosis, you know. I learned in neuroscience that it milks dopamine neurons for all they're worth, and can confuse—

He interrupted: *Bee-caaauuse, Jean. Bee-cause look. I would be sitting here like this, and all of a sudden, I would hear the voices. Then I would move my head like this, and I could not hear them no more. Then I would return my head to the initial position, and I could hear them again. So obviously it was some kind of radio-wave—or electromagnetic—technology that those fuckers were using to beam voices into my head. They lost the signal whenever I moved abruptly.*

My first thought was that my father was misinterpreting the diodes and resistors of reality. He was trying to find a coherent story in the chaos, and the most compelling narrative he found was that the CIA had targeted him for illegal experiments. But then I realized it was presumptuous to assume I understood my father's experiences better than he did. For years, as I sought to recover my father by conjuring him in myself, I had been seeing him through my eyes. For once, I wanted to see him through his.

•

I started researching Project MKUltra, a covert mind-control project begun by the CIA in 1953. For nearly twenty years, CIA operatives slipped hallucinogenic drugs to unwitting civilians, causing them to hallucinate while operatives pursued them in large, intimidating groups. They targeted social outcasts: drug addicts, prostitutes, immigrants and other minorities who would self-censor or whose complaints would be dismissed as insane. MKUltra sought to determine if this combination of induced hallucinations and stalking could dramatically alter the personalities of subjects.

Prompted by a *New York Times* investigation, the U.S. Senate formed the Church Committee, which exposed MKUltra and other illegal operations by the CIA and other intelligence and national security agencies within the government. Those agencies appeared to abandon mind-control research.

But in 1980, the journal *Military Review* published an article, "The New Mental Battlefield," calling for renewed experimentation in "mind-altering techniques" such as "manipulation of human behavior through use of psychological weapons effecting sight, sound, smell, temperature, electromagnetic energy or sensory deprivation." Had the CIA or some other government agency developed more sophisticated mind-control weapons at the turn of the millennium, perhaps to alter the personalities of religious extremists and combat terrorism? My father told me he was one of thousands of Targeted Individuals tortured by the CIA in the early 2000s. I discovered forums, YouTube testimonials and ebooks from Targeted Individuals. I learned that in the late 1990s, the Air Force started testing the Active Denial System, which remotely transmits millimeter waves to create intolerable burning sensations in enemy targets, according to *Wired* reporter David Hambling, who obtained documents under federal sunshine laws. "The beam produces what experimenters call the 'Goodbye effect,' or 'prompt and highly motivated escape behavior.' In human tests, most subjects reached their pain threshold within 3 seconds, and none of the subjects could endure more than 5 seconds," said a 2006 *Wired* article. The "painful electric shocks" my father described sounded a lot like the Active Denial System. Perhaps my father was telling the truth.

•

I responded to a Craigslist ad offering a pirated operating system. A young Asian-American with dark circles under his eyes brought it over and installed it. Jay looked like a character from a book, hunched mysteriously in his hoodie. I was curious about him. I asked him to meet me for lunch. At a seafood restaurant he chose, Jay confessed he was a crack addict. This alone was not a problem, he claimed, because crack was an acidic compound, beneficial for the body. But the CIA was torturing him with radio waves. Sometimes, if he wrapped himself up in aluminum foil, he could protect himself from their intervention. But it's not like he could wear aluminum foil all the time. People would think he was crazy.

I gawked at Jay. I told him about my father.

It's happening to a lot of people, Jay said, shrugging matter-of-factly, and suggested that I read a 2007 *Washington Post* article called "Mind Games," which features the testimonies of Targeted Individuals from across the United States.

How do you know you're not hallucinating? I asked.

That's a fair question. I considered it. But imagine this. I'm sitting around, minding my own business, and bam, *I'll hear voices. Then I'll move my head like this and,* bam, *they stop. So I have to conclude they're pinpointing my location in space or something.*

Jay insisted on paying for our meal. His illegal business netted about $500 daily in cash. He lived in an ocean-view Marina del Rey penthouse, bought gourmet dog chow for his terrier, shopped at Whole Foods and smoked crack. When I got home, I read the *Washington Post* article he recommended. In the piece, the national security correspondent Sharon Weinberger delves into the history of clandestine mind-control research in the United States. In the 1960s, the Pentagon's Project Pandora tested the effects of microwaves on human behavior and biology. In the 1990s, the U.S. government started looking into V2K, or voice-to-skull technology. In 2001, Dennis Bushnell, the chief scientist at NASA's Langley Research Center, "tagged microwave attacks against the human brain as part of future warfare." In 2002, the Air Force Research Laboratory patented a technology that uses microwaves to send voices into people's heads. Weinberger concluded: "Given the history of America's clandestine research, it's reasonable to assume that if the defense establishment could develop mind-control or long-distance ray weapons, it almost certainly would. And, once developed, the possibility that they might be tested on innocent civilians could not be categorically dismissed."

•

I listened to Jay's stories with rapt attention, being perhaps the first sober person to entertain the possibility that he was telling the truth. Like Jay, Papi chose me as his confidante, calling on a regular basis, probably for the same reason: no one else had ever bothered to listen. My father's logic wasn't exactly bulletproof, but he clearly did not have Schizophrenia, which my neuroscience books described as a degenerative and debilitating disease. It appeared that Papi no longer hallucinated. Temporary drug-induced psychosis was more likely. But my father hadn't smoked crack in years and maintained, adamantly and articulately, that the government had subjected him to years of torture.

•

Mexico continued to exert its gravitational pull on me. Footsteps north of the border, I discovered a forest cluttered with car tires, plastic bottles, Barbies and dog carcasses carried in from Mexico by the Tijuana River. I trekked through the knee-deep sewage with trash bags tied around my legs, investigating cross-border pollution for an environmental-journalism class assignment, which I later sold as an article to an alternative weekly. Papi drove me to a Tijuana slum where much of the garbage originated. We stopped for mangoes, driving with the windows down so that Papi could smoke. I ate the sticky fruit, carving off pieces with a knife as he told me about his battles with the CIA. When we arrived at the canyon, I launched into my interviews, accosting squatters as if I were a paparazzo, causing them to clam up in confusion. Papi sighed, rolling his eyes. *You can't treat people like that,* he said. *You have to be a person first, then a journalist—watch me.* He approached a man at a fruit stand. He pulled his Marlboros out of his back pocket, placed a cigarette between his lips and asked the man if he had a lighter. The man procured a match. My father offered him a smoke. The man declined. After taking a long drag of his cigarette, Papi asked the man how long he had been living in Los Laureles. I tried to memorize my father's posture. Without hunching over and in spite of his height, he made himself almost disappear. His limbs were loose and comfortable. He nodded slowly as he listened. He was close to the stranger, but angled slightly, squinting one eye.

After a minute of small talk, Papi leaned back a little. He casually told the man why we were visiting. Would the man mind answering questions for a news article? I did not know it at the time, but I would go on to use my father's lesson throughout my career—in the mountains of Mexico's most dangerous states—convincing smugglers, illegal drug growers and murderers to confess their secrets.

●

My mother was launching a private practice in San Diego. After two decades of working for men who compensated her less than her colleagues, she decided to work for herself. Her last boss owned a multimillion-dollar home in San Diego and a ranch in Lima, Peru. He vacationed at his leisure. Meanwhile, my mother was struggling to pay off her mortgage and pay for tuition at my university, one of the nation's most expensive. When her boss had finally offered her a raise so she would stay, she said: *You can't afford me.* Dr. Del Valle left with her chin up. Her patients followed. Her income quadrupled. She hung a large black-and-white portrait of her bespectacled father in the waiting room, inscribed with the words *This Practice Is Dedicated to Luis Del Valle.* She remained single. Jeannette hadn't fallen in love with a man since Marco Antonio. She felt fulfilled on her own. She had sent both of her daughters to college—Michelle had decided to pursue her artistic ambitions after all, enrolling in San Francisco's Academy of Art University. Both of us were doing well. My mother had achieved her own version of the American dream.

●

The summer after college graduation, I interned at the Los Angeles bureau of the *Wall Street Journal,* where I wrote stories about marijuana dispensaries and other local issues. A few days before the annual Electric Daisy Carnival, the largest anticipated rave in U.S. history, I pitched a story about it to the bureau chief, Gabe. Deaths at a San Francisco rave had caused officials there to call for a ban on the events. I was pretty sure the same would happen in Los Angeles. Gabe guessed I was looking for an excuse to rave; he turned down the story. The night of the event, I dressed up as a fairy and smeared my mascara to make it look like I'd been crying. I approached a security guard near an exit and told him, in an anguished voice, that I had left the festival because I believed my friends were in the parking lot but they were actually inside. I shivered and hugged myself. It worked—the security guard let me in. More than a hundred people were hospitalized that night. A fifteen-year-old girl died, allegedly of an MDMA overdose. When an outcry for prohibition ensued, Gabe asked if I could still churn out a piece. I could.

•

At the end of my internship, I learned that the Mexico City bureau was seeking a correspondent to cover Mexico's and Central America's soft commodities, like coffee and sugar, for the newswire and the newspaper. I had recently watched the film *Blood Diamond*, in which Leonardo DiCaprio's character dies on a mountainside while exposing corruption in the mining industry. I was desperate to die young in a similar dramatic way, on an altruistic mission. My conversations with my father were making me aware of my privilege as an American with a private education in the planet's most powerful country. I wanted to unshelter myself. The prospect of doing so in my father's birthplace seemed a dream come true. I could explore my paternal roots while exposing corruption in commodities sectors. I applied for the Mexico City opening. A hiring manager informed me the position required at least four years of reporting experience; I didn't qualify. I asked Gabe for help. He made a few calls to vouch for my abilities. After a few weeks, the job in Mexico City was mine. I was heading to my father's country. Papi bought a one-way ticket to go with me.

Part IV

HOUSE OF COLD

My father balances on a tree near Uruapán, Michoacán, in September 1987.

CURSE

As a little boy, you scrutinized the world with ochre eyes. You had an intuitive understanding of simple machines and you built them: wagons, slingshots, animal traps. Living creatures and complex machines like cars shared a mesmerizing characteristic: self-generated movement. What was the mechanism behind it? You threw open the hood of your stepfather's car and ran your hands over the metallic maze of the engine. You fiddled with pumps and filters and coils. Some aspects struck you as remarkable in their simplicity. You tinkered with toys and televisions. They had been tossed on the Tijuana streets, broken or dysfunctional. You dissected them until you mastered them. Then you fixed them.

You could have been an engineer. But it was the calamities of human beings that most concerned you. If you could figure out the secrets of human *life*—its *whys* and *hows*—then you could fix people. You dreamed of becoming a surgeon.

At night, your parents' fighting kept you awake. You hid under the covers, heart thundering like a freight train along old tracks. Screams. Smashing plates. Curses and threats. Weeping. When you slept, you had nightmares of discovering your mother's corpse in the kitchen. One morning, as she served you breakfast, she stared at you with a monstrous, bulging black eye. Your stepfather had slammed the telephone into her face. It was horrifying. You loved your mother more than anything in the world. You craved her warmth, her touch, her love—but she gave it to you in clipped gestures and cutoff looks, like humiliating secrets. Sometimes you feared she saw you as the disgusting symptom of a terrible sickness she would not name—she refused to tell you where you were from. It was too shameful, too awful to mention.

You knew Don Jesus was your *padrastro,* not your *padre biológico,* because one day your mother's friend asked her, *¿En qué año conociste a Jesus?* And you overheard your mother reply that she had met him in 1958. You were born in 1956. You concluded that Jesus was not your blood, and probably not Alejandro's, either. Your brother was born at the end of 1958. You had long wondered why Don Jesus had always ignored you and Alejandro, while showering his youngest son, Jesus Jr., with affection. Sensing a change in your attitude—perhaps greater confidence born of understanding—Jesus began to pay attention to you. He disciplined you with his belt. He whipped you and cursed at you, treating you like the repulsive creature you often feared you were.

Decades later, when I am reading Tarot cards for you, I pull the card of the Devil. I try to explain that it isn't a bad thing—only that blocked natural impulses must be embraced in order to move forward. I tell you about Baphomet, the Sabbatic goat of lust who represents the triumph of matter over spirit, a carnal creature who isn't necessarily evil—he has merely and paradoxically become vulnerable to material impulses because of his unhealthy suppression of them. You interrupt me: "The *lust* thing. *That* is very relevant. Sometimes I think I'm the way I am because I was the product of pure lust. My mother's lust . . . not love or destiny or anything good. Pure lust. Hers and my father's."

I want to tell you her story—the story she told me about Mario Perez, a story she has never told anyone else. But something holds me back.

"Papi, what are you talking about? Your mom was innocent," I say simply.

"She was never innocent. She was never innocent."

Your first memory is of being left alone in a house because you wouldn't stop crying. The walls began to move toward you. The air curled itself around you like a snake. You couldn't breathe. You broke a window. Crawled out and walked to a bench while the tears dried on your face.

One day, you asked your mother for a doll with yellow hair. You had seen little girls in your neighborhood cradling Goldilocks *muñecas,* caressing their cheeks, running fingers through their curls. You were overwhelmed with a desire to do the same—to express that level of tenderness for something. But when you made your request, your mother gasped with horror, as if you had blasphemed. "You don't know how badly I wanted a *muñeca,*" you recall decades later, laughing at yourself. "When you were born, it was like my dream came true: I finally had my little doll."

As you grew, you ignored your desire for affection. You had to cultivate toughness. You had to learn to move. When your stepfather tried to beat your mother, you threw yourself between them, to protect her. But she did not always protect you. Once, Jesus called you into his bedroom and demanded that you remove your shorts and underwear. He was drunk. When you refused, his face turned bloodred like *carne cruda,* and he unbuckled his belt. He whipped your face, your arms, your shoulders, the backs of your legs. Your mother observed passively, having decided to be selective with her battles. *Strip naked!* Jesus roared. You crawled under the bed, terrified, and he dragged you out by the shoes. Finally, you pulled off your shorts and underwear and stood there, exposed, trembling. Your stepfather doubled over with laughter, pointing. He said he had never seen anything so small. You were five or six years old.

Why are we broken? How can I fix us? What is the secret?

You knew, from the machines you dissected, that often what seemed inscrutable could be mastered through careful study. In the

backyard, you built a large wire-mesh cage with shelves for jars of creatures you captured in the desert. You cut lab coats, surgical caps and
masks from a large white sheet you found in a dumpster. Dressed in
medical costume, you sliced open spiders, snakes, lizards, tarantulas,
frogs and scorpions with Alejandro, your medical assistant, who
handed you tweezers, needles, strings. You were averse to hurting
mammals and birds, but you believed that anything cold-blooded was
fair game, so long as you tried to keep the animals alive. You sought to
determine how hearts pump blood, how intestines digest food, how
brains form thoughts. You surveyed fluid-filled bags, entwined tubes
and elixirs, coaxing mysteries from their labyrinthine conglomera-
tions. Then you sewed the creatures closed and set them free.

Blood did not make you queasy. From a young age you had accompanied your stepfather to the *carnicerías* where he chopped the meat of
cattle and pigs. You scrubbed blood off the floors with rags, organized
merchandise, wiped windows after school and on weekends. Jesus let
you keep your earnings. You saved each coin for medical school.

One day, you found an enormous toad by a river. It was the largest
amphibian you had ever seen. It stared at you with almost human eyes.
You brought it home running, clutching it to your chest. In your
laboratory-cage, you asked the toad's permission to proceed, and as
you held it down it seemed to relax, submitting to your scalpel. You
saw its slimy heart reverberating in its chest, impossibly fast, like yours
when you lay awake at night terrified. In a fit of inspiration, you
pinched the heart between your fingers and plucked it from the toad's
chest, severing its connections to the circulatory system. The bloody
bead seemed to pulse the secret of life into your palm. As you at-
tempted to decipher its speech, blood filled the lines of your hand. The
heart stopped beating. You shoved the heart back inside the toad,
sewed shut the little animal's chest and performed cardiopulmonary
resuscitation. It was too late. The frog was dead. You felt guilty, evil,
horrible. You buried the toad with tears in your eyes.

Recounting this decades later, you become out of breath. You look
at everything in the room except me. Your forehead fills with lines and

your eyes become heavy and you say: "I wouldn't have done that if I had other *means.*"

You sought to operate on dead creatures, but carcasses were hard to come by. You abandoned your experimentation and visited the library for anatomy books instead. As you scrutinized those tomes one evening in the living room, Don Jesus stumbled through the front door, reeking of alcohol. You kept your eyes on the textbook, tense with fear of his drunkenness. You felt warm liquid splashing the back of your head. Your stepfather was urinating on you. You ran into your bedroom.

You sought refuge in the library, staying in its dusty rooms to consult the books on medicine. A thin brunette noticed you. She introduced herself as Elizabeth. Unlike your brother Alejandro, who broke hearts even before his voice turned deep, you were terrified of women even at the age of fifteen. Girls provoked in you an anxiety so profound it paralyzed your capacity for conversation. At school, your classmates teased you for your awkwardness. You preferred to be alone—reading, thinking, learning. But when Elizabeth asked you to walk her home, you agreed. You were mesmerized by the graceful curve of her neck, the sway of her hips, her large brown eyes. You walked beside her, speechless as she sung her thoughts into the air. She showed you her house. *Come over later, yeah? Just whistle here by this window.* That evening, you obeyed. She crawled out the window and led you to an empty parking lot around the corner. She lunged. For hours, she moved her lips against yours, explored your mouth with her tongue. You loved kissing her—her purring limbs, her smell of flowers—and hoped you were doing it right. You returned the next evening to kiss her again. On the third night, your whistle failed to bring her to the window. A fat girl emerged from the house next door. *Elizabeth isn't here! Were you looking for her?*

You nodded, mute.

Do you want me to tell you the truth?

You waited.

She ran off with another man. A man, who's, well, an older man. She told me you just take her and make her horny but don't do anything to her. This other guy knows how to satisfy her. He has a truck.

You were mortified. It wasn't until your eighteenth birthday that some brothers who lived down the road took pity on you. *Vente, pinche Marco!* they said. *Vamos a desquintar este guey!* We're going to de-virginize this guy! They took you to Calle Revolución. They grabbed a prostitute and said, *Desquinta este cabrón!* De-virginize this fucker! They paid for your very first time.

·

Your first real friend, Charlie, completed the corruption. He was hired at a *carnicería* where you worked alongside Don Jesus. Charlie was the first person who made you feel comfortable. He treated you like an equal, confiding his exploits, inviting you to parties to drink and smoke weed, which eased your social anxiety. When he caught you collecting pennies off the floor of the *carnicería* and delivering them to the owner, Charlie laughed in your face, pocketing $20 and $50 bills from the cash register. Nobody noticed but you. You marveled at his confidence. Whenever a pretty girl ordered a piece of meat, Charlie grabbed his crotch and said, *You mean this piece of meat?*

Charlie made you question the value of morality. The universe did not reward good intentions, he argued. Success was tied to greed. Principled behavior led to poverty. You realized as he spoke that your ambitions had nothing to do with morality or money. Cash seemed an empty pursuit. Ethics was a fixed concept; the world was not a static place. Of course you wanted to be good—your mother had instilled in you that desire—but you sometimes feared it was impossible, like you were innately evil, dirty, vile. What you valued above all else was exploration, inquiry, discovery. Movement—constant movement, mental and physical, internal and external. The owner of the *carnicería* had always complimented how swiftly you mopped the bloody floors and wiped the grimy windows, how spotless you left them. You moved white chalk along the blackboard at school, scribbling neat solutions, and the teacher stood agape at your speedy acuity. It was movement that inspired you; that is why you took joy in both your body and your mind, in cerebral calculations, in connecting disparate objects and information. And yet, it seemed you were doomed to be an outsider because of this. Only Charlie appreciated you. When you confided in him your dream of becoming a surgeon—to uncover the secrets of life—Charlie encouraged you, calling you *chingón*.

You decided to become Charlie's accomplice. You took money from the cash register. You had no interest in unearned money, but you enjoyed the thrill of discovering you could break rules and not get caught thanks to the speed of your hands. You helped Charlie rob boxes of butter from a parked commercial transport vehicle.

You continued to study. Tijuana didn't have a medical school, so you made plans to attend the Universidad Autónoma de Guadalajara. You had aunts in Guadalajara who had offered to let you live with them while you attended college. In 1973, while you were a junior in high school, your mother revealed that she had secured permanent residency in the United States for the family. Jesus sold the house, and everyone except you moved across the border. You had no interest in *los Estados Unidos*. You felt it was an imperialist nation that abused its power across the planet. You had read about the country's involvement in Vietnam, the military dictatorship it had installed in Guatemala in the 1950s, its meddling in Mexico's affairs. You stayed in Tijuana, sleeping on a neighbor's couch, intent on making your way to Guadalajara. When you graduated from high school, you took a bus with your life savings—a few thousand pesos—in your pocket. You visited the admissions office for information. The tuition, you discovered, was hundreds of thousands of pesos beyond your reach. Your grades weren't good enough for a scholarship; you had never managed to get straight A's while juggling classes and jobs. It would take you decades to earn enough money for medical school—at least while working in Mexico.

You decided to follow your family across the border to accumulate U.S. dollars until you could pay for medical school. You were hired as a burner at NASSCO. The shipyard was a spiderweb of steel, black cords falling from the sky like tentacles. The Coronado Bridge arched blue over the bay. Thousands of dusty-faced men worked with cigarettes dangling from their lips. Seagulls the size of dogs soared in search of scraps. Through the whistling, blowing and beeping of machines, the roaring of torches and sandblasting, the barking of sea lions wafted in from the sea.

You guided your oxygen-acetylene torch along steel, spitting columns of fire that sparkled and hissed. You kept your gloves in your back pocket. You cut shapes and eliminated imperfections from the plates, immersed in showers of flame. You worked expertly, with agility. You grew into a striking man with a copper complexion. Molten metal dripped on your arms, boring holes to the bone. Injured men lined up at a medical station where nurses cleaned and bandaged wounds, then sent men back to work. One day, while hauling a heavy hose backward on an upper deck, you stepped through a hole in the floor. Time slowed: You dropped the hose, threw out your arms and arrested your fall at the height of your chest. You looked down. Darkness curled around your lower body from as far down as the bottom of the ship. You scrambled back onto the deck. Coworkers were less fortunate, plummeting to their deaths. Crushed corpses were hauled out on stretchers.

You saved every paycheck. You enrolled in biology and chemistry classes at a community college in Chula Vista. You stopped seeing Charlie as often as before, too busy to join in his mischief. One day, you received a call from an old acquaintance from the *carnicería,* who informed you that Charlie had overdosed on heroin. His corpse had been found in a hotel room. Your only real friend was dead.

An old chasm widened inside you. It was heavier than your body, threatening to consume you. I can almost feel it, Papi—stretching across countries, from San Diego to Tijuana, to the backyard of an old house, where the blood of animals failed to yield secrets. You absorbed yourself in toil. Movement, movement. Only when you were feeling yourself in your flesh did the doors to black-hole gravity close. You toiled at the shipyard, in the classroom. But your beginner's English made it difficult to keep up in school. You took your textbooks to the shipyard, using every free moment to decipher them, until a foreman caught you and threatened to fire you.

One night, you had a terrible dream. You awoke sweating and sobbing, certain you had foreseen an unspeakable future. "It was a revelation of some sort, that I—I blacked out," you explain decades later. "I blacked out. I blacked out. But nothing that has happened in my life has been so devastating. It's like something I don't even wanna—it was so traumatic." Your mother took you to a *curandera*, but you refused to pay the exorbitant fee for the cleansing. You started meditating. You read books about Eastern philosophy. As you erased thoughts and emotions from your mind, you felt yourself spinning inwardly and outwardly. You were connecting with the essence of the universe, perhaps God himself.

You befriended a machine operator at the shipyard, Joe, a short kleptomaniac with bulging tattooed muscles. He picked fights with lazy gringos in the shipyard. His comedic, careless personality reminded you of Charlie's. He was a drug dealer, and sold grams of cocaine in little vials. The white powder made you feel confident on the weekends. Joe invited you to barbecues at his house. *I stole a pair of beautiful Chihuahuas,* Joe bragged. *A male and a female. You've gotta see 'em.* They were ugly, like all Chihuahuas, but you pretended to be impressed.

You thought Joe was crazy, and the feeling was mutual. Once, you went fishing on a boat Joe had stolen. About a mile from the Coronado Islands, you became seasick. You bid Joe farewell and jumped into the water. Joe cried out in terror. *Are you crazy? You'll drown!* You felt immediate relief, and swam the breaststroke through the water. The ocean stretched past every horizon around you. The vastness was exhilarating; you felt yourself expanding to match it. Your body was as efficient here as on the decks of ships. When you grew tired, you simply floated on your back. You swam until you felt rocks under your palms. You crawled onto a small stretch of sand, saltwater catching sunlight on your eyelashes. You stretched your tanned limbs, watching birds overhead.

Joe told everybody about your stunt. *You know what this* puto *did? He just jumped out of my boat in the middle of the fuckin' ocean. He swam like ten miles to the Coronado Islands. He's a lunatic!*

One weekend, you stopped by Joe's and knocked at his door to see if he wanted to play pool. Nobody answered. A neighbor emerged from a nearby house and informed you that Joe had been killed. His body had been found on the sidewalk with bullets in his back and his face.

You asked yourself: *Why did my two friends die? Why does everyone I love suffer or drop dead? Is it me? Am I causing their deaths by getting too close?*

Your head was filling with too many questions; knowledge wasn't coming quickly enough to let your brain breathe. You needed answers, information; you needed understanding to relieve the pressure in your skull. But school was becoming impossible. One day, when you couldn't figure out why your teacher had marked your answer to a certain exam equation as wrong, you tried to articulate a question in your accented English: *I do the equation again and I again have 105 grams,* you said. The teacher was a white lady who instinctually distrusted you. She sneered, walked up to the blackboard and reproduced the equation in front of everyone. She underlined "105 gr." Enunciating each word as if speaking to a child, she said: *The answer is 105 grams. But I marked it as incorrect because you wrote "gr" instead of "g." The abbreviation is "g."* In Tijuana, "gr" was an acceptable abbreviation. You tried to explain. She interrupted you, accusing you of making excuses— you were lazy, you didn't want to accept responsibility for your mistakes. It was humiliating. In Tijuana, instructors saw you as gifted. Here, they treated you as if you were stupid. The whole education system seemed engineered to inspire in you an unbearable sense of inadequacy. Worse, it was slow—in a monotone, meaningless way. The formalities and structure and redundancies forced students to crawl through facts as if through molasses, and become exhausted before absorbing a single thing. You decided to quit. You didn't need a college degree. You didn't need to play by made-up rules. You would become your own teacher. You would gobble up knowledge quickly, with the efficiency you brought to building oil tankers. You decided you had set the bar too low with your childhood ambitions. You would teach yourself medicine—not just traditional medicine, but homeopathic medicine, Chinese medicine, *curanderismo*. You would become an expert in everything. You visited the library for books about biology and world wars and economics. You became fluent in English. You used your savings to buy a house, the Cutlass and a motorcycle.

•

You were speeding on a Honda CX650 when you saw a curvy girl with long black hair at a bus stop. She was eye-catching. You stopped and offered her a lift. The girl blushed and accepted the ride. You were now aware of the allure you held for women, in spite of your ongoing anxiety. Maria was a cross-border resident of Mexicali and San Diego, studying in the United States and spending weekends south of the border. You started dating. She was a shy, sweet girl, cooking and cleaning at the house you had purchased in Lemon Grove, studying with you in the evenings. You rarely spoke; you were comfortable in silence, enjoying each other's company. But one evening, as you cuddled in bed, she stared at you with intense uncertainty and an evident desire to speak. A whirlwind of secrets swirled behind her lips. Finally, she yielded: *I have to tell you something.*

What? you asked.

There's something wrong with me. She inhaled a shaky breath and continued. *If I get mad at someone . . . if I get really mad at someone . . . something bad happens to that person. Always. Always.*

You laughed dismissively—*Me estás jodiendo*—and then you fell asleep.

Maria left for a cousin's birthday party in Mexicali. You promised to pick her up at the Tijuana bus station. But on the morning of her return, you awoke to realize you had slept through your alarm clock. *Híjole, ya me está esperando,* you thought. You ran to your motorcycle, forgetting your helmet. You sped south on I-805. A rock had rolled into the middle of your lane. You noticed it too late. Decades later, you tell me: "If you start to think about it, she was already waiting for me. Like half an hour, maybe an hour. She was real angry. Like, *This mother-fucker isn't coming to get me.*"

The pavement scraped the skin from your elbows, knees, shoulders, knuckles, cheekbones. Someone called 9-1-1. After a few hours in the emergency room, you hopped back onto your mangled motorcycle, drugged on painkillers, wearing bandages. You pulled up to the Tijuana bus station. Maria was waiting. *I'm sorry,* you said.

Maria told you she wanted to get married. *My cousin tells me you're just using me for sex,* she said. She looked at you with black, angry eyes. Although Maria was nice and pretty, you didn't see a future with her. You told her you weren't ready for a commitment. A few days later, she turned to you and said: *I'm pregnant.*

That's impossible. Do a test.

What are you going to do if I am pregnant?

I dunno. Do a test.

What do you mean "I dunno"?

I dunno. Let's go to the doctor, let's find out.

I want to know now what you're going to do!

You're not pregnant. We always use protection.

She wept. She told you she was through with you. You dropped her off at her cousin's on your motorcycle, then sped home, relieved. You heard the tiny sports car a split second before it hit you. Your body smashed into the windshield and bounced into the street. The tires skidded toward you. You slid along the flesh-eating asphalt. The car stopped an inch from your face. The driver stumbled out and stepped on your body in a drunken stupor. You were still conscious. *I'm going to faint, I'm going to faint,* you gasped, hyperventilating. The drunk gawked at you, then sprinted back to his car and sped away. By the time the ambulance arrived, you had lost consciousness.

"If that hadn't happened to me, I would say *mal de ojo* doesn't exist," you tell me years later. "But it does exist. *Mal de ojo* exists."

Mal de ojo is a curse caused by a look filled with negative energy, such as a glare, a scowl, a frown. You had never believed in the power of curses—you were confident that if they existed, disbelief or pure mental effort canceled their efficacy—but after the two incidents on the motorcycle, you concluded that curses, especially *mal de ojo,* were real. But Maria was not the first person to curse you. Surely, you thought, you had been cursed long before you met her, long before you arrived in the United States, perhaps even long before you were born.

CIA TORTURE

The second millennium came. You had two daughters and a hand-ful of dead dreams. You discovered crack cocaine, which resem-bled a piece of calcite from the guts of the earth—pure and promising. The drug made you feel you were in touch with God himself. You had never been convinced by your mother's Catholicism, but the existence of some kind of divine being was undeniable. You had felt it while meditating as a teenager, and again while smoking crack. It seemed more real than anything in this world, a blissful bodily filling and eras-ing, contradiction embodied.

But then, one day, you started hearing voices in your head, light-ning bolts in your chest. You noticed people following you. You turned to the Internet, and discovered a vast community of people reporting the same experiences: Targeted Individuals, or TIs. You read about Project MKUltra, about how between 1953 and 1973, the CIA con-ducted covert mind-control experiments combining LSD and intimida-tion techniques such as gang stalking on involuntary subjects in the general population. Was the CIA doing something similar now with electromagnetic or radio waves? You noticed a correlation between the torment and your crack use, and finally you figured it out: the CIA was trying to eradicate your drug addiction with its mind-control technology. Success would prove to them that their weapons were effective in dramatically altering human behavior. The simultaneous genius and evil of the possibility infuriated you; you became hell-bent on thwarting the project.

You smoked crack with fervor. The government punished you with what felt like a remote Tasering of your coronary muscles, causing you to collapse and writhe in pain. You called the *San Diego Union-Tribune* and requested to place an advertisement. A female representative typed as you dictated the message: *Desperate cry for help, period. Unconsenting victim of aversive behavior conditioning. Seeking lawyer, activist, civil rights group and reporter.* The representative hung up the phone. When you called back, she hung up again. You concluded that the newspaper was working with the CIA.

While flipping through the channels on TV, you noticed something strange: channels without a signal synchronized with your thoughts. A horizontal line through the center of the gray static wiggled wildly if you were having agitated thoughts and went flat if you stopped thinking. When your brothers visited, you showed them how the line danced when you spoke and went still with your silence. *You're crazy, man,* they said.

You felt a constant electric current through your body: a cold, hard, painful feeling, like particles of ice in your veins. If you touched anything metal, you felt immediate relief, as if the current was dissipating. This gave you an idea. You drove to my mother's house with a magnet and a piece of copper wire. You wanted to prove to Jeannette, scientifically, that something was happening to you. You held up the copper and the magnet, tied to a string. The copper caused the magnet to move wildly on its string, a physical impossibility unless the copper had a strong electric current running through it. Here was evidence that *you* were charging the copper as you held it.

"Mom saw this?" I ask you years later.

"Yes," you say, emphatically. "But I guess she's not *analytical*."

When I ask my mother about the demonstration, she says she has no memory of it. "I don't know, maybe I ignored him. . . . It's not like you can take somebody like that seriously."

"So you're saying it may have happened?"

She shrugs. "When you don't believe something, it doesn't matter if someone tries to prove it to you—you don't believe it. But knowing he was using hallucinogenic drugs . . . how could you believe him? Your father was very smart, but unfortunately he messed up his brain really bad with drugs. What he thinks is real is not real. What he thinks happened did not happen."

Downtown, among other crack addicts, you were believed. Surrounded by homeless people, you leaned your head back and placed a penny between your eyebrows. It instantly jumped off you, as if zapped by your corporeal current. The witnesses backed away in fear and amazement.

Most of your friends were black men who lived on the streets. They were the only ones who listened to your theories and believed them. They, too, were uncooperative lab rats of CIA mind-control experiments. You smoked crack together, talked about the fucked-up world together, drank beers, played cards, walked on the beach. You soaked up their street slang, eager to speak like them. To this day, your language features a riveting hybrid of their rhythms and book-nerd Spanglish.

Sometimes the torture did not feel like torture. You discovered enormous, ethereal shapes—sapphire spheres, crystalline cubes, mutated pyramids—floating above your head. They seemed both divine and dangerous. They looked like doorways to parallel worlds. But you couldn't figure out how to open them. When you touched them, they became disfigured. They possessed a consistency between wax and clay, molding around your fingers. If you scratched them, their substance collected under your nails.

You were unwilling to give up crack; you weren't going to let a corrupt government dictate your behavior. But every time you smoked, the gringos commented annoyingly in your head, *Look at him sitting there,* and *Watch him light up the pipe,* and *Let's see how long he can handle this one,* then zapped you with their icy rays. You collapsed on the ground, writhing as if with a seizure. You broke several crack pipes with these falls, until finally you stopped buying the glass kind and got a wooden pipe, as suggested by one of your friends. At night, the voices tormented you without cease, making threats and insulting you, and finally, crazed with insomnia, you decided to end your life. You were living with your mother at the time. You walked into the bathroom and filled the tub with water. Then you plugged the hair dryer into an electric outlet. You crawled into the tub, weeping and trembling, and as you reached up to pull the hair dryer into the water, your mother burst in through the door. She hauled you out of the tub, soaking herself as she summoned Santa María and blessed you with the sign of the cross.

She drove you to the Bayview Behavioral Health Campus. A psychologist asked if you were hearing voices. You shook your head. "But she fuckin' wanted to *insist* that I was hearing voices. And I *did* hear voices," you say, laughing. "There was a TV playing over there in the room and I said, 'Do you hear that TV? Well, I hear it, too. But that doesn't mean I'm "hearing voices."' There's a technology in which they can make you remotely hear voices, and it has been *documented*. You can *read* about it."

At the clinic, the voices stopped. You were released. You decided to cross the border into Mexico. You were determined to be the most recalcitrant victim the CIA had ever known. You would not let them win! You drove your dark green VW Jetta into Baja California with a month's supply of crack in a glass jar and your life savings in cash. Rebelliously, with the windows down, listening to jazz, you sped through the desert on the Transpeninsular Highway, inhaling deeply and defiantly from your crack pipe. Finally, you were free. Free of voices, free of electric shocks, free of stalkers. You drove joyfully, skirting iguanas and roadkill, watching as the ocean transformed from a dark savage blue into a celestial aquamarine. You lost sight of the sea for several hours, then it reappeared, now on the east, the Gulf of California. You saw sunlight dancing on the sky-like water, glittering through walls of mutant cacti that leaned and grasped and twisted in on themselves in a crazed paralyzed dance. You were anxious to get as far from the United States as possible, and did not plan to check in to a hotel until reaching La Paz, at the southern end of the peninsula.

After several hours of driving, you felt an itch on your cheek. You turned your head. You leaned closer to the passenger's seat. It was unmistakable: the headrest was zapping you. Cursing, you pulled into the next Oxxo—the Mexican equivalent of 7-Eleven—and bought aluminum foil. You wrapped a long piece around the headrest, trying not to tear it with your trembling hands. That seemed to stop the unpleasant sensation. But as you reached for your keys to put them in the ignition, they swung away from you with a sudden motion, as if repelled by your flesh. You held them in front of your face and watched as the keys, rather than hanging loosely in accordance with gravity, moved toward the dashboard. You forced the keys into the ignition, started the car and stepped on the gas.

Back on the road, you saw a military checkpoint up ahead. You consulted your rearview mirror for an escape. A black SUV with tinted windows and American plates was tailgating your car. You took deep breaths, using the meditative techniques you had cultivated as a young man. You rolled down your window. A Mexican soldier asked where you were going. Praying he wouldn't notice the empty beer cans and drugs strewn around you, you tried to explain that you were heading to La Paz for a short vacation on the beach. You checked the rearview mirror again. Two gringos in casual clothing were emerging from the SUV. They seemed to be friends with the soldiers at the checkpoint. They were chatting amiably.

I need you to step out of the car, the soldier said.

You opened the door, sweating, trembling. The soldier led you away from the car, asking innocuous questions about where you were from and what you did for a living. You glanced over your shoulder and saw four people crawling into your back seats, including one of the white men from the SUV. "It was like they were putting something in there, a piece of equipment or something," you tell me decades later.

After a few minutes of small talk, the soldier told you to enjoy La Paz. "I went back to the car, closed the door, and everything was intact," you recall. But as you drove south, you noticed a difference: the whole car was buzzing with painful electricity. About five kilometers outside the beach town of Loreto, you parked your car on the side of the road. A new moon hid in the night sky. You sprinted into the desert with your crack. You walked until you reached a precipice. You could hear the ocean roaring beneath. You could not see it, or tell where it ended or where the sky began, but you knew it was there, a noisy liquid blackness blending into the mute vacuum of unlit space. You sat at the edge of the cliff, feeling your way downward as the wind whipped your skin. You wanted to lose yourself in the blackness, wanted to hang from the barren mountainside against those elements—pinned by the wind between sea and earth, fire on your pipe. You slid until you arrived at a thick barrier of brush. You lit up, warmth gushing through your veins. You melted into the night.

·

You woke up to the chirping of crickets. As you walked to your car, you saw two flashes of red light in the distance. Simultaneously, two electric shocks penetrated your chest. The second shock, sustained, sent you thrashing to the asphalt. You were sure you were going to die, it was so extreme, like an electric chair enacting a death sentence. But it stopped. You stood and sprinted to your vehicle.

Sobbing, you sped belligerently into Loreto. You drove into trash cans and telephone poles. You threw empty beer bottles out of the car. You tossed the whiskey, the crack jar, the pipes, the empty bags of peanuts. You hit your brakes randomly, spun the steering wheel, made your car screech and spin. You threw your head back and screamed. You were determined to get arrested. You felt you were the victim of a grave injustice. If the CIA wanted you to stop smoking crack, they should have put you in jail—not violated your civil rights in your home country. You pulled up next to another driver and offered him twenty dollars to lead you to the police department. He obliged. About a dozen police officers stood in front of the station. "I got out of the car and I was crying. 'I want you to arrest me!' *'Quiero que me arresten!'* And all of them were trying to be real nice. 'Why? Do you have drugs?' I told them I had been doing drugs, drinking, making a mess, throwing garbage all over the streets, speeding around the city. 'I'm a danger to other people and to myself and I want to be arrested.'"

One officer invited you into the passenger's seat of his patrol vehicle. You insisted that he handcuff you and throw you in the back. He acquiesced. Inside the jail, officers counted the thousands of dollars you had brought, recorded the exact quantity and stored it in a locker for you. Then they put you in a cell. You found an empty milk carton on the floor and used it as a pillow. Finally, you could sleep. The CIA would not bother you in jail. They had left you alone at the mental health campus. You had placed yourself exactly where you belonged. But as you were about to drift away, you felt an iceberg growing in your heart, causing you to choke and gag on the floor. The torture stopped. You gasped, trying to recover, then it started again—this time stronger than ever before. "I passed out like two, three times," you say. "They went on and on like that . . . until I said: 'Kill me, *please*; I'm ready to go.'" Each time, the torture stopped just when you were certain you couldn't take it anymore. You stumbled to your feet, gasping and sobbing. You punched the concrete wall of the jail cell, breaking a metacarpal bone. Blood dripped from your knuckles. You fell to your knees. Another shock sent you facedown to the floor. "I felt like they were pulling my soul out of me—I got really—it was terrible. Terrible. Terrible." You sigh, voice quivering in recollection. "I don't even know why I'm telling you all this. It fucking sucks, man."

You shake your head. You look down at your trembling hands.

"Does it depress you to talk about it?" I ask.

"No, it's just dumb; I can't convey it to you properly, it's—I don't understand why you don't write fiction," you say. "You can make up better stories than this."

FLIGHT

I submit a Freedom of Information Act request to the CIA for records related to Marco Antonio Guerrero, resident alien of the United States, and include a signed authorization and certification of identity from my father.

The CIA responds promptly, informing me that my request is "denied pursuant to FOIA exemptions (b)(1) and (b)(3)." FOIA (b)(1) applies to "information currently and properly classified, pursuant to an Executive Order," and FOIA (b)(3) applies to "information that another federal statute protects," including the CIA Act of 1949, which exempts the agency from disclosing its "organization, functions, officials, titles, salaries, or numbers of personnel employed."

In response to a separate request for records regarding experiments using electromagnetic and/or radio-wave technology on residents of San Diego County anytime between August 1999 and August 2004, the CIA says its primary mission is foreign intelligence and therefore finds my request inappropriate.

"The information you request, insofar as we can discern, has nothing to do with the primary mission of this Agency, and therefore, we regret that we are unable to assist you," the agency writes.

I send requests to the FBI, the Drug Enforcement Administration, the Department of Justice and the Defense Advanced Research Projects Agency (DARPA). All respond that they have no records or decline releasing them based on exemptions.

•

It has been a decade since the national security correspondent Sharon Weinberger first gave a voice to the so-called Targeted Individuals, featuring their testimonies in the *Washington Post* article "Mind Games." I call Weinberger while writing this book and ask her personal opinion about their theories. She has continued to cover national security agencies and authored the book *The Imagineers of War*, about DARPA. Could the CIA, DARPA or some other government agency in fact be experimenting on innocent people? It's unlikely, Weinberger replies. She has found no hard evidence to support the claims of Targeted Individuals. But she maintains that they are not "crazy"—that's not the right word to describe them. "I guess that was my point, that to just say these people are crazy is not, in the most part, correct," she explains. The Targeted Individuals she interviewed sought logical explanations for their experiences. They did research. They were critical of unscientific claims. They printed out patents and academic papers. "In many ways, they had a sanity that was sort of impressive," she says. "Instead of just saying they're obviously all crazy, what if we just put aside the veracity of their claims and try to understand it on their own terms?" She says she was baffled when interviewing psychologists because they expressed no interest in the details of their patients' allegations of persecution; their narratives were dismissed and medicated. "That, for me, is sort of mystifying; I mean, you're studying—this is your career. It seems odd and unscientific not to be interested in [their stories]."

For months after her article was published, Weinberger found herself inundated with emails from self-described Targeted Individuals who wanted to thank her for "exposing" their plight or to request her assistance. She still receives about an email a day about "Mind Games."

•

Back in San Diego after your trip down Baja California, you purchased a one-way ticket to Amsterdam, certain that the Netherlands, unlike Mexico, would not let the United States torture innocents. Once you arrived, however, you encountered a problem: taxi drivers—in your experience, connoisseurs of their city's underworlds—informed you that crack was impossible to find. One driver took you to a plaza where a powder cocaine vendor prowled. As you cooked it in your hotel room, you smelled something strange—some kind of nerve gas. It made your heart rattle. You ran downstairs to request a new room, gasping: *There's some kind of gas leaking into mine.* A hotel employee came to inspect it. He backed away from the door, coughing, confirming your belief. The new room was better. But three-dimensional geometric shapes sprouted all over the furniture, tiny brown versions of the portals to parallel universes you had seen before. You plucked them off the furniture and collected them in a jar, grateful for concrete evidence of what was happening to you. One of them was a four-sided pyramid with the top chopped off, and when you touched it, you felt a massive electric shock in the area of your brain stem. You had never felt a shock there before. It was unbearable, an iceberg erupting in your upper neck, enlarging it to the point of rupture. You ran downstairs crying for help. The torture intensified and you collapsed.

You awoke in the hospital. A radiologist held up your X-ray, showing you the broken rib. It stabbed your right lung with each breath. You beseeched the doctors for pain medicine but they refused to administer it, as if colluding with the CIA. You stumbled out of the hospital in agony. You hailed a cabdriver and asked him to take you to a heroin dealer. You were desperate for an anesthetic. For the first time in your life, you injected the black tar into your veins—like your first friend, Charlie.

You spent days searching for crack. A taxi driver told you it was widely sold in Belgium. You bought a ticket to Brussels. A tattooed Moroccan led you through alleyways and turned to you with a bag of perfect white pieces. You nearly jumped into the sky with joy. Returned to Amsterdam. Smoked in your hotel. Felt earthquakes ripping apart your brain.

You writhed and cried on the floor, digging your nails into your neck, trying to stop the torture by extracting your brain stem. The intensity augmented. You were drooling and screaming. It felt like the government was cutting off the circulation to your brain while simultaneously zapping you with electricity.

This was it. This was your limit. You could fight no more. You fumbled for your suitcase and ran outside. You hailed a cab, sobbing. You gasped at the driver to take you to the airport. Sitting in traffic, you begged the CIA to stop torturing you. *I give up!* you shouted at the top of your lungs. *Leave me alone! I will never smoke crack again!* You threw your crack from the window. *Calm down, my friend,* said the driver, a compassionate Indian with an accent. *I know how you feel. I was using once, too.*

Outside the airport, a group of concerned strangers surrounded you as you convulsed on the ground. *He's having a heart attack!* an American traveler shouted in English. *Call an ambulance!* An angry security officer dismissed the onlookers. *He's just a drug addict,* the officer said with disgust. The American traveler kneeled and said to you: *Sir, I've called an ambulance; everything is going to be all right.*

The torture halted just as the paramedics hooked you up to an electrocardiogram. They could detect no abnormalities. The officer talked to them in Dutch; the paramedics left. You stumbled into the airport and caught a flight to San Diego. You experienced no shocks on the plane, which protected you with its casing of aluminum alloys.

•

Back home, at your mother's house, you were sober. A terrible heaviness penetrated your limbs. It was like the ocean swelling inside your bones, your veins, bloating you with *toneladas* of itself. You felt dead, or rather possessed by death. Perhaps it wasn't the CIA hurting you all along. Perhaps it was demons, or *el Diablo* himself.

You looked up at a metal crucifix on the living room wall and it filled you with hope. What a beautiful shape it was: a negation affirming, a yes and a no. You walked over to it. Pulled it down. Carried it into the kitchen. Turned on the stove. Took off your shirt. Pulled tongs from a drawer, used them to hold the crucifix over the fire. Once it was glowing red, you brought it to your bare chest, right over your heart. You screamed as it burned. Kept it there—you wanted it to make a permanent mark. It would protect you. It would negate the evil inside you, and create space for something good. You stared out your mother's window at the ocean. Near the water, the sky was the color of blood. You smelled your cooking flesh. Pulled the tongs away. Blood dripped from a cross-shaped wound on your chest. You breathed a sigh of relief.

•

You became a taxi driver. Drunken groups of teenagers regularly stumbled into your cab offering you Ecstasy. You refused, afraid to re-incur the wrath of the CIA. But you wondered how long your sobriety could last with so much temptation.

One day, a fellow taxi driver named Nelson told you about a trip he made to Bangkok, where he slept with beautiful Thai women for twenty dollars apiece. He lamented that he couldn't do drugs, though, because they weren't available. *Drug dealers are executed over there,* he explained. He ran a finger across his neck.

It occurred to you that if you went to Thailand, you would have no temptation whatsoever to do crack, and you would have the best distraction: women. In less than a week, you were on a plane to Bangkok, carrying notebooks filled with lists of the best places for pretty girls. You headed straight to Nana Plaza, a three-story sex complex where you bought slim girls in their twenties with thick legs. They remarked on the horrible cross-shaped scar on your chest. You lied that it was from a motorcycle accident.

You rented a scooter for about five dollars a week, flying through the city, soaking up exotic sights and aromas, past the Temple of the Emerald Buddha with its dazzling murals, past the palatial Wat Arun, which glowed like a golden version of the Ivory Tower in *The Neverending Story*, past the banks of the Chao Phraya River and the floating markets of Khlong Lat Mayom.

Everybody seemed happy in this country. The vibe was great. When the monk police stopped you for running a red light, they accepted your apologies and cigarettes with amused chuckles. They posed for photographs with you. But it was not long before you grew tired. You couldn't sleep when prostitutes spent the night, fearing they would rob you of all the cash you had brought. It was exhausting. For the first time in years, you discovered in yourself a desire for emotional intimacy. But the mere thought of love made you so anxious you started drinking whiskey. Intoxicated, you drove your scooter to the beach resort of Pattaya. In the hotel lobby, you observed that the receptionist was attractive. *Let's go to my room,* you proposed, your voice slurring.

She asked you where you were from.

I'm . . . from . . . Italy!

"Right away, she was all infatuated because I was an Italian man," you recall. She went to your room and you slept together. Afterward, she wanted money. You felt hurt. *I don't want a prostitute,* you explained. *I want a girlfriend.*

The receptionist thought about it for a few seconds, then agreed. But her haste made you suspicious. She seemed easy, even shallow. After a few weeks, you got tired of Pattaya and the receptionist. You hopped on a train toward the border with China, your backpack stuffed with bottles of Johnnie Walker. One of your happiest memories took place in a mountain village filled with rice paddies, mushroom pastures and bowls of glistening honey. "It was the best honey I ever tasted, like flowers' perfume," you say. Around a campfire, you pulled out your whiskey and got the locals drunk. In the morning, you woke up by the embers, where you had passed out. A local woman appeared with your wallet in her hands. You had dropped it on the road. Not a cent was missing.

Wow, thank you! you said, surprised by their honesty.

When you were leaving, all of the townspeople crowded around you, trying to persuade you to stay.

We have a girl for you, a wife! someone said. *She's in the rice fields.*

You were tempted, but you felt restless. You traveled east to Vietnam. You joined a group of expats at Saigon's Duna Hotel, where local girls hunted foreigners with money. Phuong, a twenty-two-year-old with a plain Mongolian face, told you she had moved to the city from a remote rural village when she was a child. She grew up selling gum on the streets. She spoke English; when she learned you were from Mexico, she asked you to teach her Spanish. Phuong had to hear a word only once to remember it. She was enchantingly sharp. Like you, she had a drinking problem. One day, she became belligerent. She stood up at the hotel restaurant, cursing at the expats in incomprehensible Vietnamese. She ran outside, where it was pouring rain. You followed her.

What's wrong, Phuong? Let's go back inside; you're going to get sick!

I want to go home.

You offered to take her on your scooter.

It's too far. An hour outside town.

I don't care. I'll take you.

She hopped on and you sped through the rain to her mother's modest lakeside house, which was filled with so many mosquitoes they entered your nose with each inhale. You spent the night. In the morning, you were covered in mosquito bites.

You asked Phuong to be your girlfriend. She showed you a picture of a fat gringo who sent her $400 a month. *I belong to him,* she said sadly. You showed her a picture of me and my sister that you kept in your knapsack. *I belong to someone else, too,* you said, jokingly, to convince her that you didn't care. You moved into her mother's house. The two of you kept a pact of sobriety. You cooked and went shopping together. At the market, Phuong picked out the fattest ducks for dinner. She watched with a hawk's eyes as the sales boy strangled, plucked, skinned, chopped. Once, she spat and screamed when he handed her the plastic bag. With a blush, the boy handed over additional bloody chunks of duck. *He tried to keep the liver,* she explained. You fell in love.

One day, when you were alone with Phuong's mother, she looked at you with a somber expression. *You a very nice man. But you, you gonna be gone. Gone. Gone,* she prophesied. She was crazy. You were never going to leave. You were going to stay here and live happily ever after with Phuong, maybe even start a Mexican restaurant. You had never felt so happy, so comfortable.

Then you discovered that Phuong's fat old man had come for a visit. You left the city in a fit of jealousy. You say of Phuong's mother: "It was like she saw into the future."

•

You traveled to Kuala Lumpur. You stayed only a few days because whiskey was hard to come by. You jumped onto a train to Cambodia, swimming every day in an abandoned green pool. Once, while riding your scooter in Phnom Penh, an enormous group of prepubescent girls blocked your path on the road, offering oral sex for a few dollars. Disturbed, you headed to the Philippines, where you spent New Year's alone, drinking, depressed by the festivities. You took a deep breath and decided to go home.

•

Back in San Diego, you stayed at your mother's house. You built a cage for her multiplying lovebirds. She had acquired two large mutts: Pechocho and Muñeca. You took them on runs. Your calves swelled. Your skin browned. You stopped drinking. You purchased a digital camera and lighting equipment. You transformed your bedroom into a studio. You planned to become the professional photographer you had once desired to be.

One day, during a run with the dogs, you noticed Pechocho was losing weight. You increased his food rations, figuring he was not getting enough calories. But he continued to shrivel. Within weeks, his rib cage protruded from his sides. You stopped taking him on runs. It was confusing. Pechocho was a good, young dog, only three or four years old. Weeks ago he had been in perfect health. Now he seemed to be dying. One day, his hind legs collapsed and he dragged them as he walked. You knew you needed to take him to a veterinarian. But you felt feverish and exhausted, and decided to wait until you felt better. Pechocho died before that happened.

His death mystified and frightened you, especially when Muñeca began to show identical signs of deterioration. You knew you had to act quickly, but every day, you became more sick. You felt so heavy you could hardly move your limbs. Your hands shook with the effort of the simplest gesture. You saw Muñeca at the patio door, bones jutting from her torso and limbs, her back legs collapsed on the floor. She stared at you with cloudy eyes. It was like looking in the mirror.

When Muñeca died, you forced yourself to haul her carcass to your truck, sweating and gasping from the effort. Whatever had killed the dogs was killing you. You needed to get Muñeca autopsied. You dropped her off at an animal diagnostic laboratory. Days later, you received the report. "They said they couldn't perform the autopsy because the dog had been in such an advanced state of decomposition," you recall.

This seemed impossible. You had taken her to the lab literally hours after her death. What could have caused her body to rot so thoroughly, so quickly?

You asked for blood and urine and fecal tests from doctors on both sides of the border. All claimed you were perfectly healthy. You typed different diseases into Google and made a squiggly list of symptoms, pencil trembling in your hand. You thought a tick with Lyme disease had bitten you and the dogs during one of the runs. Or maybe a fungus or bacterium was eating you alive. You created folders on your computer and filled them with PDFs of scientific papers on Lyme disease, H. pylori, amoebiasis, adrenal fatigue and more. You printed out the documents and highlighted large sections. You researched cures—goldenseal, gentian, wormwood, hawthorn, yucca root. You were interested only in natural solutions; the pharmaceutical industry was repellent to you. On sheets of paper you had used to diagram renovations for your mother's backyard, you scribbled questions and theories. You printed out studies about epidemiologies, microbiologies, enzymatic reactions and more.

You wondered if the CIA was experimenting on you again, or if perhaps they had done permanent damage to your body during the previous period of torture. You were determined to find a cure—you wouldn't let the government or nature or whatever win. Your parents had stopped using a house they owned in the Mexican beach town of Rosarito, due to rampant bloodshed among warring drug cartels. You moved into the abandoned house, a few blocks from the ocean. You started an experimental garden in the backyard, planting crops with curative properties. You toiled in the dirt, pushing past the pain in your limbs, the growing exhaustion, imagining that as you dripped sweat you were also expelling the illness. You strung bamboo sticks into small square-shaped enclosures that served as trellises. You stacked healing flowers on a pyramid of shelves. You prepared teas and tinctures in the kitchen. You used yourself as a guinea pig. Your cabinets overflowed with combinations of powders, pills and potions. You varied dosages and amalgamations, diligently recording each regimen and its results. You tried everything until you found a cure: black walnut husks.

After a few days of consuming their ground-up powder, newfound vitality gushed through your veins. Finally, you felt normal again. The effect was long-term. When your mother's favorite Chihuahua, Habibi, began to go blind, clouds forming in her beady eyes, you flew to Missouri, rented a car and bought black walnuts in bulk. Back home, you grated the husks to make a powder that you placed in empty plastic pills. Per your instructions, your mother fed the pills to Habibi by hand, folded up in little pieces of ham. Habibi regained her sight.

•

One day, your stepfather developed an open sore on his foot. He visited doctor after doctor. The sore kept growing, in spite of the powerful antibiotics prescribed to him. It looked like Jesus was going to lose his foot. His days at the Butcher Block were becoming unbearable. He could hardly stand, let alone walk. You did some unconventional research and concluded that your stepfather needed sessions in a hyperbaric oxygen therapy chamber. You took him to a place in Tijuana. The sore on his foot began to shrink. The sore vanished. Jesus was healed.

●

I remember the first time I told you I wanted to write a book about you. I was listening to you recount your life at a bar in Tijuana. Your chameleonic eyes matched the reddish brown of your Victoria bottle. I was nervously peeling the damp label off my own Victoria. You paused to take a sip of your *cerveza* and I confessed: "I want to write your story." You gasped and gulped and coughed. Your eyes watered and their whites reddened, causing your irises to appear rust-colored, congruous with the sunset sky outside the windows. You pounded your fist against your chest. When you could breathe again, you shook your head and said:

"Absolutely not. Maybe if someday you become famous, and respected, you can do it. Otherwise, nobody will think twice if"—you lower your voice—"if the CIA kills you."

I paused, trying to think of the best response.
"Pa, if I write your story, you'll be immortal," I said.
You rolled your eyes and squeezed indignation into your brow, saying you didn't give a damn about superficial bullshit like the perpetuity of your insignificant ego, but I could see the grin growing on your face as you spoke, the grin you were trying but failing to suppress. If you remain forever beyond my grasp, Papi, at least I could determine this: you were human, just like me, dying to live among the gods.

Part V

HOUSE OF JAGUARS

A staircase winds down a mountain toward a hidden beach in Los Tuxtlas, Veracruz, in May 2012.

EL MONSTRUO

I moved to Mexico City on September 30, 2010. My father's country had never been bloodier. Drug cartels were diversifying their portfolios with human trafficking, murder for hire and kidnappings for ransom. My job was to report out of coffee plantations and cocoa farms, where corpses accumulated in clandestine graves. Abuela Carolina touched her fingers to my forehead, chest and shoulders, in the sign of the cross. My mother wept.

Mexico had terrified me as a child. Now it loomed magnetic on the southern horizon. From the back of the Aeroméxico plane, I saw the capital. The protruding peaks of Popocatépetl and Iztaccíhuatl were the eyes of the terrain. The city—like all cities in Spanish—struck me as feminine (*la ciudad*). It was evident in the curve of her back, in her maternal embrace of the dead. Every year, she sank a few more inches into the buried swamp of the ancient Tenochtitlán. Buildings of all shapes and colors rose from her skin. The unapologetic chaos of the landscape was congruous with the man she had conceived, the man awaiting me, the man I had come here to understand. I was plummeting into an alternate universe, into the dream of the city itself, where the laws of fairy-tale physics reigned.

Papi had long showed me how to palpate borders for a "beyond." I had found it everywhere. The United States had its own brand of fantasy, with its UFO sightings, mind-control programs and drug-infused raves. But the magic of Mexico was different. It was earthier, more organic—as elemental as nature, and as merciless. It recalled an old garden a young father built, a *jardín* that swallowed life and made it nil. The sight was exhilarating. It felt like coming home.

•

Papi hadn't seen the capital since he was an infant. He had grown impatient as I struggled to stuff my library and thrift-store dresses into suitcases, and had left two days before me from Tijuana. He told me he'd get the lay of the land. He greeted me at the Mexico City airport by the baggage terminal, arms crossed in front of his chest. He looked like an emblematic figure in his element. He had grown a medium-length salt-and-pepper beard and black hair he kept in a little loop at the base of his neck. Abuela Carolina's half brother, Goyo, and two of Goyo's children stood with him. Papi had moved here to "keep me safe," according to him. This gave my mother and grandmother comfort, but I knew it was a vain promise. My father couldn't join me on reporting trips, and the capital was safe compared with the rest of the country. Still, his concern made me happy. It enhanced my sense of invulnerability.

How could a fearless girl ever be vanquished, with her fearless father at her side? We had ventured into the unknown together, in quest of *¿Por qué?* The beasts and demons in this land were real: flesh and blood. Earth-hewn creatures, feeble foes. Death was for mere mortals. I had pushed past the boundaries of quotidian reality, into the story I had longed to live as a child: I was a protagonist in a book about my father, and, as such, I could bleed and die without ever truly perishing. I felt immortal within the perimeters of the pages I was living.

We drove to a Mexican restaurant and ate from steaming plates of meats with melted Oaxaca cheese. After dinner, I checked in to Hotel Habita in the upscale neighborhood of Polanco. It was a ten-minute walk from the news bureau. I would start work the next morning, a Friday, which happened to be my father's birthday: October 1.

Alone in my all-white hotel room, I sprawled out on the king-size bed and ordered room service: an extravagant dessert of brownies and *galletas,* which came on a porcelain plate with raspberries. While sampling the sweets, I turned the pages of the day's *El Economista,* reading, among other things, about a mudslide in the state of Oaxaca that had killed a family. It seemed so far away.

•

The news bureau was in a three-story house with pseudo-baroque quarry windows. A dark stone staircase spiraled up to the hardwood floors of the living room, where I met my editor, Tony, a laid-back British man with a wheat-colored mustache. He showed me to my desk, which was in one of the bedrooms. *I guess you can start by calling the agriculture ministry,* he said. I was one of only two women in the bureau of nine people. A calendar featuring images of buxom women in bikinis hung in the coffee room.

•

My first interview was with the spokesman for Mexico's Ministry of Agriculture, Paco. We met at Vip's, the Mexican version of Denny's. Paco was a thin, olive-skinned man with glasses, an aspiring poet. He folded his hands on the table and asked: *So, did you always want to be a journalist?* I confessed that I had once dreamed of writing novels. He furrowed his eyebrows. *Novels?* Paco leaned forward and lowered his voice: *Mi niña, living here, what you write won't have to be fiction. In Mexico, things happen that don't happen anywhere else.*

•

Papi celebrated his birthday at a *mariscos* restaurant in Polanco near my hotel. Family members I had never met came from the outskirts of the capital. They sat around my father, watching him with captivated eyes as he described life on the border: how the Rosarito fishermen near his house sell fresh *pescados* on the shore, how the northbound lines at the ports of entry stretch for miles but can be bypassed on a motorcycle in minutes. I had never seen anyone look at my father in the mesmerized way of our relatives—as if he were a saint or a celebrity. Their faces informed me of what mine must have looked like gazing at my father sometimes. He turned to me, tipsy and happy. He told me he was planning to look for his Mexico City birth certificate. He thought it might lead him to his biological father, whom he had never met. The man was probably dead by now—he'd be nearly a hundred years old, based on the few details Abuela Carolina had revealed to him. But he was curious to see where the search might take him.

Yes! I'll help you investigate, I said, excitedly. *Oh my God, Papi, what if we find him?*

One of his eyebrows twitched, a flame flickered in his eye. He made a sound like *agh,* then took a swig of his beer. He shrugged.

I don't really care, Jean. I probably won't find him. I just figure I might as well try.

I had noticed a pattern in our conversations, and I wasn't sure how to eradicate it. He spilled his guts, I asked questions, he seemed to enjoy my curiosity, and then, out of nowhere, one of my questions— its excessive emotionality—would irritate him, and he would look at me like I was an annoying teenager, causing me to panic. Afraid of losing my father's friendship, I would cheerfully steer the conversation in a new direction.

I got up to go to the bathroom. At the end of the table, a dark-skinned young man with spiky blue hair and an eyebrow piercing gave me a piece of paper with his phone number on it. He was my cousin Rodrigo, a *taxista.* He wanted me to call him whenever I needed a ride. He confessed he had stolen his cab, like the criminal *taxistas* who express-kidnap gringas like me. *Never wave down a taxi on the street,* Rodrigo said. *You can't trust any of them. But you can trust me—because we're cousins.*

After a couple of hours, I started looking at my phone. One of my colleagues, Nick, had invited me to drink mezcal at his apartment in the expat hub of Condesa. Nick was a handsome young man with curly brown hair, thick-rimmed glasses and light brown skin faintly freckled on the nose. He covered the drug war. We had spoken over the phone before my arrival about what I should expect from the bureau. When I told Nick my father was coming with me to Mexico City, he confided that he had never met his own father. I was eager to cultivate a friendship with Nick, who felt like a kindred spirit. A few minutes after 10:00 p.m., when I noticed that my father was drunk and happy again, I whispered to him that I was leaving. Papi had situated his birthday dinner in Polanco for my benefit, had just relocated to a different country to be near me. The disappointment was evident in his face. *It's not safe for you to walk at night! Plus, your hotel is too far,* he said in Spanish, too tipsy to sound authoritative. An uncle offered to take me on his motorcycle. Papi seemed placated. I stayed neither to order him a piece of cake nor to sing "Feliz Cumpleaños."

•

I spent the night smoking Lucky Strike cigarettes with Nick and two of his expat friends. They were all book lovers living abroad to avoid becoming ensconced in the privilege of first-world countries. They discussed the links between Mexico's violence and U.S. drug use in hushed voices, like characters in a novel: through inquiry, through calculated risks, they would solve the Big Questions. I was living a dream, surrounded on all sides by people like me. I felt I had to tread lightly—as if this world's foundations were made of water and I might fall through. I called my cousin Rodrigo at around four in the morning. He picked me up in his taxi and drove me back to my hotel. In the morning, he took me apartment shopping. I chose a two-bedroom penthouse with a library and a hot tub in Condesa next to Parque México, the neighborhood's largest park, a few blocks from Nick's place. The rent seemed cheap because of the exchange rate—I was earning U.S. dollars and spending in Mexican pesos. I had come to Mexico to unshelter myself; I was living with more advantages than I had ever known.

•

I asked Rodrigo to show me the Zócalo. The main plaza of Mexico City gave him claustrophobia, but he agreed. We chugged Indios in his taxi and crept through traffic as Rodrigo told me about his life. He worked part-time as a security guard at a whorehouse. He felt like an outsider. The family rejected him because of his unusual style in work and fashion, he claimed. *By the way, your vintage look is very outdated,* Rodrigo said, wrinkling his nose at my frayed faux-fur coat. Ever since my father gave me a brown Vietnamese dress threaded with floral patterns when I was eighteen, my wardrobe had been dominated by the color brown. I rolled my eyes, gesturing at Rodrigo's spiky blue hair. *Okay, Beauty Queen,* I said. Rodrigo and I passed graffitied tortilla factories, hardware stores, *supermercados,* laundries. Clothing lines on balconies showcased panties, socks, T-shirts. A newsstand sold the latest issues of *El Gráfico,* the capital's most popular tabloid, featuring images of decapitated corpses beside images of half-nude women. *My best friend is a transvestite,* Rodrigo mused. *She is so beautiful, nobody believes she is a man.*

Rodrigo parked his taxi. We walked through the narrow streets strewn with Coca-Cola bottles, McDonald's bags, flattened cockroaches trailing their guts. Wedged in a slow-motion stampede, we passed food stands selling quesadillas and boiled maize.

Finally, we reached the main plaza. A towering Mexican flag rose out of the Zócalo, waving its snake-devouring eagle on the *nopal.* According to legend, the gods told the ancient Aztecs to build their civilization at the site of that apparition. Hidden by asphalt beneath our feet, I realized, was the gutted heart of Tenochtitlán. Before destroying the Aztec capital, the Spanish *conquistadores* wrote that it was as beautiful as a dream—a floating metropolis of brightly colored pyramids. Centuries later, a Gothic gray cathedral grew out of the ruins. I saw the National Palace beside it, made of the same materials as the palace of Moctezuma, who was killed by the *conquistadores*.

Here was the strange mix of incompatible symbols, the forced intercourse of contradictions that defined my father's country. It was the child of carnivorous convergence. It felt foreign and familiar—like Papi himself. The most exotic parts of Mexico struck the most personal chord. They invoked the wildness of my father in my most native memories, when he dangled me over the edge of an ocean cliff with all the confidence in the world and asked: *¿Qué miras?*

I looked around at this landscape that embodied his mystery. Half-naked shamans danced and chanted in *náhuatl;* skinny children sold Chiclets; tourists bumped into beggars, who blinked their eyes against thirsty flies. So many people stomped, sauntered and skipped over the site of the ancient slaughter that all of the skeletons beneath us, with their pulverized pelvises and crushed clavicles, were probably shaking as if alive, as if dancing. Rodrigo crinkled his face with disgust. *God, I hate the Centro,* he said. But I was in awe. Reality was punctured through in this place. I saw meaningful patterns in all of it. What I had sensed from the plane I could perceive here with clarity: The city was alive. It was alive with death.

•

Food poisoning is a rite of passage for expats in Mexico City. Bacteria and parasites lurk in the ice cubes, the tap water, the lettuce irrigated with *aguas negras*. The delicate intestines of sanitary Americans are especially vulnerable. The torture for me began during my first visit to Goyo's, where I was going to have dinner with Papi. My intestines were wringing themselves like dirty rags. The cramps were unbearable. My father guessed I didn't want to be there. Chewing loudly, pointing with his fork, he asked, *What's wrong with you?* Before I could answer, he said: *Oh I know, you think you're so amazing now 'cause you have this fancy job. You think you're better than everyone. I knew this would happen. I knew you'd get this superiority complex. You think you're the shit. It's 'cause I never used to hang out with you. Now I want to hang out with you, and you're having revenge.* He persisted without pausing for protest, the same anger he had directed at me when he was driving me to my riding lessons as a teenager. I stared at the table, steeling myself. The numbness came naturally—a habit of my adolescence.

•

Two days later, Papi brought me herbal-tea remedies he had purchased at a local market. I was writhing against waves of nausea, exploding over the toilet every few hours. I had called in sick at work. Papi said the remedies would soothe my stomach and serve as antibiotics. While brewing me a pot, he told me about a recurring dream of his: *We climb a tall mountain. When we reach the summit, a dark energy—an evil spirit or something—tells us to turn back. He says we can't be up so high.*

What does the evil spirit look like? I asked.

I don't know, I can't see it; I can only sense it and hear its voice.

In the recurring dream, Papi said, we ignore the evil spirit. We exchange defiant smiles. We spread our arms and leap from the summit. We soar over the clouds.

That's a nice dream, Pa; what do you think it means? I asked.

I don't know, my father said, scratching his head.

Every time I have a lucid dream, I go flying. There's nothing else I'd rather do.

What's a lucid dream? he asked.

It's when you're in a dream and you become aware that you're dreaming. It's cool 'cause then you can do whatever you want—like flying.

Nice, he said.

I taught myself to do it in college, after reading some stuff online about it, I said, swerving my tone suddenly, because I realized I sounded excited and potentially boastful. I strove to speak without emotion, so as not to upset him. *Just write a letter or a symbol on your hand in pen—like the letter S, for sleep—and every time you look at it, ask yourself, Am I dreaming? You can do reality tests. Look at a clock to check what time it is. Turn away and look again. If the time stays the same, it's probably reality. If the hour has changed a lot, you're dreaming.*

Huh, Papi said.

Eventually, you'll see the S on your hand in a dream and become lucid. At that point you can do anything. If you start to wake up, spin in a circle or run your fingers on the palm of your hand. That way you ground yourself in the world of the dream.

It was probably the most I'd ever spoken to my father. Normally I just listened to him talk and I asked questions. I hoped what I was saying would increase his curiosity about me—that it would make him realize we were more similar than he acknowledged. He nodded slowly, eyebrows raised.

Sounds pretty neat, he said.

My father rummaged through my cabinets for a mug, then poured his tea. He told me about relatives I had yet to meet: a brilliant teenager, Eddie, who knew the entire history of the ancient Aztec and Maya civilizations; his parents, Chucho and Diana; and his two sisters, Valeria and Vivian. The family had taken Papi to a gargantuan hill overlooking the city. He had collapsed because of the altitude. They had carried him down. He said they were his favorite people in the world, and that he was planning to move in with them to give Goyo some space. He brought me the mug of tea. I took a sip.

Do you like it? he asked.

Yes, it's good, thanks.

He stood there in silence for a while, staring at me awkwardly, then said he had things to do. He left abruptly.

•

Back at the bureau, I called my father and thanked him again for the tea. It had cured me almost immediately. *Come over tonight,* I said. *You can make dinner at my place.* I knew that cooking always gave my father satisfaction. He agreed with enthusiasm, and offered to pick me up from the bureau in his rental vehicle. When I jumped into the passenger's seat, he launched into an angry monologue. I was surprised. We had exchanged such pleasantries over the phone. Had the traffic ruined his mood? Had I entered his vehicle with a rude air of entitlement? My father criticized me almost without stopping to breathe: I was spoiled, self-centered, shallow, stuck-up and seemingly endless synonyms for those words. I felt a static in my chest, a ticking in my head. I wanted, desperately, to defuse the situation. But his words were cannonballs, obliterating me, like my mother's accusations of Schizophrenia. I sought words in my brain with which to battle his. They exploded from my chest: *You're acting insane!* I cried, full of poison. Never before had I told him he was "insane." His voice wavered. He continued at a lower volume.

I kept my distance when we arrived at the grocery store Superama, which was next door to my building. Guilt thrashed in my guts, but I couldn't find the words to convey it. My father picked out halibut, vegetables and a loaf of French bread. We rode the elevator into the penthouse. When we saw the kitchen, we froze.

Shards of broken plates were scattered across the floor. My roommate, a British freelance journalist who had moved in that day, had stacked them on the edge of the sink, and they had fallen when the flimsy building shook with passing traffic. But I didn't know that at the time. My first thought was that my new roommate was mentally unstable. It was my father's first thought, too. As we stood in mutual fright, my father broke the silence. He began to laugh maniacally. In a high-pitched voice, he spoke as if possessed by my spirit:

> *I think I'm so smart! I think I can judge people just by looking at them! I am going to study neuroscience so I can screen my roommates better and understand everything! Ha ha, he he. I hate you, you piece of shit father! I am way better than you because I have a real job and a real life! I wish you would get out of mine! You're a nobody!*

I realized, with his last line, that he was quoting something I had said eight years before. I felt my insides go cold. Slowly, I responded: *Yes, actually, you're right. I want you to leave.*

He poked the button for the elevator, cradling three heavy bags of groceries. The doors opened. The doors closed. The elevator descended. He was gone.

I fell to my knees and cried, overwhelmed with contradictory emotions. I contacted my roommate, who explained what had probably happened with the dishes. I descended the elevator and walked to Parque México. I sat on a bench and smoked a cigarette under the trees, staring at the darkness in front of me. My father and I were supposed to be bonding. But every time we were together, one of us ruined everything. I returned to my place and dialed his number.

What, he said.

Are you calmed down now?

I calmed down the second I left your apartment.

Good, I said, casually. I considered apologizing, but thought better of it. Presuming out loud that Papi was capable of hurt feelings might further infuriate him. *So when are you gonna come cook for me?*

He grunted. *When you clean your kitchen. I can't cook in a dirty kitchen. I hate women with dirty kitchens.*

But my father never did come. Our disastrous first interactions in Mexico City had set the tone of our new relationship. We avoided each other for weeks. In November, Papi felt so exhausted he could barely get out of bed. His left foot was mysteriously paralyzed. It dragged behind him as he walked. He had been feeling sick since climbing that mountain with Eddie and the other relatives—the one where he had collapsed because of the altitude. He said he was going back home at the end of the month. *But you haven't found your father yet,* I protested. He claimed he didn't care. The prospect of his departure filled me with despair. It occurred to me that perhaps Papi *was* essential to my safety in this country; I feared I would be naked without him. I begged him to stay. But it was too late—he had made up his mind.

•

Rodrigo drove me to Papi's *despedida*. The farewell party was on a steep hill in the slums outside the capital. Inside a shared patio, my father was dancing to electronic music with a little girl. I had never seen Papi dance with anyone. He had certainly never danced with *me*. He spun her around, laughing with genuine, carefree enjoyment. His paralyzed foot dragged awkwardly. The little girl giggled with delight.

I felt a mortifying wave of jealousy. I tried to smile like a normal person as more than a dozen unknown relatives rushed to greet me. Plates of steaming, delicious food appeared in front of me: chicken bathed in mole sauce, *arroz blanco,* cheesy beans, spicy shredded beef, crunchy *chicharones,* soft *maíz* tortillas. My father's dance partner skipped over and introduced herself as Vivian, Goyo's great-granddaughter, among the relatives my father had moved in with in Ecatepec. She was ten. She fired off questions more quickly than I could answer. I told her she would make a great journalist.

She's my little doll, my father said, pinching her face.

Vivian's brother, Eddie, approached me. He was a lanky fifteen-year-old with brown skin, thick black hair and crow's-feather eyebrows that looked villainous and wild. He was the cousin my father had described as a "brilliant teenager" who knew everything about the Aztec and Maya civilizations. Eddie was writing a book about parallel worlds and extraterrestrials. The world doesn't have three dimensions, he explained, but four—the fourth, he said, is not yet visible to most people.

Do you know why the ancient Maya calendar ends in 2012? he asked.

I guessed: *The apocalypse?*

He grinned with his teeth and his eyes, so dark they looked obsidian. *Everyone is going to become aware of the fourth dimension, and the world is going to acquire a fifth dimension. Some people are going to be able to fly into it.*

Suddenly, Eddie leaned in close and asked, in a low voice: *Jean, do you think your father is a shaman?*

I laughed. *What?*

I think he is a shaman. He has seen the fourth dimension, Eddie said.

I squinted at my father on the other side of the room.

I guess he does look like a shaman, with that beard, I said.

Eddie's father, Chucho, stumbled to my side. Chucho wore a hat and a fur coat similar to mine. He had the same crow's-feather eyebrows as Eddie. He wrapped one arm around my shoulders and lifted his *cerveza* with the other.

You know, I have to say, your father is one tipazo. *He may not be a perfect person, maybe not even a good one, but he's a* tipazo, he said.

Chucho took a swig of his beer.

Do you know what tipazo *means?* he asked.

I nodded. It means "big type" or "true character."

Juanita, we're fucking crazy, he said, calling me Juanita because Jean was too difficult to pronounce (Cheen? Yeen? Yahn?). *We never plan anything. Fuck planning. I'm going to call you at some point—maybe next week or the following one—and I'm going to say, "Juanita. Three hours. The jungle."*

Papi approached us with a Marlboro in his mouth. Chucho's wife, Diana, called Eddie and Chucho into the kitchen.

So, my father said, *what do you think?*

About what? I asked.

He exhaled a ring of smoke. *About the family. I told you they were amazing, but you wouldn't listen—you were always busy.*

I felt guilty. I had spent my first several weeks in Mexico City prioritizing my job and social life and had neglected my family, with the exception of Rodrigo, who was always nearby in his taxi. *You were right. They are amazing.* I paused, then added: *I wish you weren't leaving.* When I looked at my father's face, tears were welling up in his eyes. My lungs stopped mid-inhale. I had never seen my father cry.

I'm just so glad— His voice broke. He took a deep breath. *I'm just so glad that even though I'm leaving, you have them here. To show you what a real family is like. So you can experience what I was never able to give you.*

He grasped my shoulder, hard, as if his life depended on it. The water in his eyes made his amber irises appear to glow. *I hope you know,* he said. Papi stopped to gather his voice. *I hope you know I love you.* I felt warm water on my face before I realized I was crying. I wiped it away. Perhaps my father had told me he loved me when I was a baby, but I couldn't remember him ever saying it until that moment. I told him I loved him, too. I pulled him onto the dance floor, afraid he would resist. But he was pliant. Standing in front of the speakers, I clasped Papi's hands in mine and jumped. He jumped, too. Neither of us could salsa or merengue. But it didn't matter. My cousins were playing an electronic remix of a song by the Doors. We leaped up and down in sloppy synchrony. *Let's fly,* my father cried, his eyes holding on to his tears. *Let's fly.*

BLOOD EDEN

I moved into a moldy two-bedroom in a Colonia Roma complex where Che Guevara was rumored to have lived while plotting the Cuban revolution. Termites crunched on the walls; the ceilings crumbled. Cockroaches crawled in and out of my clothes. I thought: *This is where I should be living, not that fancy penthouse. This is the real Mexico.*

An exchange student from Bolivia became my roommate. Rodrigo spent all day reading Russian literature and smoking cigarettes. He was a tortured soul, grasping his forehead in misery, but somehow also cheerful, whistling and humming in our apartment. He had striking emerald eyes and walnut skin. Although he was very handsome, we were too alike for romance, we understood each other like twins. We developed an idyllic platonic rapport. I cooked and washed the dishes; he took out the trash. He killed the cockroaches, which darted like enormous black bullets with antlers even after he stepped on them. "It's not dead yet," I told Rodrigo, watching the roaches drag their entrails. He stomped again. "It's dead now." I wiped up the guts with paper towels.

My cousin Eddie came over regularly. Like his father, Chucho, he called me Juanita. He was the most spiritual person I had ever met. He was not interested in videogames or sports or girls, like other teenagers. He spoke about energies and magic and the nonlinearity of time. Eddie was a riveting storyteller and as proficient as an old professor on various subjects. We went horseback riding in La Marquesa, a national park in Estado de México, an hour's bus ride from Mexico City. I gave him a crash course on riding—heels down, shoulders back—and we galloped through the trees, plunging into canopies of flowers so low and thick we had to hug our horses' necks. Afterward, we ate blue *maíz* quesadillas that old *campesinas* cooked on stone *comales*.

One day, Eddie told me the story of his grandmother, Goyo's daughter, the niece of Abuela Carolina. Maria Antonieta was the kindest, most positive person in the universe, a beautiful, benevolent octopus holding together disparate strings of sinners and drifters, with patience and understanding, before she fell into a depression and possibly committed suicide. Her body was found in a sewage canal, drowned in the *aguas negras* of Ecatepec, months before my father and I arrived in Mexico City. She died the day she was supposed to start a residency at a mental health clinic. *I can't digest the thought that she killed herself,* Eddie said. *I tell myself she was heavily medicated, that she was walking past the canal, that the thought crossed her head and she was falling before she knew what was happening. She hated water; she was terrified of it.*

Eddie told me her death cast a gloom over the whole family, over the world. He began to doubt the existence of things like magic and the afterlife. Then my father came to Mexico City, a beacon of spiritual light, inspiring ecstasy and hope in everyone he touched or beheld. *I knew he was different from the moment I saw him,* he said. *It was his eyes. Just by looking at me, he took away my sorrow about my grandmother's death.* Eddie told my father about his fears and troubles, and my father spoke sage words about spirits and parallel worlds that bestowed on Eddie a renewed faith in the meaning of life. He loved my father, and didn't mind that Papi showed no interest in staying in touch after leaving Mexico, ignoring Eddie's emails. *Mystics always have that in common: solitude,* my cousin said. *Any bonds they have to this world—people, mate-*

*rial belongings—separate them from their spirituality. Mystics have to eradi-
cate all of their terrestrial links because what ties you to this world keeps you
from achieving a maximum spiritual state. And it's sad, it shouldn't be that
way, and it's not that you want it or even understand it, but your body, your
very flesh and soul demand it. Solitude. No one will understand you. But I
understand your father. I know that he would have been an incredible dad,
loving, stupendous. But his nature . . . goes beyond common sense and desires.*

Eddie's descriptions of my father struck me, simultaneously, as as-
tute and absurd. I had seen Papi's enchanting side, but I had never
heard him wax poetic about spirits or parallel worlds. Eddie claimed
my father was an expert in the Kabbalah of esoteric Judaism, specifi-
cally the Sefirot of the Tree of Life—the ten channels through which
the unknowable reveals itself to conscious humans. Papi had mentioned to me that he was studying the Kabbalah. But when I asked for
details, he changed the subject. My father spoke to me almost exclu-
sively about his grievances. And if I volunteered information about *my*
woes, it was fuel for criticism. I couldn't express emotions without provoking his contempt. I had to be journalistic 100 percent of the time.

I was upset about my father's departure from Mexico City, and jealous about the fact that he evidently preferred talking with Eddie rather
than with me. I started reading *The Divided Self* by the Scottish psychiatrist R. D. Laing. The book's analysis of Schizophrenic patients sounded
to me like Eddie's descriptions of my father, without the mystical over-
tone: "His longing is for complete union. But of this very longing he is
terrified, because it will be the end of his self. He does not wish for a
relationship of mutual enrichment and exchange of give-and-take between two beings 'congenial' to each other. He does not conceive of a
dialectical relationship." Laing argues that "schizoid" symptoms de-
velop in individuals who seek to eliminate in themselves natural impulses, such as a desire to be touched. The repression causes a
splintering of the self, and the person becomes divided from himself
and others. He despises his own desires and the desires of others. Fleeing intimacy becomes a survival strategy. "The individual experiences
himself as a man who is only saving himself from drowning by the

most constant, strenuous, desperate activity," Laing continues. "Engulfment is felt as a risk in being understood (thus grasped, comprehended), in being loved, or even simply in being seen." But Laing rejects clinical diagnoses: "There is a common illusion that one somehow increases one's understanding of a person if one can translate a personal understanding of him into the impersonal terms of a sequence or system of *it*-processes." I still refused to reduce my father's beliefs to brain-chemical imbalances. But the idea of Papi as a shaman struck me as overimaginative, to say the least.

You know, Papi used to smoke crack, I told Eddie. *If he saw the "fourth dimension," it was probably a hallucination.*

Eddie's mouth dropped open. *Juanita, don't you know? The* curanderos *throughout Latin America use substances to open doorways in their minds.*

I sighed. I had listened to my father's stories for hours on end. *He* had never concluded he had shamanic powers. Still, I had to admit it was strange that my entire Mexico City family viewed him with a kind of spiritual reverence.

On Mexican Independence Day, I joined Eddie's family on a hike of El Cerro de San Pablo Tecalco, a mountain outside the capital. We drove halfway up, then hiked so high we were standing above the fireworks. A few clouds hung far beneath us in the lower levels of the sky. Eddie asked me to follow him on a dirt trail into the dark. As we walked through the cacti and prickly shrub, we came across a green pond. Eddie dropped to his knees and dipped his hands into the green water, splashing his face, taking vigorous sips. I grimaced. The water looked unsanitary. *Drink these magic waters with me, Juanita,* he said. *These waters will awaken your powers—but only if you believe.* Eddie looked at me with such earnest expectation I felt I had no choice. I cupped some of the water in my hands and took a meager sip. I burped and gagged as it trickled down my throat. It made me sick for weeks.

•

Back in San Diego, my father overdosed on tinctures of black walnut, wormwood, clove, goldenseal, gentian and more. The mysterious illness that had killed Pechocho and Muñeca was back. It had returned in Mexico City. His paralyzed foot regained its capacity for movement when he left the capital, but every bone in his body ached with an impossible density; Papi felt so weak he could barely support his weight. At first, he suspected Mexico City bacteria and parasites, but he had tried countless antimicrobials. He experimented with potent new concoctions, combining this mineral and that seed. His neat cursive writing filled stacks of notebooks. He reviewed existing folders of research on his computer and made new ones with labels such as "Antibiotic therapies" and "Detox." None of his herbal remedies worked anymore. Months went by. Depressed, full of self-loathing and frustration, Papi once more turned to whiskey.

•

At a national coffee conference, I met a man named Francisco Piedragil. He had bloodshot eyes, an Aztec nose and snow-white hair tied in a loop at the base of his neck. His skin was the color of cocoa seeds. He was the president of Cecafé, the Guerrero state coffee council, managing federal funds for the growers. I asked him innocuous questions about coffee subsidies. *You're asking all the wrong questions,* he said. He spoke not with scorn or in rebuke, but in confidence, as if we were co-conspirators. He leaned in so close I could see the individual hairs in his chaotic gray eyebrows and smell the whiskey on his breath. *You should be asking me about how the opium poppy farmers in my state are switching to coffee because of the high prices. I'm leading the effort.*

If I had heard him correctly, he had just handed me the commodities story of my dreams. Why he had chosen to confide in me, an inexperienced gringa, was a mystery to me. In retrospect, I have no doubt it was precisely that—my youth—that served as a lubricant on his inhibitions. But at the time I was not willing to see it, nor do I think it's important now, except to show that Piedragil was a man with big dreams.

I asked Piedragil if he would show me where this crop shift was taking place. *Of course,* he said. *The town is called Eden.*

•

I flew to Acapulco and took a cab to Hotel Copacabana, where Piedragil was going to pick me up in the evening. I jumped into the ocean and swam, then dried off and typed a daily-turn story for the newswire about the month's coffee output in Guatemala. When Piedragil arrived, he wrapped me in an aggressive hug, laughing as if we were childhood friends who hadn't seen each other in years. He smelled of cigarettes and undeodorized armpits—my father's smell. Night had fallen; Nick had told me not to stay in Acapulco after dark. The former tourist hub had become one of the most dangerous cities on the planet due to unprecedented cartel violence. But I was hungry, and Piedragil wanted to have dinner on a terrace by the beach. We smoked cigarettes and drank Victorias—the only clients in the restaurant. Piedragil told me his story. He spoke in a low, deliberate voice that bewitched me. He had grown up a guerrilla in Guerrero, setting fire to Nestlé coffee husks in protest of the multinational corporation's presence on the sierra. Now he fought the drug traffickers, an obstacle to the *campesinos'* ambitions for peace. He described the mass graves in the mountains and traced the bloodshed to the demand for drugs in *los Estados Unidos* as well as the "pointless war on drugs" waged by corrupt Mexican officials on behalf of *los gringos*. An hour passed, then two. His words merged with the rustling breath of the ocean winds. Around 9:30 p.m., we ordered dinner. A man in a red outfit, with horns and a tail, appeared beneath us on the beach. He poured gasoline into his mouth and blew on a torch, causing the fire to roar and expand. He stared at us, eyes wobbling on his wet, red, blistered face. He was drunk or dying. Piedragil dropped coins in his direction.

The waiter arrived with a plate of large shrimp doused in red sauce. Piedragil ate the shrimp with his hands, detailing how he had persuaded the *campesinos* of Eden to abandon the illegal drug trade to plant coffee instead because coffee was selling for record-high prices that year. Many had begun to win regional and national awards for the quality of their beans, even though they were *naturales*—normally considered inferior to *lavados,* which undergo an expensive washing process. Still, violence reigned among the *campesinos.* "They look at death like they look at sleeping," Piedragil said. "It's no big deal to put someone to sleep."

"Why do they see it that way?"

"It is the culture of Mexico. Especially in Guerrero. They are dragging behind them centuries of repression. Those who are alive today are the children of the fiercest killers. The fearless ones. The ones who have seen spirits with their own eyes, and aren't afraid to lose their lives. They see death as a dream."

His hands were covered in red sauce. He looked at me, one eye more pale than the other in the candlelight.

"But don't worry," he said, reading my mind. "If someone wanted to kill me, I'd be dead already."

He smiled with his teeth.

•

Piedragil dropped me off at an empty hotel on a dirt road. My bed crawled with tiny ants; a flattened cockroach adorned the wall; the room's only window refused to close. That night I dreamed of poppy flowers. I dreamed of being filled up with them. Their round bulbs entered my body through every crevice and pore, so my flesh stretched and expanded. Then I exploded. I woke up nauseated in the morning.

The road to Eden was bumpy the whole way. The producers gathered in their town hall, and Piedragil instructed them to speak freely. Then he vanished. I stood in front of the men, trying to remember my father's casual pose. I offered them cigarettes, but they declined. Whenever one man opened his mouth to speak, another man cut him off: "We're past all that. We shouldn't talk about the poppies—only the coffee." I tried breaking the men up into groups, encouraging them to talk among themselves, but the town-hall structure had ruined any chance of comfort. I was going to have to wait for another opportunity to interview them.

When Piedragil returned, he announced it was time to eat beans at the house of the town's poorest and oldest woman, La Doña. But first, we were going to have a drink with a *campesino,* who had slaughtered a pig for us. We could not eat twice, but we could share some mezcal to show our gratitude to the *campesino.*

All of the men gathered in the *campesino's* empty concrete living room on plastic chairs. Piedragil and I poured everyone mezcal in plastic cups. Piedragil spoke to the producers in his slow, captivating way. The producers leaned forward, spellbound.

"If you want your coffee to be successful, you've got to make it taste the same every time," Piedragil said. "That way, consumers will say, 'I like this brand.' Mezcal for example. Mezcal, they say, is the drink of the gods—because you always drink it and end up with your butt cheeks pointing toward Heaven."

The men guffawed. One cleared his throat and said: "I have a fear. Well, it's not so much a fear as an anxiety. You have helped us so much, Piedragil. What is going to happen with the new administration? What if we don't get a council president who cares about us as you do?" Piedragil shook his head. "I'm not such a good person. I get paid for what I do. The problem is some people get paid and don't do their jobs."

"But he's asking what we're going to *do.*"

Piedragil's hawk's gaze swept across the room.

"You've got to make yourselves *alive.*"

The room was silent. I saw goosebumps on the men's arms, on my own.

"Look," he continued. To help himself see, he put on his glasses—two pairs, each missing a lens. "The only relationship more powerful than a friendship is that which you have with an accomplice. All you have to do is understand that you produce some of the best coffee in the world, and that you are *accomplices* in this."

I needed to use the bathroom. While walking to the door, I noticed a producer with a young face and kind eyes standing near the back—one of the men who had tried to share information in the town hall but had been interrupted. I approached him and whispered: "If I come back tomorrow, alone, will you take me to the opium poppies?"

He nodded.

"What's your name?" I asked.

"David."

Outside, two roosters fluffed their feathers and rammed into each other, fighting. There was so much anger. A burst of it, an explosion. Their feathers were red and shiny in the glare of the setting sun. The bathroom was a hole inside a wooden shed. I squatted over it. When I returned to the *campesino*'s living room, most of the men were gone. Those who remained were trembling in their seats. Piedragil's assistant, Mayra, was standing up. She was a curvy, dark-skinned woman with curly hair; her eyes were wide with terror.

She said: "But they have guns, *licenciado*."

Piedragil shrugged and said: "So what? We have our hands."

I blinked. "*¿Qué está pasando?*"

"Nothing, *mi niña*. Take a seat and drink some mezcal while I teach you the three rules of life. Never get scared. Never get nervous. *And always be soft.*"

"It's time to go dine at La Doña's," he continued. "I wish I had three stomachs so that I could eat pork *and* beans *and* chicken, in three different houses. But alas, I only have one, and it is a stomach that, like the rest of me, is governed by the heart. Poor Doña has been waiting for me."

As we walked out into the dusk, Mayra explained in a shaky voice that one of the producers had been contacted by radio. "They told him two trucks carrying seventeen armed men were descending the mountains from the neighboring town of Paraíso. A few days ago, men came from Paraíso, threatening to kill everyone if they didn't continue planting poppies. They're coming back."

"What? Are you serious? How long will it take them to arrive?"

"I don't know," Mayra said. "I know nothing. Piedragil won't listen to me."

Piedragil marched ahead of us. We followed him to La Doña's house. I grabbed my phone to call my editor, but I had no service. In La Doña's candlelit kitchen, the white-haired *campesina* served us beans and tortillas. Mayra and I gulped down our food, desperate to depart. Piedragil was too busy talking to eat. Mayra took his fork and stuffed his beans into her mouth. He didn't seem to notice. "It's time to go," she said.

"Don't you see I'm eating? We must eat in peace! We mustn't let others terrorize us!"

La Doña offered more beans.

"No thank you," I said, my stomach in knots.

"Yes please!" Piedragil cried, holding up his empty plate.

"Piedragil, didn't you tell me we had to leave before dark?"

He waved my question away with his hands. "It's already dark! Night has fallen! What difference does it make? If you're worried, we can stay here. Right Doña? We can spend the night with you?"

I searched my bag for a cigarette. I stood and said I was going to smoke outside.

"Smoke here! La Doña—the girl can smoke in your house, can she not?"

La Doña assured me with a smile that I could. Piedragil leaned forward in his chair. "Panic," he said. "*Panic* causes people to make the most stupid mistakes."

I lit up my cigarette and took hard drags, glaring at Piedragil. I wasn't *panicking*. I was pissed. Piedragil was knowingly endangering me. He was breaking the rules of this place, overthrowing my sense of the plot. The old man with the chaotic eyebrows was supposed to have whisked me to safety as soon as we got word of the approaching criminals.

La Doña's husband spread his arms wide open and declared that he was going to go to bed a very happy man, having spent the evening with a *güera* (white girl). I forced a smile at him through my second cigarette. Then I stood up and declared: "Piedragil, we are leaving.

Now. My editor expected me to be in touch hours ago. I am sure he is worried about my safety at this point."

Piedragil stared at me in silence. Then he sighed. "Okay. Let us go," he said sadly.

We sped away from Eden through the pitch-black night, crammed in the bed of the Cecafé truck. The cold wind whipped my face as I clutched the rim of the truck. I could see nothing anywhere.

•

The next day, one of Piedragil's employees dropped me off at David's house in Eden. David informed me the men from Paraíso had turned around the night before. He smiled: "Maybe they heard a gringa was here."

I followed him into the forest on foot. The landscape was so thick with vegetation we had to break branches to make a path. "So whose flowers are we going to see?" I said, pulling spiderwebs from my face.

"He's just a man," David said. "He's not here this week. That's why we can go."

"So it's not your plot?"

"I stopped planting when Piedragil came."

We crossed a river using a fallen tree. We were surrounded by coffee bushes with bright red berries. David stopped by a cacao tree and plucked off the large yellow fruit. He cut it in half with a knife from his pocket. Large brown seeds lived in its fibrous, spiderweb-like substance. He plucked a seed and ate it. Then he held out the plant for me to try one. The juice of the spiderweb stuff was mildly sweet. *Spit out the seed or it will make you light-headed,* he said. The terrain became so steep we had to crawl on all fours, using moss to hoist ourselves up. We passed plantain trees and stacks of wooden logs. I gasped when I saw a giant stinkbug on the path. David picked it up. *He's harmless,* he said, placing it on his arm. *All he does is stink if you scare him.* The creature limped up his arm. It was missing a leg. It looked like tree bark.

After we had hiked for about an hour, the trees gave way to a vast clearing: bulbous pink flowers rose up out of the green. An extensive sprinkler system cloaked the clearing in a mist. Bees dipped in and out of the opium poppies. Their bulbs burst at the seams with black sap. "The bees—don't they go crazy?" I wasn't sure of the word for "high" in Spanish. He told me the bees went crazy, but not as crazy as the squirrels who ate the coffee berries.

"Wait here," he said. He walked to the center of the field, scanned the forest, then beckoned me with a hand. I heard twigs breaking behind him. A man holding a rifle appeared with a dog. The dog ran toward David, but then stopped to urinate on one of the poppies. I held my breath. David spoke to the armed man for what seemed an eternity. The tension in their faces was not dissolving. Eventually, I couldn't take it. I walked forward with a ditzy smile, hoping my blonde hair and green eyes and petite stature would save us. *"Mucho gusto, señor,"* I said, sticking my hand out to shake the stranger's. He looked at me with a bewildered expression. "Do you mind if I take a few pictures? I'm not identifying the town. It's a story for a financial newspaper about coffee prices." The man seemed to relax, realizing I posed no threat. *"Está bien, no hay problema,"* he said.

•

In December 2012, Piedragil's body was found facedown on a pile of coconut husks in a garbage dump near Acapulco, hands tied behind his back, blindfolded. He had multiple gunshot wounds. I saw the photograph of his corpse in one of the Mexican tabloids. He looked more asleep than dead, as if passed out drunk on the bed of coconuts. He wore *huaraches* and his usual earth-toned clothes: green shirt and brown pants. I remembered his words in Acapulco: "If someone wanted to kill me, I'd be dead already."

DROWNED

On April 23, 2011, during what is known in Mexico as *Semana Santa*, or Holy Week, I sped through a heavy storm into the known territory of bloodthirsty Zetas: Los Tuxtlas, Veracruz. I traveled with Rodrigo and three other friends, including my coworker Paul, a blond, blue-eyed adventurer who covered Mexico's economy. He and Nick had become two of my closest friends in the capital. Nick had refused to come with us to Los Tuxtlas, saying it was too dangerous. Paul had laughed. He was carefree and lighthearted, the opposite of Nick, who was introverted and serious. Paul had secured a transfer to Brazil, where he had longed to work for years. The trip was a goodbye journey. Paul's departure weighed on me. I had a secret crush on Paul, perhaps because he was the first man I had befriended in years who seemed utterly unmoved by me in any romantic sense. When I tried to charm him by discussing what I believed were fascinating subjects, such as quantum entanglement and out-of-body experiences, he rolled his eyes. I was not used to censoring my amorous feelings, but I knew there was no point in making confessions to Paul. He seemed to tolerate my friendship only because I enjoyed traveling, like him.

In a *National Geographic en Español* article that year, a mutual friend had written an enticing description of Los Tuxtlas, the northernmost tropical rainforest of the Americas. The volcanic region was home to a dwindling population of jaguars, and the central town of Catemaco—which means "burned houses"—had gained a reputation as the national and international epicenter of black and white magic. The article included a frightening photograph of a *brujo* sacrifice that involved cutting the head off a black cat, but the other images made the region look as verdant and beautiful as the rainforest near Uruapán and the coast of Colima, where my parents had gone on their false honeymoon. I hoped to encounter *brujos* in the rainforest; the boys were eager to see jaguars. "I'd rather die than live afraid," someone said as we drove through a storm. And in the solemn silence that followed, every person in the vehicle nodded, one after the other. So ignorant and young were we—was I, with my fearless smile.

Everyone knows Holy Week is the worst time to go to the beach in Mexico. Families occupy every square foot of sand. But Paul and I were determined to find an uncrowded beach in Los Tuxtlas if one existed. We were confident in our investigative abilities. I believed we could find not only an uncrowded beach but a hidden one, full of foliage, like those in the photographs of my parents' trip in southern Mexico.

We walked through the streets of Catemaco until we came across a stone building that lacked a front wall; the fog drifted in and out as though the building were breathing. We entered and discovered a drinking establishment. We ordered a pitcher of beer at the bar. I asked the bartender, a German expat, if she knew where to find a secret beach.

"She wants a beach with unicorns and waterfalls and fairies," Paul said with a smirk. The woman smiled mysteriously. She leaned forward and drew us a map on a napkin.

"A few minutes after the signs for Playa Jicacal, you'll see a dirt path leading into the jungle. Take that road until it ends. You'll see an abandoned hotel there. Get out of the car and look for a staircase leading into the jungle."

•

The next morning, we drove for hours along the coast, following her directions. Every beach we passed was so crowded with people you couldn't pitch a single tent. "I have a gut feeling you're going the wrong direction," I said. "Oh really?" Paul said. "Since you have a *gut feeling,* then you must be right. From now on, I won't make a single turn unless your gut tells me to."

He made a sudden U-turn. His friend Brian sighed from the back seat. "There is so much sexual tension in this vehicle," he said. "Will you guys just have sex already?" The others cringed in awkward silence.

We searched for the secret beach all day, and at some point I fell asleep. When I awoke, we were on a bumpy dirt road under a canopy of trees. Amber sunset light drifted through the dense green canopy in thick lines. Butterflies the color of butterscotch floated in the air. At the top of a mountain, three dusty white buildings rose out of the earth by a stone well. Spiders had spun webs in place of windows. We parked, got out of the car and heard a rustling in the trees. A Mexican man with a missing arm emerged from the rainforest. *"Buscan la playa escondida?"* he asked. We nodded yes, we were looking for the hidden beach. "That way," he said, pointing with his intact arm.

A stone staircase spiraled down the mountain. We followed the crumbling steps and saw the sea. It was lapping the verdant sides of the mountain. The wind lashed my face with the taste of salt and the smell of *mariscos.* We descended farther. At the base of the mountain, the steps spilled us onto the secret beach. The sand was covered in a pearly carpet of crabs that we displaced with each step. "Ladies and gentlemen, we have just found the only Mexican beach without a soul on it this weekend," someone said.

Darkness crept over everything. We hurried to pitch our tents and gather dry wood for a fire. A chorus of insects made a foreboding sound, like an E-flat that seemed to rise endlessly in pitch. Strange, glowing insects that were not fireflies emerged from the dark. They were black, bee-size bugs with two blue lights in front of their bodies. When they drifted into the smoke of our campfire, they fell into the sand and their lights flickered off, as if they had fainted. "Look, it's the fairies you've always dreamed of!" Paul joked. He scooped up a few that had fallen into the sand. He blew on them gently, getting the sand off their wings, and their lights came back on in his palms. Suddenly, even he was perplexed. "Those lights are their *eyes*," he said. We watched the creatures as they glided over the sea, then twisted in and out of the foliage on the mountain. We tried to keep them from the smoke, which seemed to make them sick.

In a mystified tone, my friend Becca said: "They're protecting us."

Brian snorted. "Either that or they're warning us."

•

The next morning, Becca and I dove into the Gulf of Mexico. We took our bikini tops off to feel the cold water against our naked skin. Gold particles of light winked in and out of sight around us. On the mountain behind our beach, a clearing in the jungle revealed a herd of grazing sheep. *It looks like a scene from the Bible,* I thought, breathlessly. I threw my head back onto the water. I had the sensation of reaching a summit: I had found a secret paradise in my father's country. I closed my eyes and reveled in the feeling of expansiveness that the ocean gave me. This was the meaning of life: moments like this—careless, weightless, free.

I opened my eyes and turned toward Becca. I felt disoriented. She was much farther than she had been a few seconds ago. I could no longer feel the ground under my feet. I tried to swim toward her, but my efforts gained me not an inch. I was moving away. I realized, with consternation, that a rip current was sucking me out to sea. How many times had I gone skinny-dipping off the coast as an intoxicated adolescent? Nothing had happened then, and here I was, a sober adult, caught in a rip current. I told myself to remain calm and conserve my energy. I knew I had to swim parallel to the shore. I did the breast-stroke north along the beach. The ocean pulled like a conveyor belt toward the horizon. I grew tired. Becca, the only person who realized what was happening, stared with her mouth agape. The waves became turbulent, blinding me, gagging me. I let go of my bikini top.

Panic gripped me. I had never understood the meaning of panic until that moment. I had heard of people suffering "panic attacks" and had often referred to my own feelings as "panic." I thought it referred to a sort of exaggerated anxiety. But when panic gripped me—and "gripped" is the right word—I discovered its true meaning. Panic is an animal that hides in your organs; it shreds you with its teeth, from the inside out. Rationality turns into a foreign language. The most horri-ble possibility becomes the only reality.

I knew immediately it was the panic that was going to kill me, not the rip current, if I didn't get it under control. But the knowledge that my life suddenly depended on my ability to slow my pulse made it impossible. I started hyperventilating the ocean into my lungs. I then understood fully—not just intellectually and emotionally but *bodily*—what the word "drowning" means.

Calm down, I screamed in my head, trying to remember the medita-tive techniques I had taught myself in college. But the phrase "mind over matter" suddenly struck me as incomprehensible. My heart was exploding in my chest. Water was penetrating my lungs. I was ex-hausted. We were a fifteen-minute hike from our rental vehicle and a forty-five-minute drive from town. None of us had a flotation device. No one had phone service. With every breath of oxygen I took, I heard the gurgling of water in my throat—a terrifying sound with corpse-like connotations. Every neuron in my brain begged me to keep fight-ing, and every cell in my body screamed that it could not. It was the ultimate mind-body battle; both were losing. The blue Gulf of Mexico seemed to stretch out around me immensely, indomitably, in all direc-tions, rising and falling like a panting creature, a predator intent on devouring me. After a few minutes, the inevitable became clear: I was not going to make it out of this alive. I hadn't yet written a book, I hadn't mothered a child, I hadn't done a single thing to improve this world. I would die in my father's country, senselessly, at the age of twenty-three. This was the end of my story.

•

The *taxistas* of my father's birthplace often asked me why I moved south to a country marked by northbound migration. *Why would you abandon* los Estados Unidos, *a country so many dream of, to come here, to this Hell?*

For my job, I always responded.

The answer was, of course, more complicated than that. There were many reasons: to understand my father, to unshelter myself, to expose corruption, to find adventure, to feel alive. How petty all those reasons seemed now. All of them had led me here: to the Gulf of Mexico, off the coast of Los Tuxtlas, where I would drown.

•

Waves like animate limbs rose out of the sea and thrust their way into my throat. I coughed and swallowed to keep them out of my lungs. *Meditate, meditate, meditate,* I thought. But the ocean was ruthless. It kept entering me, mindlessly, without intent yet embodying an inescapable cause-and-effect that involved sinking and suffocating me. The sea had a solely material purpose: to fill me. The thought of its vast, unthinking body, wrapping itself around the entire planet, stronger than all ships, all whales, all continents, positioned itself inside my bones with all its weight.

I sank. The discovery of my insignificance drained me of strength. I submitted to the sea. I meant nothing to the soulless universe, no more than cattle—like the sheep grazing on that faraway hill. How stupid I was, how absurd my pursuit of my father. I sobbed. My tears were a surprising comfort, a maternal caress on my cheeks. I thought of my mother: my beautiful, protective, hardworking mother. After everything she had sacrificed, she would be informed that her daughter had drowned. My mother had never wanted me to come to Mexico. She hated unnecessary danger; she despised futile questions. Her will was always to survive. Her focus was life, the immediate, the known. My father gravitated toward the opposite: death, the faraway, the unknown. In my obsession with the parent who rejected me, who rejected everything, I had become the mirror of a phantom. My obsession had dragged me here, off the coast of Los Tuxtlas, beyond a border I could never recross.

In the end, it was my connection with my mother that felt most real. I sensed her in my skinny limbs, in my frantic, pounding heart. And through that link, something dawned on me: I was my father's reflection, yes, but there was a distortion in the mirror. The distortion in the mirror was my mother. She had inflected my death wish with a need to survive—to embrace the fighting animal within me, regardless of its insignificance. *No, no, no,* I thought, or felt—a surge of refusal through every cell in my body. My mother coursed through my veins like a drug. I broke through the surface of the sea. I could see Paul treading water up ahead.

"What's going on?" he asked, trying to sound casual.

I gasped that I was drowning. His face was full of fear.

"You're going to be okay," he said, uncertainly.

"Please don't leave me," I begged.

The current was still pushing us into the horizon. The beach looked like a paradise you'd never be mad enough to swim to.

"Don't look at the shore," Paul said. I tried to grab him, but he swam away. He reached out from a distance and gave me his hand. "I need you to back-float."

Back-floating had always been difficult for me. The absence of muscle or fat on my bones made floating nearly impossible without vigorous movement. Earlier that morning, I had actually said to Becca: *I couldn't back-float to save my life.*

I turned onto my back. The sea reached its fingers into my mouth. Then the fistfuls came. I swallowed. I begged my stomach to be big enough to contain the whole ocean if necessary. Paul placed a palm under my back, holding me up with one arm, swimming with the other. My breasts were bare on the surface of the water. Here I was: naked, mortal, mammalian. Paul warned me every time a wave was coming so I would hold my breath. Sometimes it worked. Most of the time, the water penetrated my throat. I looked at the shore: it was farther than it had ever been.

•

Time passed. The ocean filled me. In what felt like another universe, Paul was saying: "I can feel the ground under my feet." He let go of my body. I clung to him impulsively. "Brian, your shirt!" he cried, dragging me onto the sand. Brian ran for a shirt. Rodrigo was pacing back and forth. Becca was sobbing. "We thought you guys had drowned!" she cried. I crawled away from the shore, pinning myself against the mountain, as far from the water as possible. I coughed and gagged and puked the sea.

As I lay gasping on the beach, I realized that something strange had happened to me, something I wouldn't understand until reading *Moby-Dick* months later. I didn't feel grateful to be alive. In fact, I didn't feel alive at all. Although Paul had clearly saved me, I felt dead. "The sea had jeeringly kept his finite body up, but drowned the infinite of his soul," Herman Melville writes of the sailor Pip after he sees the ocean stretching out forever in all directions, and goes insane.

•

Paul left for Brazil a few days later. The near-drowning had so thoroughly messed with my neural wiring that my belief that my life depended on Paul extended beyond the incident, and I felt certain that once he left the capital, I would die. He let me sleep at his apartment the night before his flight out of Mexico. I lay beside him, watching the glittering Mexico City skyscrapers from his open windows. Their lights remained on all night. I couldn't sleep. My body was filled with a highly unpleasant electricity. Suddenly, Paul pulled me against him. I

froze. *Does he think I'm someone else?* I wondered. *Is he dreaming?* I tried
not to breathe or make a sound. I didn't move until the sun came up.
We said goodbye without smiling or crying. Paul told me, after leaving
Mexico City, that in all his years of surfing he had never experienced a
rip current so wide and fast as the one in Los Tuxtlas. He wasn't sure
he was going to be able to save me. But, he said, "I knew from the time
I swam into the current that I wasn't coming out of the water unless it
was with you." I could no longer say I owed my life to God, to my
parents, to destiny. I was alive because of a young man's decision to
swim into a rip current.

⋅

I tried writing about what had happened, but I couldn't find its meaning. In my journal, I wrote: "When confronting death, what keeps you
alive isn't your soul. Because your soul dies very quickly. What keeps
you alive is the animal in you. The part you share in common with
livestock." I perceived the part of me that had endured as primitive and
instinctual. My spirituality, my inquisitiveness, my adventurousness—
those parts were dead. I had flashbacks, panic attacks and recurring
nightmares. My lungs felt compressed to the size of fists. I tried to
stretch their muscles by sucking in more oxygen, but they stayed small.
Something very disturbing started happening at night. I later learned it
had a name: sleep apnea. As I slept, my brain stopped sending signals
to my lungs to expand, and my throat collapsed. Carbon dioxide rose
to dangerous levels in my blood, prompting my nervous system to
send emergency signals to awaken. I sat up, suffocating, struggling
with all my might to breathe against the harsh grip of some invisible
demon squeezing my airways. I gasped and gasped until I felt a whistle
of air enter my throat. My throat opened, slowly, until finally the
demon let go. The demon was death. It had taken me into its jaws and
I had escaped, but I wasn't supposed to escape. And so death kept
hunting me. Fear dominated and drained me. I was drowning in the
memory of the drowning.

•

That year, Papi was diagnosed with polycythemia—the excessive pro-
duction of red blood cells. He had to get a pint of blood drawn once a
week, a phlebotomy. But it didn't cure him of the mysterious illness—
he was a stone the weight of a supernova. He kept drinking profuse
amounts of whiskey, the only thing that made him feel better, killing
himself to kill the sickness or curse or whatever it was. One day, at the
Tijuana clinic where his blood was drawn, he begged the nurse to remove more blood. She refused. When she left the room, he took the
needle and stabbed himself, sucking up syringeful after syringeful.
Again and again, he eliminated blood from his body, squirting it into a
trash bin until finally he felt lighter, better. He hopped into his jeep and
drove across the border to visit his mother. He passed out on I-5. His
jeep hit the median and flipped over twice. Miraculously, it came to a
halt right-side up without hitting other vehicles. The final impact shook
Papi awake. He assessed the damage and drove on.

•

I was determined to fix myself. The idea that I had lost my fearlessness
was unacceptable to me. I needed to recover it. I took swimming
classes at the local gym, pausing in the middle of laps to grasp the side
of the pool and calm my panic attacks. I went on a guided excursion in
Malinalco, Estado de México, jumping from the tops of small waterfalls into river rapids below—which induced panic attacks so increasingly terrible I had to be escorted out of the canyon early. I took guitar
lessons. I climbed mountains. I learned to ride a motorcycle and bought
a black Yamaha FZ16. I drove the motorcycle to work, cutting my
commute from forty minutes to ten by weaving through the Mexico
City traffic. But it was useless. Fear thrashed inside my body. I felt rigid
as a *concha de mar*, empty of everything but the ocean's echoes. On the
summit of a volcano called Malinche, I felt the unconquerable pull of
the abyss on my limbs. I curled into a ball on the slope, battling the
vertigo I had never before felt, and I cried.

•

My nightmares were always the same. I'm back at the secret beach. The sea level begins to rise. I turn toward the mountain, and use the foliage to climb. At the top, I encounter corrugated steel gates that rise to the end of the sky. Paul is behind a foggy window on a locked door. I beg him to open it. The ocean is lapping at my feet. He shakes his head. "You're going to have to find your own way this time," he says. But I can't, and I drown.

•

The tomatoes in Papi's backyard blackened and shriveled. The comfrey and other curative crops sagged and stank. The coastal wind carpeted his rotting garden with salt. Papi drank bottle after bottle of whiskey. His skin became the color of *maíz amarillo*.

•

I went to see a psychologist in Polanco. She diagnosed me with post-traumatic stress disorder and recommended EMDR therapy: eye movement, desensitization and reprocessing. Mimicking the rapid-eye-movement (REM) stage of sleep, in which we dream, EMDR is a guided and conscious imitation of dreaming. The therapist asks the patient to meditate on the traumatizing experience while exposing her to bimodal stimuli and steering her away from negative associations. I reimagined myself drowning as the therapist moved her fingers in front of my eyes, left to right, left to right, and asked me to describe what I saw. After several sessions, I began to observe that my body was glowing as I drowned. A golden light was buoying me—a magical light from my mother. I had never been in real danger. I was never meant to drown. My mother had been protecting me. This "realization," however imagined, eradicated some of my worst symptoms: my flashbacks and my panic attacks. I had reframed my recollection of the trauma. But my nightmares and sleep apnea persisted. I felt depressed, exhausted and, worst of all, afraid.

•

Papi poured powders and potions into his whiskey. He awoke feeling refreshed, and began to revive his *jardín*. But the improvement never lasted. The mysterious disease always returned: his hands shook, his legs became so heavy he could hardly take a step. He crawled up the stairs and collapsed on his bed. His body shook with unknown crashing energies. All night, the turbulence kept him wide awake.

•

While walking back from the cinema one evening with a friend, I noticed a taxi pull over beside us on the curb. A man leaped out with a gun, shouting, "I'll kill you! I'll kill you!" in Spanish. I thought he intended to kidnap us. But he just wanted our money. I handed him my purse, my phone, my jacket, almost joyous with relief. Back in my apartment, I curled up on the floor and succumbed to violent tremors. I coughed and shuddered. I desperately needed to cry, but the tears wouldn't come.

•

I went to a club in Polanco with a handsome, shaved-headed Venezuelan. We danced. My legs and arms felt too heavy; I couldn't enjoy it. We decided to go back to his place. I tried to wave down a taxi in my golden Bebe dress and heels, and fell through an open sewage hole in the sidewalk. I opened my arms in time to arrest my fall at the height of my chest. I looked down at the nothingness stretching all the way to the swamps of Hell. The Venezuelan hauled me out with his muscular arms, gasping at the sight of my bloody shins. *Vamos al hospital!* he cried. I shook my head. I wanted to go home, to crawl into my bed and stay there forever. This was an omen if ever there was one: Mexico wanted me dead, and would swallow me whole if it had to.

•

I flew to the coastal town of Puerto Escondido. I needed to force myself back into the ocean. I could no longer live with this fear. But I had barely checked in to my hostel when the electricity in the port went out. It rained for the first time in months, a torrential pour that wouldn't stop, with lightning and thunder. The next day, the sea level started to rise. I stood on the shore as the waves crept closer and closer and enveloped my feet. Even the locals were dumbstruck, taking pictures of the water on their phones, calling their friends and relatives: *"¿Estás viendo esto?"* The flooding consumed restaurants on the beach, sent families running to cars. Purple clouds spat lightning on the sea. I went online and checked the National Hurricane Center's website. The probability of a hurricane in the next forty-eight hours was forty percent. A few hours later, it was at sixty percent. My return flight wasn't for another week, but the sounds of the waves cracking like the whips of an angry God and the thunder and howling wind hurling itself against my cabin walls made my body ache with terror. The owners of the cabin complex told me they were leaving that night; there were no other clients; I would be alone. I tried to sleep. My body trembled with fear. *What if the ocean reaches my cabin doors? What if it takes me again?* I believed the flooding was tied to my presence. *Don't be silly,* I told myself. *That's nonsense.* Suddenly: a knocking at my cabin door. I could see a human silhouette in front of the window of the flimsy wooden wall. I held my breath, paralyzed. Who could it be? I reached under my pillow and grabbed my phone, checking it for service. It had none. If the figure forced its way into my cabin, it could do anything to me, it could rape and kill me, it could drag me into the ocean, nobody would know. I prayed for the shadow to disappear. It knocked again. *"Qué quieres?"* I screamed. No response. I checked my phone a second time. Still no service. Knock. Knock. I wept. I stared at the window; the shadow was shifting its weight. After a moment, it turned around and disappeared in the direction of the sea.

I bought a flight back to Mexico City the next morning. In the Associated Press, I learned an American had died on the same beach the same day I had stood watching the lightning on the water. The waves had pulled him out to sea and drowned him.

•

Melville writes:

> Consider the subtleness of the sea; how its most dreaded creatures glide under water, unapparent for the most part, and treacherously hidden beneath the loveliest tints of azure. Consider also the devilish brilliance and beauty of many of its most remorseless tribes, as the dainty embellished shape of many species of sharks. Consider, once more, the universal cannibalism of the sea; all those creatures prey upon each other, carrying on eternal war since the world began.
>
> Consider all this; and then turn to the green, gentle, and most docile earth; consider them both, the sea and the land; and do you not find a strange analogy to something in yourself? For as this appalling ocean surrounds the verdant land, so in the soul of man there lies one insular Tahiti, full of peace and joy, but encompassed by all the horrors of the half known life. God keep thee! Push not off from that isle, thou canst never return!

I had pushed off the isle in pursuit of my father. How similar was his country to the sea—its properties and its myths—all-consuming, unfathomable, full of corpses and secrets, sickening, indomitable, capable of driving souls insane. How strange, that the Spanish word for "swim"—*nada*—is the same as the word for "nothingness." The sea had consumed me; in my quest for my father, who had introduced me to *el mar*, I had discovered its true meaning: *Nada*. Nothing. Nonexistence.

My childhood and drug-induced perceptions of nothingness as the most fertile ground in the universe were, after all, hallucinatory. Life was not full of meaning and mystery. Lives were droplets of blood in a sea of nothing. Humans were dreaded creatures, remorseless tribes, dreaming themselves into existence.

"There is no quality that is not what it is merely by contrast," wrote Melville so many years ago. I highlighted and starred this sentence in the book.

I moved to Mexico because I believed, like Melville, that the poetry of a sunset is in the entanglement of night and day, in the limbs of light yielding to the dark. I moved to Mexico to unshelter myself: to discover death and, through it, life. What I didn't expect was that discovering death would make me terrified of living—that my capacity for joy would recede into the past, irretrievable.

•

I returned to Los Tuxtlas on the anniversary of my near-drowning. I took two friends—a Puerto Rican art curator, Maria Elena, and a Mexican programmer, Ro—and brought a large piece of cardboard, a knife and a marker. I was determined to give the deadly beach a name: one that would give it a positive connotation in my mind. On our first day in Los Tuxtlas, we camped on a popular beach. We awoke to find that Ro's red vehicle had been mutilated. The name of the Zetas drug cartel had been inscribed in massive letters on the hood of the engine, the roof of the car, the bumper and each door with a blade: ZETAS. ZETAS. ZETAS. ZETAS. ZETAS. As we drove, searching for the hidden beach, we saw a military checkpoint up ahead. Maria Elena tossed me her bag of marijuana, beseeching me to hide it: *You're the only white person here,* she said. I stuffed it into my bra, heart pounding. The soldiers, with AK-47s, asked us to step out of the vehicle. I held my breath, terrified I was going to Mexican prison. They searched Ro, interrogated Maria Elena and left me alone. After determining we weren't Zetas, they informed us we had been marked for death. They advised us to ditch the car.

We walked to a supermarket to purchase red nail polish and red lipstick. We filled in the letters, drew random symbols over them, poured sand on them. We drove until we found the hidden beach. As we descended the spiral stone staircase, we saw a Mexican family in the water. They were moving east at an impossible speed. A rip current was pulling them into the horizon. We ran down the steps. I had brought a life vest. I could save them. But by the time we reached the sand, the family had reversed course—the mother was hauling her sons onto the beach. They were gasping for breath, gagging and coughing. One of the little boys joked, in Spanish: "Go on in, the water's great!" I smiled and jumped in with my life vest. Afterward, trembling with the horror of what I had just done, I used a fallen bamboo stick to erect my sign, which read: *Playa de las Hadas*. Beach of Fairies. On the back, I wrote, in Spanish: *Beware of rip currents.*

•

Several days later, I flew to San Francisco for my sister's graduation ceremony at the Academy of Art University. My sister had grown into a beautiful young woman, with her scarlet-dyed hair and enchanting gap-toothed smile. She produced surreal works of art featuring charming gap-toothed creatures. Michelle had episodes of depression, but she had a vibrant social life in San Francisco, promising artistic prospects and a crazy-eyed mutt with a natural mohawk. Our parents, our two *abuelas* and I watched her get her diploma. We visited her in her apartment. Michelle showed us a portrait she had recently finished: our father dressed in colorful shamanic robes, balancing in his palm a stringy, melting blackness. It was the image from her recurring childhood dream. She had finally purged herself of it.

We had dinner at the San Francisco Grand Hyatt hotel restaurant. I was supposed to share a room with my mom and Abuela Coco that night, while my father and Abuela Carolina shared the room next door. But Papi wanted to go drinking with me and my sister, so I exchanged places with Abuela Carolina. After barhopping, my father and I said goodbye to Michelle, walked to the hotel and fell asleep. Papi jolted me awake with a scream. He was hearing voices. He searched the room, returned to bed, whimpered, tossed and turned. In the morning, I saw his cross-shaped *cicatriz*.

•

In June 2012, a young journalist, Armando "Mando" Montaño, moved to Mexico City. We had befriended each other during an internship at the *Seattle Times* while we were both still in college. Mando had been following my posts on Facebook, "liking" my pictures, saying he was eager to work as a journalist in Mexico and explore his roots—his father was also Mexican. He was two years younger than me. After securing an internship at the Associated Press, he asked for my advice on where to live. I had moved back to Condesa while my roommate, Rodrigo, was visiting relatives in Bolivia because I could not stand the cockroaches of Roma by myself. I suggested my new building, where a rental services company called Live in Condesa grouped foreigners in large, vaguely themed apartments (artsy, party, studious) and provided a housekeeper.

Mando's parents were worried about the country's violence. But they believed he would be safe with me; they had met me during a visit and trusted me. I heard Mando reassuring his mom over the phone: *Mom, I'm going to be fine—I'm with Jean!* I showed Mando around the capital, feeling its allure for the first time in months. *Your life is my dream,* Mando said. He took pictures of me on my motorcycle, posed for some of his own. We curled up in bed, exchanging stories of boys we had loved, of journalism dreams. I confessed I was thinking about quitting my job. It had been a dream come true for a while, allowing me to report out of Guatemala, Honduras, Costa Rica and Mexico, spending time with the poorest of *campesinos* and the richest of commodities traders. But the stories that most mattered to me—about people instead of prices, about corruption instead of market trends—were the ones the editors in New York either turned down or altered beyond recognition. Mando encouraged me to become a freelance writer. *Sí se puede!* he said, laughing in his openmouthed way, black tresses dancing. On the weekends, we went to clubs in Roma and Condesa. The gay boys loved him, with his Clark Kent face and tempestuous limbs. *I feel like I'm seeing Mexico City for the first time again, through your eyes,* I told him. For the first time since the near-drowning experience, I felt oxygen in my veins.

On his fourth Friday in the city, I was tired after three consecutive weekends of clubbing. All I wanted to do was sip hot chocolate and binge-read in my bed. I informed Mando I would not be joining him at a party of expats that evening. I had to cover Mexico's presidential elections on Sunday, and wanted to be well rested. My editors were sending me to the headquarters of the Institutional Revolutionary Party (PRI) to shoot video of Enrique Peña Nieto. They expected he would win. Mando informed me that the Associated Press was sending him to the PRI headquarters on election night as well. *If only we were being sent to the headquarters of the PRD,* he sighed, referring to the Democratic Revolutionary Party, whose candidate had vowed to root out government corruption and help the poor after decades of policies favoring foreigners and lighter-skinned Mexicans. Peña Nieto, meanwhile, had run on promises to open up the oil industry to foreign investors for the first time in nearly a century. American traders were excited. Global spectators saw Peña Nieto, who resembled a black-haired Ken doll, as the man who would modernize Mexico. Mexican youth saw him as a puppet of the *dinosaurios* of the PRI. The PRI had ruled the country for more than seven decades with impunity and violence, massacring hundreds of protesting students ahead of the 1968 Olympics in Mexico City. The party's fall to Vicente Fox of the National Action Party (PAN) in 2000 had seemed like irreversible progress. But now the PRI was making a comeback—and many of my sources in New York were delighted.

Mando and I made plans to meet Sunday at the PRI headquarters. He blew me a kiss goodbye and headed out the door. The next morning, I woke up and checked my emails in bed. I had one whose subject read, simply, "Mando." I clicked on it.

> Jean, this is Mando's mother. I heard about the accident and I
> just wanted to touch base with you. The AP buo chief and
> colleagues are investigating. Do you know anything?

I called Mando. He didn't answer. I ran upstairs and found the door to his apartment wide open. The housekeeper was mopping the floor. I walked into his bedroom. It was empty. But there was an energy there, by the bed. Crouching. Loneliness. Fear. I backed away, sick to my stomach. *Surely, I'm projecting,* I thought. I returned to my apartment as questions raced through my head: *An accident? Like, a car accident? Is he okay?* I ran into one of my roommates, a Spanish girl with straight brown hair and bright blue eyes. She told me she had gone barhopping with Mando and other friends. Around midnight, she encouraged Mando to go home. He was so intoxicated he could hardly stand. She accompanied him outside to wave down a taxi. *You put him in the taxi alone? Was it a safe taxi? Did you get the plates?* She couldn't remember.

I called Mando's mother. She said Mando was "dead." The adjective felt like a piece of raw meat in my brain, impossible to digest. *I know this must be hard for you to hear,* she continued with the incredible calm of traumatic shock. *His body was found in an elevator shaft in a building on your block.*

I knelt on the floor and braced against a noise passing through my body. I sobbed without tears; the relief of shedding them had become largely inaccessible to me after Los Tuxtlas. Mando's mother asked me to call the Associated Press and help them coordinate with the police. I promised I would. I stumbled into the bathroom, turned on the shower and let it soak me as I heaved.

On Sunday, I stared at the video screens in the media room of the PRI headquarters. My roommate called and said, crying: *The police say the official cause of his death was asphyxiation. He was crushed by the elevator.* A mob of reporters rushed past me. Peña Nieto had just been declared the next president of Mexico. He was going to make a speech outside. I followed with my camera, trying to get to the stage. A security guard stopped me. *Passage is closed as of an hour ago,* he said. I tried to argue. But as I spoke, I could hear my voice getting increasingly hysterical, and I found it suddenly very hard to breathe. The booming sounds—of screams, of drums—were strangely rhythmical. It was unmistakable: I was hearing Mando's heartbeat, accelerating as he ran out of air. I knew exactly what it felt like not to be able to breathe. I knew how painful it was: the terror, the loneliness. The pounding got faster and faster. It ran together into something primordial. The figure of Peña Nieto flickered on a stage, blurred, growing, monstrous, like

an Animorph becoming a beast. Cameras flashed. My vision blackened. People laughed. Panting. Panting. Mine. I was surrounded by
paramedics, breathing through an oxygen mask on the outskirts of the
chaos. An ambulance was parked beside us. "You're fine," one of the
paramedics said. "Just breathe. Just breathe."

•

A young man pulled my body out of the sea. But my flesh was so
dense I couldn't feel myself in it, only darkness. I was erasure embodied. I had caused Mando's death by getting too close. I could feel him
at night, clawing my back, begging me to hear him. *I'm sorry,* I wept.
I'm sorry, I don't know how to save you.

•

I visited my father in Rosarito. His door was blocked by a maze of
unused bags of fertilizer covered in seagull droppings. His yard was a
mess of rotting plants contrasting devastatingly with the intricate constructions he had made for them: complex trellises and shelves and
enclosures. He said: *It isn't the polycythemia, it's too horrible to be that; it
is some kind of radiation, it's Lyme disease, it's cancer, it's a curse, it is something so heavy and dark that there is no room for myself.*

I knew exactly what he meant.

The past had shifted my center of gravity behind me. I could no
longer move forward without turning around. I decided to quit my
job. I couldn't save my friend. I didn't know how. But perhaps I could
save my father. Perhaps I could save myself. I needed to disentangle
our threads, a knotted mass of unknowns. I needed to give Papi a
story—*his* story. Maybe then I could stop living his life. I had to finally
deal with my chief motive for migrating to Mexico—Papi, the past—to
free myself.

On February 28, 2013, I rehearsed my resignation over breakfast. I
feared my boss would argue with me about my decision, and I wasn't
sure how to defend it. Journalism was a struggling industry plagued by
mass layoffs. I worked for one of the few news corporations with

money—I enjoyed raises and bonuses and trips through Latin America. I loved my supervisor and coworkers. What if I never found such a great job again? Suddenly, I received a text message from Tony. He informed me that Pope Benedict XVI had just resigned—the first pope to do so in nearly six hundred years. He asked me to film the reaction in the Zócalo. The coincidence of being asked to cover a resignation as I was rehearsing my own flooded me with relief. It felt like a sign that I was moving in the right direction, even if I was potentially committing career suicide. The Pope was stepping down due to a lack of strength in his "body and mind," validating my need to address my corpse-like feeling. *I can't work here anymore,* I told Tony that day. *I'm going to write a book.*

Abuela Carolina had mentioned something to me, casually, in conversation: *My abuelita was a witch.* I remembered Eddie's words: *I think he is a shaman.* Echoes. Mirrors. Repetitions. Time rhymes to tell us secrets. Perhaps the witch could teach me something about combating black magic, if in fact it was black magic that plagued us: my father, dying of mysterious diseases; me, plagued by death. I had followed Papi's footsteps into a cursed world. Both nature and nurture had failed to reveal the exits. Maybe the supernatural could show us the way. I felt the only way out of Hell was through the graves of our ancestors.

Part VI

HOUSE OF FIRE

My great-great-grandmother stands beside her pentagram in Tlaltenango de Sánchez Román, Zacatecas, in the 1940s.

THE ROOT

Come, Papi, to the turn of the twentieth century: to the sowing of our rootlessness. Railroads multiplied up and down your country, writhing and stretching like snakes, thousands upon thousands of new miles of steel tracks, man-made vertebrae catalyzing, growing, connecting . . . and in the state of Zacatecas, in the rural town of Tlaltenango, a love story between a very old man and an adolescent clairvoyant girl, or *clarividente*. Your great-grandfather, Gregorio Valenzuela, was in his seventies: the past incarnate in a country where less than ten percent of the residents were over fifty. He was the same age as the dictator with abscessed teeth, Porfirio Díaz, who was robbing peasants of their land and selling it to Americans. *Extranjeros* owned ninety percent of the value of Mexico's industries, and nearly a third of the land. The gross domestic product swelled like a beating black heart, pumping oil for the first time. The *campesinos,* or countrymen, found themselves as nomadic as their Mexica ancestors had been before spotting the eagle and serpent on a cactus—the prophesied site of their empire in the 1300s. Already there were rumors of a revolution coming; no man was immortal, and in your very young country, the ancient dictator's impending doom was discernible, to say the least.

Gregorio's agedness was a fact often remarked upon as well. The villagers called him "San Gregorio" because of his saintly air. He was a descendant of Spanish immigrants. His eyes were blue or green, no one alive remembers which. A lengthy snow-white beard grew from his face. He was a cattle rancher with a family of grown daughters. He lived in Rancho de Encinillas, alongside dozens of Spanish families and their mestizo and indigenous *peones*. The outer walls of every adobe house were decorated with pots of pink and purple *flores malvas,* watered by the women. Each house had its own cobblestone well. The ranch is now pure ruins, crumbling adobe façades. But in the late 1800s and early 1900s, it was bustling, with families tending cattle and cultivating maize, barley, lentils, sweet potatoes and sugarcane.

Gregorio's mestiza mistress, Juanita Velasquez, was probably the daughter of *peones*. She had hair as black and sleek as obsidian. She had striking cheekbones, *pómulos,* protruding from her face like plump sapodilla fruit, casting shadows over her eyes. I don't know how she and the wrinkled San Gregorio became entangled. Perhaps Juanita never loved the old man. Perhaps the spirits told her to be with him. She bore Gregorio three sons: Trinidad, Isidro and Antonio.

Antonio, their youngest son, was born on June 13, 1901, at two in the afternoon, the product of an autumnal conception. His irises were the color of the sun. He was your grandfather, and he was not yet walking when Juanita ran away to fight in the revolution. War had not yet been declared, but there were revolts in the north, including a notorious battle in Chihuahua that involved the magical intervention of a young sorceress, Teresa Urrea, age eighteen. A magazine called *Regeneración* was circulating throughout the country, full of apocalyptic messages to fan the flames of agrarian discontent. Perhaps Juanita had read it; I found a letter she wrote Antonio at the end of her life that indicates she was among the few Mexican women then literate. The details remain in darkness, and it may always be so. Everyone who knew her as a young woman is dead.

They say history repeats itself. They say, too, that everything happens for a reason. But the redundancy of events seems purposeless. What is the use of repeating experiences if people never learn from their past? Perhaps these echoes have an aesthetic reason for being, as in the rhythmic repetition of poetry. Can it be, Papi, that you are part of a rhyme?

After Juanita ran away, abandoning her sons, San Gregorio paced up and down the dirt roads of Tlaltenango with a distraught expression, cradling the youngest boy, your *bebé abuelito*. If San Gregorio died, his sons would be left to fend for themselves at a time of revolution and chaos. San Gregorio walked and walked as if to ward off death, Antonio in his weakening arms. Martyr-like, he wandered daily. But no man is immortal, and soon the old man ceased to wake up with the dawn. The boys were orphaned just as the revolution turned *el campo* into the Devil's backyard. Though it was the first time the boys saw so many corpses, it was not the first massacre on their homeland. The decomposing flesh of humans had long fertilized the crops here, where the waterfalls wetted the mountains, and the maize stalks towered on avian claws.

Four hundred years before, in the early 1500s, word reached the valley that bearded white men with godlike powers had come from the direction of the sunrise, landing in the Yucatán Peninsula, then conquering the mighty Mexica empire at the center of the country. (The Mexica were later renamed the Aztecs.) The leader of these wizards, Hernán Cortés, was alleged to be Quetzalcóatl, the sacrifice-hating god who had long ago disappeared into the eastern horizon, promising to return on the date Ce Acatl, which coincided with 1519: the year the *conquistadores* arrived. At the time, more than a hundred languages were spoken in Mesoamerica. The cultures of the different societies were diverse, with a common thread: an obsession with time and outer space. Their buildings harnessed the light of celestial bodies in active dialogue with gods and the past. The ancient Maya were aware of the concept of zero—nothingness—hundreds of years before the Europeans discovered it through the Middle East. But the white-skinned *conquistadores* subjugated them with ease because the Meso-americans perceived the Spaniards as gods. An indigenous princess from Tabasco, named Malintzin, fell in love with the second coming of Quetzalcóatl. She persuaded diverse groups of natives to ally themselves in Cortés's favor. To this day, her name is used to curse Mexicans who prefer foreigners over their own: *malinchista*. It is as common an insult in Mexico as "materialist" is in the United States. Moctezuma, the leader of the great Mexica, refrained from turning his once-invincible army against the white *magos* until it was too late. The Spaniards destroyed Tenochtitlán, the floating city.

Tlaltenango, with a mere hundred cottages, was a modest land compared with the powerful Mexica capital. The Caxcans of Tlaltenango were among the seminomadic tribes called "Chichime-cas" by the Mexica, a derogatory term likening them to canines. The Caxcan men and women ran through the mountains to hunt snakes and other creatures for restorative broth, and sometimes settled for a while to grow *maíz* and *chiles* and *frijoles* on the wet banks of the rivers. The valley of Tlaltenango, which means "walled land" in the indigenous Caxcan language, was a porous ground of canyons and cliffs. The Caxcans were animists, and surely appreciated the symbolism of the earth's permeability. They believed all elements of nature, from wind to scorpion, were sacred, with connections to a parallel world. Their *curanderos* used the plant life to heal the ill. They danced and chanted to manipulate the fabric of reality.

The *conquistadores* came in a thundering stampede. Led by a man later described as the most evil in the history of the Conquest, they brought colossal dogs with bloodthirsty tongues, strange creatures called *caballos* and weapons more precise than any known force of nature. Nuño Beltrán de Guzmán left a carpet of corpses in his wake. His men unleashed deadly plagues for which the natives had no immunity. Unlike the great Mexica, the Caxcans resisted the cruel gods for decades. They were accustomed to movement, and their limbs were fast and agile; they learned to ride *caballos* and outmaneuvered the Spaniards on the rocky terrain. It was a long, hard battle, but by the 1540s, the wizards with light-colored irises were victorious once again. And as a consequence, men like your great-grandfather Gregorio, with his white skin and blue/green eyes, existed in this town nearly four centuries later, and women of largely indigenous blood, like your great-grandmother Juanita, still awaited an opportunity for vengeance.

After their father's death, Antonio and his brothers became scavengers, beggars and hunters, catching snakes like their ancestors and cooking them over improvised campfires. When word reached their half sisters, one decided to give shelter to the youngest, Antonio. At the age of five, your grandfather became a *peon* for his half sister. In exchange for a bowl of beans each evening and a straw *petate* to sleep on in a horse barn, he milked cows, mucked stalls, harvested corn, transported cattle to and from the main pueblo. His half sister almost never spoke to him; he ate with the animals. Decades later, he would remember the gnawing hunger he felt growing up, the gaunt and grimy faces of his vagrant brothers. Sometimes he sat sunburned on the dirt, exhausted, dripping sweat in damp underwear, flies licking his throat and lips. By his eighth birthday, he was a smoker, making his own cigarettes by rolling tobacco in leaves of *maíz*.

One night, when Antonio could no longer stand the hunger, he snuck into his half sister's kitchen to steal a pinch of honey. He unscrewed the jar's lid and saw the rich nectar inside. Unable to control himself, he dipped in both hands and desperately licked them as he scurried back to his stall, unaware he was leaving an incriminating trail. He was beaten the next day and deprived of his daily *frijoles*.

For the boys, there was never any hope in the revolution; for the ranchers, its glimmer faded quickly. It is believed that Francisco I. Madero, the aspiring sorcerer who replaced the ancient dictator, got the idea for the revolution from his dead brother, who spoke to him. A spiritualist wave of thought had spread across the nation, inspiring everyone from wealthy elites to *campesinas* like your great-grandmother. It combined indigenous *curanderismo*, or healing, with Western practices such as Tarot readings. Madero, a tiny man with dreamy eyes, was too busy communing with spirits to keep his promises, such as restoring stolen lands to the poor. And so the early 1900s brought never-ending discord between competing revolutionary factions. Bullets permeated the air like lead insects. Rebels looted businesses and lit aflame fields of *maíz*. The river that ran through Tlaltenango turned red. The betrayals among brothers that characterized the Spanish Conquest once again prevailed among the *campesinos*. To make matters worse, the United States kept meddling, helping a bloodthirsty military general, Victoriano Huerta, murder the mystical Madero, then replacing Huerta with a bespectacled *norteño* named Venustiano Carranza.

When a battle broke out in Tlaltenango, Antonio ran into the mountains and ducked behind some brush. The sound of hoofbeats overcame him. He leaped out of his hiding place to avoid being trampled. A soldier dismounted with a rifle in his hands. *Hold my horse, boy!* he cried, handing Antonio the reins. The soldier opened fire at an approaching mob. Antonio heard a crack at his side. The horse fell. Thick dark blood poured out of its splintered skull. Your grandfather ran for his life.

The revolution, some historians would later say, was a hallucination. A mirage. Like all fantasies, however, it possessed a great power: it bestowed the belief that a better life was possible. Stories about the United States began to spread. Like *el campo* for crops after a soft rain, the tales said, the United States was ever fertile for the dreams of men. Few spoke of the United States as the culprit of their woes. The northern country was their only salvation. *Hay que ir al Norte,* the storytellers said, pointing at Heaven, *a los Estados Unidos.* It sounded idyllic, a soft whisper with so many *s*'s, a secret promise. Antonio knew that anywhere was better than his tough town of Tlaltenango. Someday, he would hop on a train on one of those new railroads, and he would walk across the border to the other side: to *los Estados Unidos.*

•

What is a crossing? The *conquistadores* who crossed the sea brought with them the symbol of the cross. The crucifix represented atonement, a reminder of God's love for man despite his sins. But the cross symbolized other things before that, and today it has a multitude of contradictory and complementary meanings: addition, multiplication, rejection, cardinal directions. In runic divination, the cross can prophesy either a gift or a hardship, depending on the angle at which the two lines intersect.

How often this symbol comes up in your story, Papi! Border crossings. Crossings into madness. Crossings into trance states and parallel worlds. Crossings of ethnicities. Crossings into life and crossings into death.

Months before the *conquistadores* came to your country, the Italian explorer Andrea Corsali scrutinized the night sky from his ship during an East Indies expedition. On calfskin vellum, he wrote a letter to his royal sponsor, describing in detail something he saw in the southern sky: a constellation in the sign of a cross. "This crosse is so fayre and bewtiful, that none other hevenly signe may be compared to it," he wrote. The constellation came to be called Crux. I feel as Corsali must have felt contemplating configurations in the sky. What secret do these crossings spell? Do they signify anything, or are they more mere music? A choir of crossings? Concordant conflicts? Harmonious cacophony?

•

The first recorded crossing of Antonio Valenzuela occurred in March 1923, through El Paso, Texas. He was twenty-two. His purpose was listed as: "Seek work." Widespread irrigation projects were turning the pastoral Southwest into an agro-industrial region requiring cheap labor. Most eager and affordable were the Mexicans. Antonio found someone who taught him to sign his name, and he practiced until he could do so with a little flourish on the V. As of 1917, immigrants had to prove literacy to cross the border. Corporate farm interests made sure a signature was proof enough. When he crossed, Antonio joined the largest migration in the history of the two countries, one of a million Mexicans who entered the United States between 1900 and 1930 to harvest crops in *el campo* of the Southwest. Some came to work on *el traque* (the railway), too, and in *las minas* (the mines). Your grandfather lived in labor camps crawling with roaches and rats.

Antonio crossed many times before the 1923 recorded incident, according to his children who heard his tales. From coast to coast, the border then was porous. Illegal crossings were the norm. Barbed-wire fencing had been erected along small sections of the border to keep Mexican livestock from devouring U.S. crops, but along most of the 1,954 miles between the two countries, there was nothing but dirt and vegetation. The border existed in treaties and on maps and in minds—not on the land. So although Antonio crossed at least five times through official junctures, his actual number of crossings was probably much higher. He went back and forth across *la frontera*, a zigzagging pattern followed by hundreds of thousands of migrants across the century who sought to work in the United States while living in Mexico.

As hunger had taught Antonio to be a skilled hunter, debt peonage had showed him to find amusement in hard labor. Work was something his body took pleasure in, like eating or drinking or having sex. His portrait from those days shows a strikingly handsome man. His eyes are feline in shape, with an eagle's intensity. His straight nose curves smoothly at the tip. The lines of his face are angular, aquiline, attractive. His skin looks white, but his immigration documents describe his complexion as brown, no doubt tanned from laboring under the sun. His lips are a thin, serious line, contradicted by a subtle amused tilt in his right eye. His eyebrows are nearly nonexistent, maintaining the focus on his intense yellow irises. He wears a white or beige ascot cap and matching tie.

During a Tlaltenango visit, he married a local woman named Antonia. Physically, she resembled his mother. Your grandfather could not have known that, had Juanita not materialized out of thin air at around that time. *Go into the street, your mother has returned from the revolution,* a townsperson told Antonio. He recognized himself in her perfect nose, her barely there eyebrows, the feline shape of her eyes. She had come back with a fourth son, Felipe, and was settling down to practice her *curanderismo*.

Most of Juanita's story dissolved with her flesh. I don't know what role she played in the revolution—if she conducted spells on the battlefield, carried bullets in her pockets for the soldiers or fired the weapons herself. I like to think she was the Juanita immortalized in the famous revolution-era Mexican ballad, or *corrido,* that says in Spanish: "She was always in front of the troops, fighting like any Juan . . . here comes Juana Gallo, screaming on her horse." But all I know is this: when she came back from the revolution, she became a respected healer and *clarividente.* I have no doubt she felt a strong connection to her indigenous ancestors. She turned a discerning eye toward the plant life in the forests and, through trial and error and inquiry, identified each herb that might cure a sickness, soothe a hurt or summon a spirit. She prepared potions and creams. Her neighbors came for medicine, for help communicating with lost loved ones, to find runaway livestock and buried inheritances. In her trances, surrounded by candlelight, she divined the truth so often that she earned the name La Adivina. People came to see her from faraway towns. Throughout her life, she made a living with her mystical gifts, dispensing healing potions and prophecies, and paid for her own house. She taught her son Felipe to heal with magic and flowers; when Felipe was grown, he was respectfully called *El Doctor.*

•

A black-and-white photograph of Juanita shows her resting a hand on a tree branch in the backyard of her house, surrounded by crumbling adobe walls. Her neat silvery hair is pulled back from her face, emphasizing her astonishing *pómulos.* She wears an ankle-length white dress with spacious pockets and a dark rebozo draped over her shoulders and head. A pentagram of twigs and leaves hangs from one of the branches beside her. At the center of the pentagram is a piece of paper with something illegible written on it. I have so many questions for Juanita, but she died long before I was born, even before you were born, Papi. What if you inherited her psychic sensitivity to supernatural stimuli? I imagine a shamanic gift could be confusing, even terrifying, if it evolved in the wrong context. I recall the secret prophecies you left me in your VHS tapes: *Their flowering will be brief. And in their urgent need to attract pollinators, they provide copious nectar.*

•

Juanita told your grandfather that he, like she, could read the world's hidden symbols, invisible to the unconditioned brain but decipherable for insights unhindered by space or the linearity of time. Like any language, the hidden symbols, once learned, could be spoken as well as read. She told him he could use this knowledge to *alter* reality, causing the earth to yield crops or rain or sunshine. But Antonio knew nothing about reading. What he knew about was the tangible world: how to put his muscles, his physical body, to good use. The only thing he was interested in making the world yield was money—so he used his brain to find work, the only way to make money, as far as he was concerned. He said goodbye to his mother and bride and crossed the border again. After saving up *dólares*, he came back to fetch his beloved. The two crossed together at El Paso on September 10, 1923. The migration document describes Antonio as having a mole on his left cheek and another on his upper lip. He and his wife shared an apartment in De-lano, California, with his brother Isidro and his family. Antonio's first son, Goyo, was born on June 1. Against all odds, Antonio had made a life in the United States, without recourse to supernatural influences—only his flesh and sweat. I imagine he felt proud.

One day, he came home from the crop fields to discover that his wife was dead. *She was complaining of stomach pains, but it didn't seem serious,* Isidro told him. Antonio took a train up the coastline and stopped in Amador County to work in the darkness of a mine. Earlier that decade, forty-seven miners had been burned alive in the shafts, possibly after someone had dropped a cigarette. Antonio volunteered to be in charge of the explosives. Every day his lungs filled with dirt and smoke from *cigarillos* he sucked on as he sweated underground. At night, he played cards and chugged whiskey in the camp.

Scholars know that the course of history can be altered in a single moment; philosophers know individual lives are even more vulnerable than that. But Antonio was never much of a philosopher, or a scholar. He was playing a card game with his *compañeros* and humming drunkenly. Another worker grew annoyed by the sounds and asked Antonio to stop. Your grandfather told the man to mind his own business in a manner so impolite that his colleague responded in kind. Punches were thrown. Antonio fetched a razor blade from his sleeping bag and slashed either his enemy's arm or his cheekbone (his children remember conflicting details). Then the police arrived. On September 22, 1929, Antonio was placed in San Quentin prison on charges of assault with a deadly weapon. His height was reported as 5 feet and 6.5 inches; his weight as 128 pounds. In his mugshot, his dark hair is swept back elegantly as if with pomade, but lopsided, with a few loose strands sticking up in the back. He wears a collared white shirt and a jacket.

San Quentin, the oldest prison in California, was a waterfront institution with a torture chamber, a dungeon and granite walls overlooking the San Francisco Bay. It had been built in 1854 on land once owned by Indians. More than a hundred men had been hanged there. During Antonio's stay, a twenty-three-year-old American named Gordon Stewart Northcott was executed for the notorious Chicken Coop Murders; while Antonio had been traveling up and down California working in *el campo*, Stewart Northcott had been kidnapping young boys, raping them and butchering them. Newspaper articles described the gruesome grave discovered under the boy's chicken coop near Los Angeles, as having bones, blood, bullets and strands of human hair. In modern times, Mexico has become notorious for the brutality of its drug cartels. People are dissolved in vats of acid, skinned alive, eyes gouged out, headless naked bodies hanged from bridges. In the days of your grandfather, however, such hellish violence was unheard-of in Mexico. I imagine he was astonished by the discovery of it in the United States, a country of privileged men. Why would anyone maim and massacre here? Was it boredom? Antonio realized there were two ways to view his situation: as yet another injustice or as an opportunity. Having learned his lesson, Antonio chose the latter, and directed his love of utility to the world behind bars. He befriended an inmate who taught him to read and write in both English and Spanish. San Quentin wasn't bad compared with his life as a homeless child: he had daily meals and a mattress. Isidro brought Goyo to visit.

When Antonio was released, in the early 1930s, the United States was in the midst of the Great Depression. Mexicans were vilified for stealing jobs from Americans. He was deported with half a million other immigrants that decade. He didn't want to return to Tlaltenango—there was nothing for him there, besides his strange mother—so he headed to Guadalajara, Jalisco, a tourism hub. Now that he was bilingual, he obtained a highly coveted job as a hotel tourism agent. Dressed in a fancy suit with a striped tie and the hotel's insignia, he persuaded English- and Spanish-language visitors at the central train station to follow him to the Hotel Phoenix. One of the hotel cleaning ladies, Maria de Jesus, caught his eye: she was a shy brunette with sensuous down-turned lips that gave her a regal aspect. Like Antonio, she had grown up without a father; hers was killed by the Mexican army in the Cristero War following the revolution.

On June 23, 1933, Antonio wrote her a love letter in a beige card with a blue ribbon and intricate threaded pink flowers. "May God concede that some other year, if we are alive, the two of us shall be united forever, forever. . . . I ask God with all my heart for it to be thus, for it is impossible, for me, that you not be the owner of my love," he wrote in sometimes misspelled but eloquent Spanish. Bidding her farewell with a "he who sighs and suffers for you," he signed his name with an unusual amount of flourish, underlining his name thrice with an infinity sign connected to the final letter of Valenzuela. Maria de Jesus, your *abuelita,* became his second wife.

Their first child was a stillborn girl. Maria de Jesus gave birth to five children who survived: Antonio Jr., Joaquin, Carolina, Irma and Jaime. Carolina, your mother, was born on March 23, 1938, days after the Mexican president Lázaro Cárdenas nationalized the oil industry and expropriated the property of foreign oil companies. Cárdenas was the first president of Mexico who seemed a true product of the revolution.

Nearly two decades after the fighting ended, he redistributed almost fifty million acres of land. But unprecedented population growth worked against him. Most Mexicans continued to live in poverty. Antonio rented a bare studio with an oil stove in the corner for his family. Lines formed for the communal toilet. Many residents lacked patience, so the complex stank of urine and feces.

In 1942, the United States faced a manpower shortage as soldiers went overseas for World War II. The country signed a binational agreement with Mexico to launch the *bracero* program, which initially recruited 250,000 temporary Mexican laborers to work in agriculture and railroad repair. *Bracero* means "a person who works with his arms." Antonio was hired by the Northern Pacific Railway. He joined a crew that inspected California tracks for wear, replaced railroad ties, laid switches and fixed washed-out roadbeds. Antonio sent money to Maria de Jesus, allowing her to rent a house with its own toilet. One day in 1944, the repair cart turned over and broke Antonio's wrist. The railway company paid for his surgery, then sent him back to Guadalajara with a large scar and a hefty indemnity. He bought a fruit-and-refreshment stand in front of the central train station. The family commissioned the construction of a house with three bedrooms, electricity, running water, even a boiler. They were able to enjoy warm baths for the first time in their lives. Antonio grew fat. He started lending money on interest and bought the neighboring fruit stand. He purchased a fluffy Pekingese puppy for his children. He amassed stylish suits, hats and leather shoes.

In 1950, the city announced it was going to demolish the central train station and rebuild it on the outskirts of Guadalajara. Antonio protested. Officials promised him a fruit stand at the new location. But that area of Guadalajara lacked pedestrian traffic. Antonio made hardly a penny. He sold the stand and bought a cantina. The cantina didn't do well, either. Your grandfather started to gamble and guzzle whiskey. He sold his cantina for five thousand pesos. He bought another fruit stand. He drank so much that Antonio Jr. repeatedly had to take him to the hospital to get his stomach pumped. Whenever Antonio passed out, Maria de Jesus and Carolina gathered up his liquor bottles and buried them in the yard. But it was pointless. Antonio summoned strangers from his bedroom window with coins for more whiskey.

In a fit of inspiration in September 1952, Antonio told the family they were moving to Tijuana so he could start working in the United States again. He sold the Guadalajara house to a wealthy priest. Intent on traveling like the rich man he had momentarily been, Antonio bought first-class train tickets for the family and the Pekingese pup. It took five days to arrive in the border town because the train broke down multiple times. Maria de Jesus wept all the way north; blood poured down her legs; a fetus had failed to thrive.

Antonio arrived in Tijuana in September 1952. In October, he crossed the border through the San Ysidro Port of Entry to see a doctor. An immigration official wrote: "States that when he drinks Iced drinks that he can not breathe and falls down." Antonio's health had begun an irreversible decline. He would die less than a decade later in a San Diego hospital. His body was buried in a Tijuana cemetery. But first—he took his children to the border. He showed them how to cross.

•

New Spain became Mexico in the early 1800s, when the face of La Virgen de Guadalupe united pagan indigenous tribes with Catholic Criollos and mestizos. The historian Earl Shorris wrote in *The Life and Times of Mexico* that her *cacahuate* skin served as a bridge between the brown natives, the children of white immigrants and their mestizo offspring. Carrying her image, they rebelled against the Spanish-born settlers who had monopolized power. An eccentric old priest and silkworm producer named Miguel Hidalgo y Costilla led the march into battle. They won. Mexico—named after the native Mexica—was born. Betrayals came as if on cue—a signature of the country's soul since Malintzin fell for Cortés. Cousins turned on cousins. Sisters turned on sisters. A competitor executed Hidalgo y Costilla. The United States saw an opportunity to invade the new nation. President

James K. Polk sent troops south of the border. In 1848, Mexico was forced to hand over half of its territory. Today's border was born.

·

For more than a hundred years, the border existed as a 1,954-mile concept on paper without a corresponding body in the world. A porous patchwork of barriers rose in the twentieth century, mostly around cities: chain-link fence, sediment piles, steel columns. In the late 1990s, dozens of miles of helicopter landing mats from the Vietnam war were erected between San Diego and Tijuana, one of the world's busiest border crossings. After September 11, 2001, the United States spent billions of dollars on improved border security. Over the next decade and a half, hundreds of miles of steel fencing sprouted on the land like strange silver teeth: double-layered, triple-layered, topped with razor wire. As the border came to life, so did its hunger. Migrant traffic was rerouted into the desert, where the ravenousness was most extreme. There, the crossers became delirious. Amid saguaro and prickly pear cacti, they saw *diablos* and *demonios*—incarnations of *la frontera* that stalked them under an infernal sun, sending voices and visions into their minds, seducing them away from *los Estados Unidos*. Thousands died of dehydration or heat exhaustion. Most lie lost forever, hidden beneath shrubs where they sought shade.

·

You traverse the border all the time through ports of entry. You were fortunate, I suppose, that your parents immigrated in the 1970s, when it was all still rather simple. You could apply for citizenship, but you don't want to. You reject both countries. You're a new species, Papi. A new species. You dwell in a place I cannot touch.

·

On the West Coast where San Diego meets Tijuana, the border fence stretches into the Pacific Ocean. Barnacles cling to its steel column bases. They look like large, algae-covered pores; the fence is coming alive on the coast. The crustaceans greet the sea with their feathery fingers as waves bring particles of starfish and *mariscos*. The barnacles pull the marine detritus into their shells, into the fence. A rip current extends beyond the barriers into the horizon, following a channel made by the infrastructure. I remember your voice: *¿Qué miras?* Inland, the fence is steel mesh so tightly woven that only the smallest of fingers can fit through the gaps. Corrugated steel gates rise up for miles eastward, parallel to a secondary fence crowned by concertina wire. I drive east along this border, searching for you. The city gives way to desert, where barriers stop and start amid steep, boulder-studded mountains. In the Tohono O'odham Nation, home to one of the border's deadliest smuggling routes, I walk into the desert with a group of farmworkers, plumbers and construction workers who search for dead or dying migrants on weekends. Vultures circle the sky. We pass the twisting green limbs of towering saguaros and visnaga cacti with bloodred flowers. Snakes slither. Scorpions crawl. Cattle skeletons glow white on the landscape. A single white stallion stands perfectly still. I see an abandoned Bible on the earth. I sit down and flip through its dusty pages. The text is crawling with insects—termites. They're devouring the holy text.

I brush the termites from the Bible and scan the lines of Genesis. Before forging the first humans, God separated light from dark, sky from land, earth from sea. Without borders, I realize, life could not exist. Cells would have no membranes to contain them, no wombs in which to thrive. Without borders, societies could not function. The border between good and evil is central to civilization. But borders can also be deadly.

Under a nearby tree, a human skull lies on its side. Dirt clings to crevices in the bone. A few meters away: a curving human spine. It's attached to legs in brown pants. A hand lies by a bush. The remains are scattered all over the place, as if torn apart by a coyote or some other animal. I kneel in front of the skull and study its features. It has a broad forehead, just like you, Papi, just like me. I can't help seeing us there.

•

Diverse species of borders exist in the world. Some can be touched: steel gates, the skin of our bodies, coastlines. Others can't be touched but can be drawn on maps: climate isotherms and ozone-layer breaks. Some are too abstract to delineate: between ethnicities, between languages, between dreams, between secrets and the said. The U.S.-Mexico border region expert Guillermo Alonso Meneses wrote a book called *Fronteras simbólico-culturales, étnicas e internacionales.* He argues that the word "border" did not always evoke a solid division between distinct places: "In its origins, the cultural artifact we call border, limit, boundary, conclusion, demarcation, stripe, mark, or frontier, could be a strip of territory defined by a river, a mountain chain, or the beginning of the sea. . . . These references to the place where the known ends and the unknown begins speak of a world where there were not always precise borders but rather vague confines." As the world became more connected through trade and transportation, countries scrambled to calcify national boundaries. Walls and fences between nations multiplied, writhing and stretching like snakes, thousands upon thousands of new miles of steel gates, splitting, colliding, separating.

•

Borders are the opposite of motion. They are intended to stop it: stillness materialized. But it is in human nature to behold in borders the temptation of the beyond. Curiosity extends beyond the permissible, beyond the perceivable. God told the first couple in the Garden of Eden: "From any tree in the garden you may eat freely, but from the tree of knowledge of good and evil you shall not eat." He must have known what they would do.

Papi, we have crossed so many borders, so carelessly, so frequently, in quest of omniscience. Now we are caught in the fabric of their nothingness. I lie on the desert floor beside the anonymous migrant's skull, dehydrated and exhausted. I close my eyes and find myself back in the place where the roads are *caracol*. These corridors are full of water. It tastes of *sal y cigarros*. The ceiling sprouts wine-colored carpet. When I run my hands along it, I can feel the black plastic curves of cigarette burns, ouroboros shapes. There is something coming for me, Papi. It is a spider of some kind, like the one you swallowed in Paradise Hills. But it swims, it has legs like tentacles, and it speaks Spanish: *Si no encuentras a tu Papi, vas a morir.*

•

¿Papi, dónde estás? I sought you in the United States. I sought you in Mexico. But you are neither Mexican nor American. You are not Mexican-American either. You are the dash that lies between. You are in the chasm between chasms—deeper than I may ever hope to reach.

Did you lose yourself looking for your own father? I found him for you. He is buried in the south of Mexico, dead for twenty years, but I have a photograph of the man you can't recall: He sits on a boat in Xochimilco, the site of the few surviving *chinampas*—the ancient Mexica's floating gardens—in what is now Mexico City. He wears a stylish striped vest, striped pants and a collared shirt with rolled-up sleeves. He is as handsome as you, furrowed eyebrows casting shadows over his eyes. Stringy *aguehote* trees form a fortress on the riverbank, their reflections reaching toward him on the water.

Beneath him lurk the dying axolotls, Mexican salamanders that never metamorphose. Unlike other amphibians, they can regenerate any part of their bodies throughout their lives. They are pale pink or gray, with growths like tree coral on their heads. The ancient Aztecs revered them as death-defying gods. Axolotls can't be found anywhere in nature except in Xochimilco, but they are bred by the thousands in laboratories, snipped and chopped by scientists who seek to replicate their superpowers. Once, when I visited Xochimilco, a *campesino* brought me a slimy black one. He said: "Sometimes people see him all dark, and they think he's poisonous or evil, so they step on him, and beat him. They eliminate him. But he cures asthma, bronchitis, arthritis, respiratory issues, cough, indigestion, *mal de ojo,* and he's an aphrodisiac."

I bring you the photograph of your father in Xochimilco. You tell me you don't want to see it. "Some other time," you say.

I'm sorry, Papi. *Perdóname.* I know how much you hate to be pursued.

What if it is I who haunted you all along? What if it was not ghosts, not gods, not the government whose voices you heard—but your daughter's, calling your name? What if mine were the shadows that chased you?

•

In a book called *Orthodoxy,* the philosopher Gilbert K. Chesterton argues that lunacy comes not from a lack of reason but from an excess of logical ambition. Lunacy is born of his desire to understand everything—to cram the infinite universe into his finite head. "And it is his head that splits," Chesterton writes. He points out that the word "lunatic" comes from *luna.* "For the moon is utterly reasonable; and the moon is the mother of lunatics and has given to them all her name," he writes. The moon is clear and circular, like logic. It mirrors the self-devouring snake of the ouroboros. It is a symbol of erasure, a formula for nothingness. Like a country demarcating its borders, the ouroboros self-delineates and, in so doing, swallows itself.

•

The United States was born of intellectuals in the Age of Enlightenment. The white settlers believed in the supremacy of the logical mind and its ability to subjugate the natural world; they grew a country of freedom and justice on the bodies of the killed and enslaved. A high-tech world sprang forth, with portable entertainment screens and skyscrapers as tall as gods. Its military became cross-continental, sending missile-firing drones into the clouds. It was the first country to send men to the moon. It suffers one of the world's highest rates of mental illness.

•

The white *conquistadores* and the brown *indígenas* who met, mated and murdered one another to create Mexico had a faith in spirits so profound and imaginative that the concept of death was hypnotic, the abyss competitive with reality. The Spaniards, like the ancient Maya and Mexica they encountered, perceived divine meanings in everything, even logical concepts like numbers. They were seduced by what frightened them, wrapped themselves up in what they destroyed, made love to their enemies. To this day, Mexicans consume tabloids of bloodied bodies, decorate their homes with skeletons and celebrate *Día de los Muertos* on the graves of their *abuelos*. Cartel killers build shrines to Santa Muerte. The country suffers one of the world's highest homicide rates.

In *The Labyrinth of Solitude,* Octavio Paz compares the psychoses of the American and the Mexican: "The solitude of the Mexican, under the great stone night of the high plateau that is still inhabited by insatiable gods, is very different from that of the North American, who wanders in an abstract world of machines." In the United States, "the world has been created by [man] and it is made in his image: it is his mirror. But he no longer recognizes himself in those inhumane objects, nor in his fellow men. Like an inexpert sorcerer, his constructions no longer obey him."

Mexicans are fixated on the past. They find inspiration backward and downward, in the earth's cemeteries: in their future. Americans are fixated on the future. They find inspiration forward and upward, in the stars: light-years past. Both views are incomplete. Both fold back into themselves, self-devouring, like the ouroboros. The paths of logic and superstition unfold in parallel directions: beyond reality, toward delusion.

•

My mother always spoke of the United States with admiration and pride. It was a country where anything was possible, where if you kept your eyes on the stars you could reach the greatest heights. But the more American I became, the more I despised the limits of my flesh. I tore at my skin until I felt invincible—until I felt nothing but the boundlessness of my own vision. I began to understand everything: my behavior, your behavior, the "miracle" of human life. Everything was reducible to atomic numbers, electron configurations, inert facts and formulas. Reality became a set of predictable forces acting on matter. The world—once a magical, mysterious place—became as dull as an instruction manual. I hated everyone and everything.

Mexico, too, was a country where anything was possible, where if you kept your eyes on the earth you might see corpses resurrected. It was a place where the border between life and death was permeable, where hidden forces forged paths toward immortality. But the more Mexican I became, the more I lost touch with the material world. I turned into a ghost.

·

The philosopher Chesterton writes of an antidote to ouroboros illnesses: Mysticism. He describes it as a quest for truth that reveres the ultimate mystery—the contradictory nature of reality. The curiosity of mysticism never loses steam because it is fueled, not constricted, by contradictory information. It values truth over consistency. It is open to both free will and fate, prescriptions and prophecies, mathematics and miracles. Light is both a particle and a wave. Time is both linear and nonlinear. The world is both subjective and objective. "It is exactly this balance of apparent contradictions that has been the whole buoyancy of the healthy man," he writes.

From another perspective, it's the ethos of the United States and Mexico combined. Neither is correct on its own. Together, they are sane.

Chesterton calls for basking beneath contradiction as if under the blaze of a "shapeless" sun. We must not blind ourselves by staring straight at the sun, attempting to discern its contours and disentangle its rays. We must seek insights from the reflections and refractions of its light. There is power in the obliquely understood. Poetry is sane because it "floats easily in an infinite sea" rather than trying to "cross the infinite sea, and so make it finite," he writes. Poetry does not prescribe. It does not diagnose or contain. It flowers outward, rooted and free. It is creative, like conception, which biologists can describe but not explain. It is not material or magical. It is both.

The philosopher points to the shape of the cross: "The cross, though it has at its heart a collision and a contradiction, can extend its four arms forever without altering its shape. The cross opens its arms to the four winds; it is a signpost for free travelers."

Across countries and centuries, the cross has been revered as one of the most powerful shapes in nature. Éliphas Lévi, an occult scholar from the nineteenth century, said that the cross controls spirit, matter, motion and stillness. The First Cause of the universe, he wrote, is "revealed invariably by the Cross—that unity made up of two, divided one by the other in order to produce four; that key to the mysteries of India and Egypt, the Tau of the patriarchs, the divine sign of Osiris, the Stauros of the Gnostics, the keystone of the temple, the symbol of Occult Masonry."

Nature is rife with this shape: Light waves cross into cortices. Sperm cross coronae radiatae. Stringy roots burst forth from their seeds. DNA gathers in cross-shaped chromosomes.

The cross is a symbol for the language of creation. It is the opposite of the ouroboros. Rather than a singularity imbibed, it is duality yielding. *Es la contradicción en un cuerpo*—contradiction embodied.

•

The human brain is divided into two hemispheres. They communicate through a bundle of nerve fibers called the corpus callosum, but a clear fissure exists between the halves. The left hemisphere is linear and logical. It separates stimuli into categories and plans methodically for the future. The right hemisphere is spontaneous and spiritual. It is holistic and dwells in the present. The left hemisphere creates borders. The right hemisphere connects the disparate.

An American psychologist named Julian Jaynes argues in his 1976 book, *The Origin of Consciousness in the Breakdown of the Bicameral Mind*, that the brains of early humans were not fully integrated via the corpus callosum. The activity of one hemisphere was perceived by the other as external to the self: thoughts were the voices of gods. "We could say that before the second millennium B.C., *everyone* was schizophrenic," writes Jaynes. He points to one of the oldest works of Western literature: Homer's *Iliad*. "The characters of the Iliad do not sit down and think out what to do. They have no conscious minds such as we say we have, and certainly no introspections. . . . When Agamemnon, king of men, robs Achilles of his mistress, it is a god that grasps Achilles by his yellow hair and warns him not to strike Agamemnon. . . . [I]t is a god who then rises out of the gray sea and consoles him in his tears of wrath."

As the connections between brain hemispheres multiplied, humans began to perceive the gods' voices as their own internal dialogue. They merged with the divine. They acquired free will. Self-agency and the power of choice came not from logic or superstition, but from their crossing.

•

I am starting to remember what the ocean made me forget, Papi. What always scared me about the world was not the unknown, but the fear that the unknown was nothing, that mystery was an illusion, that the world was this: just this. It is not. The *whys* of the world are uncertain; therefore they are alive. They are ethereal and shape-shifting. They twist, ripple, vanish. Label an object—reduce it. Name a person—subsume him. Truth is like the most colorful things in nature (*el arcoíris, la mariposa*)—clutch them in your fists and find pure dust. But that doesn't mean they aren't real—only that they cannot be possessed.

Mysticism travels toward truth without trying to grasp it. It shatters omniscience into the freedom of discovery. The scientific method is mystical because it unites the magic of conjured hypotheses with the rigid structure of test tubes. Journalism is mystical because it is a never-ending renewal of records. Mysticism is the Migrant's Prayer, *la Oración del Migrante:* "The journey toward you, Lord, is life. To set off is to die a little. To never arrive is to arrive definitely." Mysticism is the chase for the father who becomes farther and farther away.

•

Papi, you ran from your daughters . . .
Como Juanita corría de sus hijos.
I chase you both and rediscover
La frontera entre los espejos.

•

I find Juanita's death certificate while scouring hundreds of pages of microfilm records from Tlaltenango. A scrawl tells me she died of an asthma attack on May 8, 1948, at the age of sixty-eight. The revolutionary woman? The healer? Asthmatic? I touch my throat. I know what it feels like not to be able to breathe. I know how painful it is: the terror, the loneliness. Time rhymes to tell us secrets. I don't understand what the whispers are saying. I must dwell in the uncertainty.

•

When I was a child, sick and feverish, I sometimes had horrific visions. I saw a substance that was incredibly smooth and unblemished. It was so immaculate it smothered me. When I could no longer stand it, another texture came: wrinkled and disfigured beyond comprehension. It was so flawed it gutted me. Both were unbearable to my body, which existed somewhere between the two substances. I raised my hands in front of my face and ran fingers along fingers, amazed by their physicality, which had become foreign to me: brittle, protuberant, terrestrial. I kept touching my fingers. The terror fell away.

•

Our five senses travel through a labyrinth of crossings: from skin to synapse, each part of our bodies corresponds to the opposing brain hemisphere via crisscrossing nerve fibers. Our left hands are controlled by our right brain hemispheres, and vice versa. Because the crisscrossing connections between our brain cells number in the trillions, our mental category systems are seemingly limitless. Unlike the minds of animals, human brains can combine concepts (mother, father) to create encompassing concepts (parents, lovers). This capacity—rooted in cerebral crossings—allows human consciousness to expand infinitely in all directions: like the minds of gods. Christ became immortal by dying on the cross. The cross is the *coincidentia oppositorum* of Buddhism, Taoism, Sufism and more: the unity of opposites from which all else is born. Like the counterclockwise or clockwise twist that turns a curled surface into a Möbius strip, the cross transforms finite dimensions into infinite ones by coaxing unity out of separation.

Can I use the cross to save us, Papi? Juanita reintroduced me to the magic of my youth, but unlike my sixth-grade Wiccan self, I am full of skepticism. Spells strike me as nonsense riddles, requiring absurd tools such as lambskin, eagle feathers, crowns of vervain and gold, just to invoke the power of simple shapes like the cross, the triangle, the pentagram. I want to take Occam's razor to the spell books, strip them of the superfluous. Touch would be the vehicle for the magic of forms—that is my mystical conclusion, the yield of my two cultures.

Touch. *Tacto*. It is the most elementary sense, the sense of amoebas and bacteria, the only sense crucial for mammalian conception, to create all other senses. And yet the somatosensory system, in all its simplicity, is the least understood by scientists. Its strange-named receptors seem magic spells of their own: Pacinian and Meissner's corpuscles, Ruffini endings, Merkel's disks, Krause end bulbs.

I have stripped us naked on these pages. Papi, it is monstrous of me to have done this, considering how much you hate it when I get too close. But you are the one who told me, when I was a child, that wounds need oxygen to heal. I just pressed Send on an email; I hope you read it: "I think you opened up to me because in your heart you believe in the Truth, like I believe in it, despite its ever-elusive nature. I think you know that lying, keeping secrets and refusing to acknowledge the past are what poison us as human beings. It's hiding that closes the soul. . . . What gives liberty is transparency, owning what you have experienced, letting light reach your interior, seeking to be illuminated."

Perhaps it all comes down to this: our skin. Perhaps, stripped bare, we are capable of anything. I look at my hands: small and thick-fingered, double-jointed, full of lines and veins, the hands of a very old woman, even in my twenties. My palms have more crisscrossing lines in them than most hands. One lover, a French boy, told me they were "Gollum's hands, alien." I like my hands. They have guided me through this place, where the clocks spin in all directions. They are my mother's hands.

For years, I taught myself not to feel my flesh. As I explored commodities industries, the *campesinos* placed my hands in the soil, in the crops that grow in it: *cacao, café, caña de azucar.* I saw green strings sprouting from the earth, erupting into pods and leaves. I remembered worms, and flies, and a garden bloated with bodies. Cupping *la tierra,* I found I could travel through time.

I know how to reach you now, Papi. I close my eyes and hold my hands in front of my face, summoning textures and temperatures as my guides. I feel roiling waters rippling through my body. A sound like the ocean in a conch, but much louder, fills my skull. I hold it there, even as it swells and becomes scary, even when I think the ocean is going to explode from my ears. *Papi,* I whisper. The grooves of your cross-shaped scar emerge under my palms. I remember the ouroboros of *The Neverending Story:* two snakes devouring each other's tails. In their entwinement, they cross each other several times. Papi, I think I have found the cure: it is our curse.

Part VII

HOUSE OF BATS

My sister's portrait of our father, completed while she was in college.

LARVAE

On the night of April 5, 2013, about a week after my last day at the news bureau, my father got a phone call from an unfamiliar number. He heard a woman's bloodcurdling scream. A male voice said, in Spanish: *I have your daughter.*

My father clutched his cellphone to his ear. *What?* he asked. *Which daughter?* But he already knew. Michelle was in San Francisco. I was in Mexico. I was the one who had just resigned from a large media company to freelance in one of the most dangerous countries in the world.

The stranger ignored my father's question. He demanded several thousand dollars, and told Papi that if he didn't wire over the money in minutes, he was going to slice my throat. He advised my father not to hesitate.

My father's body was an earthquake. As he tried to think it through, a seed of doubt sprouted roots in his brain. *Which daughter?* he repeated.

The stranger cursed, threats slurring into an alien language, salivary and strange. The woman's sobs grew louder.

Tell me her name! my father cried.

The anonymous man swore he would rape and kill me if my father delayed a second longer. The woman shouted in Spanish for help. *Ayúdame, Papá!* she cried. And then he almost knew.

I had spent most of my life speaking English. English was my main language. Would I, in a state of primal terror, speak Spanish?

Papi ended the call. He dialed my number. I was sleeping and my phone was on silent. He called again. And again. And again. He told himself that I was asleep, that surely he had experienced what is known in Mexico as a virtual kidnapping call—a cruel hoax to extract money without a real abduction. When I woke up at 11:00 a.m., having slept in, I noticed his numerous missed calls and called him back. After a long silence, he sighed and said: *It's not safe in Mexico, Jean. Not anymore. Go home.* He didn't understand: I could not abandon my body here.

•

Earlier that year, an American trader embarked on a journey through Latin America by motorcycle. Harry Devert was a tall and classically handsome thirty-three-year-old who planned to write a book. "Adventure is delving into the unknown," he wrote in his blog. In late January, while passing through southern Mexico, he sent his girlfriend a text message informing her that the military was escorting him out of a cartel zone. Then he vanished. For months, I followed news updates about his case with anxiety. I had never met Harry, but I identified with him and hoped he would be found alive. In the summer, his remains were found in plastic bags next to a road in the Mexican state of Guerrero. He had been slaughtered. According to news reports, drug traffickers had mistakenly believed the white-skinned gringo was working undercover for the Drug Enforcement Administration.

I emailed his mother, Ann: "I am profoundly sorry to hear about what has happened to Harry. I didn't know him, but I am a freelance journalist in Mexico from the U.S., own a motorcycle, and love to travel. I feel deep sympathy for your son. . . . What happened is terrible beyond words, but I want you to know . . . some people live their whole lives afraid . . . lately I count myself among them. . . . Your son should not have died, but he died alive."

She wrote me back. She had just found Harry's self-penned obituary in his email drafts: a permanent goodbye, as if foreseeing his death:

> I died doing what I love. . . . I was okay with this. Our time here is so short and many people I have known have passed on before their time . . . people better than myself. . . . I want to thank everyone who has kept me company along the way . . . and the many authors who kept my mind and my imagination alive when I was lonely . . . and to hug my mother . . . the most important person who has ever been in my life.

After Harry's death, Ann traveled to one of the last places Harry visited: Cerro Pelón in Macheros, Mexico, where monarch butterflies gather densely on the trees. When she saw the orange-and-black creatures, she felt she was seeing them through her son's eyes. She wrote: "The butterflies rise and settle as the sun shifts."

•

That autumn, police officers in Iguala, Guerrero, detained forty-three students who planned to march in commemoration of a 1968 student massacre. Then the students vanished. During the search, hundreds of bodies were unearthed from clandestine graves in the mountainsides—but not those of the forty-three youths. Their disappearance brought global attention to tens of thousands of other missing people in Mexico, and dragged the country's darkest problems of impunity and corruption into the light. In December 2014, more than 200,000 Mexicans flooded the Zócalo wearing all black. Flames rose from the center of their mass of silhouettes. They burned an effigy of Enrique Peña Nieto.

•

Diego Rosas Valenzuela, one of Goyo's grandsons, was abducted three weeks before the one-year anniversary of the Iguala kidnapping. He was a shy, well-mannered boy who spent much of his free time with Eddie, my cousin with the crow's-feather eyebrows. He had just turned sixteen. I had often seen him at family events. When he was twelve, he attended my father's *despedida*. A few days after he was kidnapped, his mother, Vero—who raised Diego, her only son, by herself—received a phone call and a package: two of his severed fingers. The kidnappers wanted more money than she ever possessed. Vero and her sisters gathered their life savings. Eddie's father, Chucho, left the money by a hardware store per instructions. Chucho drove up and down a highway where the kidnappers had promised to leave Diego. My cousin did not appear. The kidnappers did not call again. Vero has not lost faith that she will save her son. A mother will never give up on her missing child. Time passes. Time passes. Time passes. The hope stays alive. The dread never dies. It is a nightmare that never ends.

•

What is happening to my father's country? Piedragil blamed Mexican people. *Ven la muerte como el sueño.* In constant communion with spirits, they see death as a dream. But it's the United States that consumes the drugs behind the violence. It's the United States that supplies the cash and the bullets that spill the blood. *La culpa* must lie somewhere in between.

•

My father ordered one hundred black-soldier-fly larvae online. After sprouting wings, the creatures live only a week and do not eat. They don't touch food like other flies and therefore don't spread diseases. They live long enough to mate and lay eggs, then die. Their larvae eat like gluttons, excreting a brown elixir.

Papi planned to use their feces to revive his dying garden. He sought to create a colony of a million larvae, and sell the excess fertilizer to farmers in Rosarito. He turned a plastic tub into a composter with a drainage system and a harvesting tube connected to a smaller container lined with sawdust. He placed the grubs in the composter. He fed them seaweed from the beach. The larvae multiplied and meta-morphosed. Flies buzzed around the living room, the kitchen, his bed-room. They escaped from his composter each time he lifted the lid to drop in more food. Papi coexisted with the flies as they mated. When I visited, he snatched flies midair to point out their coal-black velvety wings.

Papi threw their fertilizer on his backyard crops, which flourished. The one hundred larvae became tens of thousands. He transferred them to a wooden enclosure outside. He fed them horse manure from a nearby ranch. Papi showed me his garden with pride. He had trans-formed the backyard into an intricate fairy-tale landscape, with curv-ing rows of crops and towering blue-tongued orange snapdragons. An impressive brown gate in an avocado-green wall led out of the *jardín* into the coastal Baja California neighborhood. Papi had built it by ar-ranging wooden panels in concentric squares around a sculpted yin-yang symbol. He told me he was collecting stray-dog carcasses to feed to his larvae, and was on the lookout for those not flattened by cars, so he could sell their intact skeletons to schools. I had never seen my fa-ther so productive. His occupation was death and deterioration, but also rebirth and renewal. In his living room, with an ocean breeze wafting in through an open window, my father and I spoke for hours. I recorded our conversations with his permission. He paused repeat-edly in his recollections to philosophize—about the origin of the uni-verse, about parallel worlds, about the meaning of life. The moonlight gave his face a ghostlike milky pallor as he spoke: "*Somos como un arbol.* We are like a tree. Like a plant. Which yields leaves, and each leaf thinks it's an individual, like—ohhh, I can do it all, I'm the head honcho—but you don't realize, as a human being, shit, I'm the leaf of a *tree.* The force . . . it belongs to the tree and the roots and the soil and something that is incomprehensible to a leaf."

•

I met my uncle Gustavo Perez—the nephew of my father's biological father—for breakfast at a restaurant in San Diego. Gustavo was eager to meet my father, but the prospect made Papi panic and so I went alone. A bald bookworm in his seventies, Gustavo brought me *Historia del Narcotráfico en México*, photos of my biological grandfather and a thirty-page document tracing our roots back to the 1800s. The document, authored by the son of Mario's twin sister, Gildarda, was a gold mine. I learned of Ildefonso Perez, my paternal great-grandfather, an entrepreneur who moved from Santander, Spain, to Mexico City. He smoked a pack of Alpines a day. "He always wore a hat and was very friendly to everyone, especially women," the document reads. "He was concerned about good nutrition and always bought lots of fruits and wholesome food." He drove a taxi, sold gasoline, designed special cartons for milk. Once, he started a farm in a town the document refers to as "Juachilko," with cows and pigs. I looked up the town; it doesn't exist as spelled. According to the document, all of the farm's creatures began to die due to "a disease of the pigs." Then the ranch ceased to exist.

The document is rich with anecdotes about every person except for the most important one: Mario. My father's father remains a mystery. He died a recluse in the nineties. I learned his nickname: *Colillitas,* meaning "cigarette butts," because he started smoking when he was ten. And the fact that he worked for years installing and repairing neon lights for businesses in Mexico City. And this: "Mario . . . was always very intuitive with mechanical things. You name it, car engines, electrical things, and anything that was mechanical in nature, came easy to him."

•

My father believes our universe was born of the implosion of a four-dimensional sun in a parallel plane. "You can have other universes," Papi said, sitting in the dark of the house in Rosarito. "I mean, it's infinite, everything continues and continues and continues. Why do we want to limit it?" Nocturnal Mexico poured in through the windows, turning us into black silhouettes. Neither of us bothered to turn on the lights. My father smoked a cigarette, which glowed each time he breathed.

I flew back to Mexico City. A self-proclaimed shaman moved into a house where I was now renting a room in a less expensive neighborhood called Del Valle. Norberto stood less than five feet tall and had dark corkscrew curls down to his shoulder blades. He claimed to be in his twenties but looked fourteen. I told him about my fear that Mexico wanted me dead. *When you look in the mirror lately, do you see anything strange?* he asked. His question was eerie because I had been avoiding mirrors.

Sort of—it's more like I sense something strange. Something sinister. Like a malevolent presence crouching behind me.

Norberto nodded as if he understood. *Someone who has died does not know they have died. You must help show them the way.* He disappeared into his bedroom and emerged with a mortar and pestle. *Close your eyes.* I let my lids fall and heard a ringing. I opened my eyes, curious, and saw the pestle sliding on the mortar. *Take deep breaths. Tell me when you see the ghost.* I closed my eyes again. I wasn't sure if the ghost was supposed to be Mando or Piedragil. I figured it was more likely Mando, as Piedragil would have accepted his death, probably even reveled in its drama. I pictured Mando surrounded by dark. Norberto told me to tell the spirit it was time to cross into the next dimension. I envisioned a bright light enveloping my friend and guiding him. I opened my eyes. It was remarkable: I felt suddenly weightless with tranquility. *Thank you,* I said.

Tienes que regresar al agua, he said, cryptically. You must return to the water.

I walked back upstairs. Norberto tended to speak in poetic riddles. I wondered: Was he using "water" as a synonym for emotion, as in the Tarot, which I had begun to study after learning that Juanita may have used the cards? Or as a synonym for the past, analogous to the underworld, as the ancient Maya used the term? It didn't matter. I felt so light, so cleansed. I didn't necessarily believe Norberto was a real shaman or that he had performed a real exorcism. But I had faith in the power of suggestion. I approached my large old-fashioned vanity mirror with its ornate gold-painted wooden frame, which I had purchased at a flea market. I was sure I would no longer fear my reflection.

What I saw in the mirror paralyzed me. I could not only *sense* a malevolent presence, I could *see* it. It was in the shadows of my face, in the engorged pupils of my eyes. The malevolent presence was *inside* me. The malevolent presence was death itself. The color drained from my face. Norberto's words echoed in my brain: *Someone who has died does not know they have died.* With a chill that turned my flesh to ice, I saw that I was the ghost unaware of having died. Paul had never pulled me out of the sea. He had never saved me. I had drowned. I had *literally* drowned—not figuratively and spiritually, but physically. Everything that had "happened" since—Mando's death, Piedragil's murder, the kidnapping phone call my father received, Papi's larvae—it was all a delusion of limbo, a dream to help me accept that I was dead.

I stared at my hands: white, rotting appendages, bloated from two years inside the Gulf of Mexico. I touched my face: dead cells crumbling. I tried to breathe, but I couldn't make my lungs expand. I was trying to inhale the sea. Saltwater leaked from my eyes. My body coughed and convulsed as the tears soaked my face. I cried for the girl I had been: the fearless girl who was like her father. I cried for the woman I would never become. I cried in mourning. The more I wept, the more I felt alive again. I was exorcising myself of the sea.

THE DEVIL'S TICK

My father resumed binge-drinking that winter. He slept cradling whiskey bottles, which he bought in bulk from duty-free stores at the border. Once again the plants in his garden died in synchrony with his slumber. His starving larvae stacked themselves into squirming mounds, rolling out of their enclosure to survive.

I flew to San Diego to celebrate Christmas Eve at Abuela Carolina's house. My father stayed in Rosarito. He ignored my calls. In the morning, he awoke to an intolerable pain in his chest. He felt he was having a heart attack. He dragged himself out of bed, pulled on his motorcycle boots and collapsed on the floor. He tried to crawl to his bike, to drive himself to a hospital across the border. But he couldn't move. He thought he would die on the floor of the Rosarito beach house, alone, reeking of whiskey.

The strength of his battered body saved him yet again. He called me to recount the experience. I thought of his grandfather, Antonio, who had crossed the border for medical help before dropping dead in a U.S. hospital. He was roughly the age my father is now. The parallels scared me. *Why are you crying?* Papi asked with disgust. *I'm not afraid of death, Jean. I'm ready for it.*

When I visited again, I saw the black tomatoes sagging on their trellises. His backyard was a mess of dirt mounds, trash crates, cluttered carts and rotting plants. He refused to go near his larvae, certain the sight of their dead masses would crush him.

•

I find a hasty, typo-laden transcription I made of one of my father's drunken monologues. I had tucked it away, pained by the phone conversation, forgetting it until now. Better than anything I have ever written, it captures our relationship. In the document, our urgencies merge us together into a single being:

> Because there's a cross line Thats hwy I wanted to have a long talk with u . . . Dont be fool dont be fooled dont be fooled by stupidites by simple explanations 'Ur father was an acoholic and he overdrank he died this and this and that was the end of it' dont be fooled. Just even if it takes u years, years to try to become yourself more of an expert on what things dont be fooled that I die today or tomorrow or 10 pm or 9 pm by the simple explanation that I was consuming excessive alcohol dont be just dont be fool by simple explanations. And try to understand more deeply what cuz thats the way I feel ok? What is happenign to me is something more. Than a simple answer. Ok? Im a very strong person u know physically ive always been and I mean just because this fuckin domino fuckin trip is not gonna u might the impression taht yeah he flip cuz he was toppled away. Its not as simple as that. Its a very complex. And all im askign is for ou to not be. That . Complacent with the simple explanation that everybody gets complacent. With the simple explanation. If im talking to u today and tomorrow im not or whatever just try to we might not even find out in a month or a week or three months try to understand ok. Try to understand its a very complex. Its a very complex very super complex system. In this life system. Like ur mother

would think like ur mother would say she would disregard everything and explain everything if I die tomorrow ur mother will have
a very simple and very symptomizing u might say explanation and
thats it and period just dont fall for that. Its not sentimentalsim just
try to undrestand try to undrestand and dont just fall for hte simple
go for the simple explanations that most ppl would give u especially
your mom. Especially your mom ok? . . . Ur my journalist ur my
record keeping ur my secretary.

·

In February 2014, I hired a moving van to ship my motorcycle and
seven suitcases from Mexico City to the Yucatán Peninsula. *Tienes que
regresar al agua.* I had decided to take Norberto's advice literally. I had
to return to the water.

I swam in the Caribbean and obtained an open-water diving certification, fighting panic all the while. I dove more than thirty feet deep,
swimming over palatial coral and caves of eels and stingrays. Electri-
cally colored parrot fish moved their lips as if speaking to me, and
sparkling schools of sergeant majors nibbled my palms. I could hardly
enjoy the beauty because of my fear. When I wasn't in the sea, I typed
from sunrise to sundown. I studied the Tarot. I did a remote reading
for Papi, a three-card spread examining the past, present and future:

PAST

Eight of Pentacles. This is the story of a man who subjected himself to
intense, focused, solitary physical toil. He came very close to reaping
the fruits of his hard labor.

PRESENT

King of Cups. This is the story of the utmost masculine confronting the
utmost feminine. It is the male archetype immersed in the world of
emotions—floating on the surface of the sea. He straddles the border
between spiritual and material. All the power of the world lies in his
hands.

FUTURE

The Devil. This is the story of a man whose destiny will be determined by whether he can embrace the parts of himself he has for so long inhibited. He has become a carnal creature because of blocks and fears. He must stop suppressing his human nature.

•

At a museum in Mérida, Yucatán, I discovered the *Popol Vuh,* the K'iche' Maya creation story, *The Book of the People.* It is often referred to as the Bible of the ancient Maya because it contains some of the few existing clues about the first sacred texts of the Americas, most of which vanished in the fires of the *conquistadores,* who believed that the strange hieroglyphs on bark codices were dangerous and demonic lies.

In the story, twin warriors—the sun and the moon—are summoned to the underworld, Xibalba, where their father was defeated long ago. The twins follow the road to Xibalba and pass rivers of blood and pus as well as the "midst of many birds." In the paragraphs of the *Popol Vuh,* I saw the slimy white trails of the *caracoles* my sister and I abused as little girls, the strange elixirs of our puberties, the midst of many cockatiels. I read on. When the twins reach Xibalba, they enter six houses and battle darkness, razors, cold, jaguars, fire and bats. They defeat the gods of the underworld and are reunited with their father. They attempt to resurrect him, but to do so they need him to speak the names of his limbs. He remembers only the name for his mouth. In the next scene, the gods of creation make humans out of *maíz.* Scholars disagree about whether the twins succeeded in saving their father, but most believe he was reborn in that most vital crop, which provided the raw material for humanity.

Lurking inside the structure of the story, I felt, was a magic spell. Across cultures and generations, magic spells have shared a salient characteristic: their use of metaphor—written, iterated or performed—to achieve a desired end. The tale of the twins was the metaphor I needed to resurrect my father. With the ropes of letters and the chains of ink, I would capture the vastness of the indomitable incomprehensible. I could change the world without touching it—like Juanita, whose name Mexico bestowed on me, who gave my father hair as black as ink.

•

The Yucatán Peninsula is made of porous limestone. Flooded caves and sinkholes known as cenotes permeate the landscape. The ancient Maya believed cenotes were literal doorways to the underworld, Xibalba. For them, the underworld was analogous to the past—to swim in their waters was to travel through time.

I learned that my apartment in Playa del Carmen was less than a mile from a cenote, and drove my motorcycle east on Calle Juárez until I saw the sign on my right: "Chaak Tun." I parked the bike next to a dusty iguana that stared at me with one eye. I pulled off my helmet. The cenote was empty except for a single employee, who led me down a gravel path and into the warm and humid cave. The opening looked like the gaping jaws of a magnificent hellscape, a scene straight from the dreams of Hieronymus Bosch: long, dripping stalactites like rows of dripping fangs, fiery orange light dancing on the blue water. The silence and stillness were total, enveloping me with a uterine beckoning. Bats flitted across the ceiling. I dove into the water.

•

On the vernal equinox, I hitched a ride to Chichén Itzá, where at sunset, shadows formed on the main stairwell of the largest pyramid, El Castillo, in the shape of a serpent: the ancient Maya god Kukulkán, their version of the Mexica's Quetzalcóatl. According to legend, Kukulkán flew into the horizon to speak to the sun. The sun burned his tongue to punish his impertinence.

On the way to the pyramids, I stopped for a swim at the cenote Ik-Kil: a true sinkhole. The green earth opened like a terrestrial throat ending in blackish-blue waters. Foliage hung from the mouth and grew on the damp fertile walls. The water was crowded with swimmers celebrating the equinox. The atmosphere was joyful, almost fantastical. I dove into the water and swam toward the center. The cenote was so deep that I could see nothing but dark blue water and inky catfish near the surface. Their slick tails slapped my legs as I swam. Waterfalls poured down the lips of the cenote. The water embraced me; the equinoxial sunlight bathed me. I threw my head back and floated, letting the waterfalls splash my face. The green was so green it throbbed. The screaming of motmot birds resonated with strings in my meat, made my blood pulse in synchrony. The wetness was baptismal, sensuous, female. I felt at home. I felt at home in the fertile climate of my mother. For the first time since Los Tuxtlas, I felt no fear as I swam. I was deriving strength from my flesh, from within my vulnerability.

•

In the first week of April 2014—almost exactly a year after my father received the fake kidnapping phone call—I got a call from Papi. He told me he had taken the miracle mineral supplement (MMS): essentially, bleach. In the instructions, the consumer is told to "activate" the supplement with citrus juice, producing chlorine dioxide equivalent to industrial-strength bleach in the stomach. It is sold as a cure for HIV, cancer, malaria. The Food and Drug Administration calls it poison. My father had decided to use MMS to eradicate his mysterious illness.

Papi was incomprehensible. He told me his tongue was swollen and white. He repeated over and over again something about a dream. I asked him what the dream was about, but he merely chanted some version of the following: *Twenty-five years ago, I had a dream. A very vivid dream. I had a dream in which it was like a revelation. It was a very revel-evant dream.* He went on like this, voicing new details with an excruciating slowness, until finally I understood: he was referring to the dream that had left him paralyzed with fear as a young man, the prophetic one so awful he had blacked out its contents. He claimed to remember its contents now: he was going to die this season. For the first time in my life, I hoped with all my heart that my father was insane.

"Papi, you're not going to die if you stop poisoning—"

"Jean. Jean. I'm just trying to *explain* to you what *happened* to me so we can psychoanalyze me."

I took a deep breath. I was speaking before I was aware of what I would say: "In the Tarot, the death card does not necessarily prophesy literal death. It just means the end of one chapter and the beginning of another. Maybe your dream means that you're going to be reborn. In *this* life. Maybe all of your psychological pain is going to disappear."

He was silent for a moment.

"Okay. Okay. That makes sense. I hope you're right."

I asked him to go on Skype and video-chat with me. He stuck his tongue out for me. It was large and white, a drowned man's tongue. I fought back my tears.

"I am totally . . ." my father said, struggling to find the next word, "totally, totally . . . totally . . . totally, totally, totally . . . totally . . ."

He repeated the word several more times.

"I don't want to say *glad*, 'cause that would be a stupid . . . *miss*. I am totally fuckin' *grateful*—and it's not the word to describe—I am totally grateful that you are my daughter, Jean. I am totally grateful that you are the way you *are*. And that I can communicate with you."

He continued: "If I die in the next fuckin' week, or the next month, be kind enough to bury me in San Francisco. There's a cemetery there where there's no tombstones. No fuckin' nothing. And you just . . . you just kick me over the side, all right? I don't wanna be lowered like fuckin' . . . royalty. Just push me over like a dump. Like a stone. Cuz that's all I am."

"That's not true. You're a human being. And a father. And a son."

"Not anymore."

He had had another dream the night before. That's why it was so hard for him to express himself about the dreams: there were two he wanted to tell me about. His poisoned brain couldn't separate them. The night before, he had dreamed of eating at an extravagant seafood restaurant. The fish he was eating were alive, but they felt no pain as he ate them. Then the manager of the restaurant approached him and informed him he had won a prize. He handed him a bundle so large he could hardly wrap his arms around it. Everyone in the restaurant stood up to shake his hand and congratulate him. Then a woman appeared. She kissed him on the lips.

"It was a *stupid* dream, Jean," he said suddenly, full of contempt for himself. And then, breathlessly, with a shred of hope: "I want to go back to that *dream*."

I burst into tears, telling Papi I wanted him to live to see his grand-children.

"What if I tell you I'm not going to live to see your children, Jean? What if I tell you I am going to be reborn as one of your sons? We all die someday, Jean. You're going to die, too. And I am going to be by your side when you do."

Please let this be mindless, substance-induced babble, I prayed as my father spoke. *I would rather have an insane father alive than a prophetic one dead.*

I called Abuela Carolina and told her I believed my father was sui-cidal. My grandmother visited him with my aunt Aimee. They cooked for him and kept him company. Papi promised to stop drinking. He did not.

•

Memory has no specialized lobe, sulci or gyrus in the brain. It func-tions through what neuroscientists refer to as "long-term potentia-tion," an increased tendency for signal transmission among neurons that fire together. Those tendencies are stored as invisible neuronal patterns prone to reactivation as recollections. Those patterns are the gravity of human consciousness. The neuroscientist Patrick McNa-mara points out in *The Neuroscience of Religious Experience* that humans can trigger religious experiences through a process McNamara calls "decentering": taking the self "off-line" by dissolving one's sense of boundaries—in other words, pushing past the patterns that glue our minds together. Some people can get lost in interior netherworlds. But narrative has the power to bring them back, he says. Like memories, like dreams in REM sleep, stories can integrate. They create new webs of neuronal connections, like the lines connecting stars in a constellation. The lines are not real, but lost sailors can see them. Those imaginary patterns guide them through the darkness.

I cannot solve the mystery of my father. I cannot save him. He is the one who must remember the names for his limbs. I can only trace my relationship with him. I prefer to believe in shamans than in lunatics. It is the great gift of my Hispanic heritage. I cannot look at the world and see mere chemical imbalances. But no human mind converses in waves and particles alone. Its native language—subjectivity—is eccentric. Brains are mystical. They perform alchemy in a place no one can measure. Yet the stories they yield exert as obvious an effect as gravity.

•

"You should be a shaman," I tell my father.

"I am a shaman" he says. "I am a shaman."

•

Papi swells to the size of a solar system. The rings of Saturn adorn his pinkies. Comets crown his head. Spells spill from his mouth like rivers. He grows. Black holes blow out his pupils. Whole galaxies entangle in his beard. Wormholes spin on his lashes. He breathes the fog of nebulae. He curls his fingers; space curves like VHS film; time rewinds and rewinds and rewinds.

•

In 2013, I read an article by a woman named Eleanor Longden in *Scientific American Mind*. She described hearing voices in her head—innocuous commentaries about her actions. When a friend told her to see a psychologist, these auditory hallucinations turned sinister. She was diagnosed with Schizophrenia.

She discovered Intervoice, an online community of voice-hearers who reject that diagnosis. They believe abnormal perceptions become maladaptive only due to negative social feedback—that the label of "sickness" is a self-fulfilling prophecy rooted in fear. Instead of trying to suppress their so-called hallucinations, the Intervoice members listen to them, mining them for metaphorical rather than literal insights. Longden learned to think of her voices "not as symptoms, rather as adaptations and survival strategies: sane reactions to insane circumstances. The voices took the place of overwhelming pain and gave words to it—memories of sexual trauma and abuse, rage, shame, loss, guilt and low self-worth." When Longden began paying attention to her voices, they taught her to cope with her past.

•

Choose the best answer for the following question from among the choices provided. The Eleanor Longden story provides evidence for which of the following phenomena?

- The power of placebos
- The existence of magic
- Both of the above
- None of the above

•

My father's medical records from the turn of the millennium no longer exist. I can't corroborate my mother's claims that Papi was "Schizophrenic," a conclusion she reached based on personal assessments. She is not a mental health specialist. But it's not accurate to call Papi a "Shaman" either. Both labels—"Schizophrenic" and "Shaman"—obscure the complex dimensionality of his in-flux reality. North of the border, Papi might be diagnosed, medicated. South of the border, he might be revered, consulted. There are exceptions to the scientific-supernatural divide, of course. Urban areas throughout Latin America have adopted the Western psychiatric approach; they lock up *locos* and prescribe lithium. In the United States, *curanderos* of the Tohono O'odham Nation rely on voices and visions to guide the families of missing migrants to skeletons. Both approaches—the scientific and the supernatural—are incomplete on their own. The former implies a purely physical mind. The latter ignores material reality. Acknowledging the power of interpretation—over the mind *and* the world—is a way to branch the two. The power is not total, but it is real. It is neither material nor magical. It is both. It extends forever in all directions.

•

I prepared my backpack for one of my final road trips: to Chicxulub, the site of the asteroid impact that caused the extinction of the dinosaurs and more than seventy percent of life on earth. I wanted to collect some sand from the beach. The sand was symbolic of the power of regeneration and transmutation—of the endless capacity of life to begin anew. I would bring some back with me to the United States and give some to my father. I could no longer live in Mexico. I wanted to be close to my family.

I headed north across the peninsula with empty plastic bottles in my backpack, stopping to jump into cenotes along the way: the bat-filled cenotes of Dzitnup, the gold-bathed cenotes of Cuzamá, the tree-lined cenotes of El Corchito and Celestún, where a crocodile sunbathed on the shore as I swam. The coastal town of Chicxulub was so alone and motionless it felt dreamlike. The contrast between the town's stillness and the explosive significance I knew it possessed produced a powerful illusion in my mind: as I walked through the deserted, postapocalyptic streets, I felt that the reality of the town hinged on my perception—that if I sufficiently willed it, I could cause the seaside shacks to morph into ships or sea creatures, as if in a lucid dream. I saw women staring out at me from windows, blinking slowly. I could almost hear their thoughts, questioning me.

The wind was gritty with sand and seashells, whipping my skin. It was so fierce that the fishermen had not gone out to sea. I found them congregated on a patio, drinking beer. They told me about *El Norte,* the name of the wind. They said it crossed the Gulf of Mexico and pummeled the northern lip of the peninsula. Lesser winds had toppled their boats in the past. I asked the fishermen about the asteroid. They had all heard of it, but they knew little about it. "How long ago did that happen? That was thousands of years ago," said one. "I'm seventy years old, but I didn't see it," another added, skeptically.

I walked to the beach and sat in front of the sea. I asked Chicxulub for permission to take some of its supernatural sands. The wind blew harder, creating a layer of broken seashells on my cheeks. I cupped the seashell-laden sand in my palms and let it drip into two bottles and a bag. I poured fistful after fistful. When I finished, I placed the containers of sand in my backpack and whispered my thanks to Chicxulub. Then I headed to the pier. Standing in the middle of its narrow length, my body battled the wind, which threatened to toss me into the turbulent Gulf of Mexico. The dominant color of the place was cream. Everything seemed to mix with the color of the sand: the wind, the sea, the sky. The crater, more than a hundred miles in diameter, was not visible anywhere, buried beneath everything. It was discovered in the 1970s by geophysicists who were on a quest for petroleum. Deep inside the Gulf of Mexico, emanating from Chicxulub, they detected a gigantic symmetrical arc that led to a bounty of shocked quartz and tektites. They found an anomaly in the earth's gravitational field. In the Yucatec Maya language, *chicxulub* means "the devil's tick" or "the demon's flea." It is incredible to me that the indigenous people gave this place such an ominous name. They could not have known about the asteroid when they named it.

CHAMÁN

The next morning, at a hostel in El Progreso, five miles from Chicxulub, I received two Facebook messages from my sister:

dude mom won a million dollars.

dont tell anyone.

I called my mother, confused. She explained in a low voice suffused with joy that she had just won the grand prize of the 2014 Ronald McDonald House Charities raffle, usually a $4 million home. She was getting a million dollars instead because not enough people had bought tickets for the sale of the house. My Facebook response to my sister vividly captures my feeling: *Seriously, this ALMOST makes me believe in Jesus Christ our Lord. LOL . . . KARMA IS REAL.*

·

Sometime that week, in near-death delirium, Papi felt moved to call his mother. *"Necesito ayuda,"* he croaked. When she came to pick him up, his skin was the color of chicken broth. He handed his mother the address for a rehabilitation clinic in Tijuana.

•

I sped east on a bus from Chicxulub to Mérida, planning to travel through Chiapas—the last place I wanted to see in my father's country. In Mérida, at Hostal Zócalo, a metal locker door came unhinged and fell four feet onto my foot. It shattered the bones in three toes. I screamed and cried for ten minutes as other hostel guests surrounded me. In the emergency room, I learned that the bones of my third toe were splintered in irreparable little pieces. *I could operate, but I would make it worse,* the surgeon said.

I was crippled in the hostel for a week. I kept my foot elevated on pillows as I waited for the profuse bleeding and the pulsating agony to stop. I considered continuing my travels on crutches. But it was impossible. Gravity made blood rush into my mangled toe when I stood, causing throbbing so excruciating I cried. A full-bodied seventy-year-old Brazilian woman who looked thirty-five took care of me, bringing me mangoes and telling stories about her husband, who she claimed was the head of the CIA. "He is always working," she sighed, peeling our mangoes with a knife. "He is *so old* but he never wants to retire. For now, I travel alone."

Back in Playa del Carmen, I lay bedridden for another week. I learned my father was in a rehabilitation center called Clínica Libre. I headed to the airport on crutches and flew north to see him, bringing some of the Chicxulub sand, which I now believed I had paid for with the sacrifice of my toe. My sister joined me at the clinic. We waited in the lobby, where an aging toucan swayed on a stick in a large black cage. It stared at us with apathy from under drooping lids. The therapist, Blanca, called us into a small room with two couches and a reclining chair. She told us our father didn't know we were coming; the visit had been organized as a surprise, as a family therapy session. She handed us both a form. On one side, we had to fill in the blanks in negative phrases such as "I felt hurt when you _____" and "I felt frightened when you _____." On the other side, we had to complete positive phrases such as "I felt proud when you _____" and "I felt loved when you _____." The goal was to make real for our father that his self-destruction was hurting people who loved him, not just himself, and thus motivate him to start taking care of himself.

My father entered the room, his skin the pale yellow of *mantequilla*. His eyes seemed faint and faraway. He lit up for a moment when he saw us. Michelle and I took turns hugging him. The therapist gestured at a sofa in front of us. Papi sat down. Blanca nodded at me. I stared at the form in my hands, dreading what I was about to do. I took a deep breath and began reading: "I felt anger when you criticized me as a teenager." I looked at my father, expecting him to become defensive, to make grunts or gestures of dissent. He did not. I continued: "I felt hurt when you failed to recognize my efforts to make you proud. I felt alone when as a child you weren't there. I felt scared each time you told me you were going to die."

His eyes grew wet. He let me talk. He just listened. Then it was Michelle's turn. "I felt sad each time you forgot my birthday," my sister said. "Especially because it was only two days before yours." With each anecdote, Papi's eyes became heavier with tears.

"Okay, now the positive," the therapist said. We told Papi about the good feelings he had provoked. "I felt love each time you opened up to me about your past," I said. "I felt grateful when you hugged me in Jalisco as a little girl, and agreed to leave Autlán." My sister recalled how special she had felt when our father had taken her to ride the trolley as a little girl. When they got off at the border, they encountered a street vendor selling toys, including a stuffed chick emerging from a stuffed egg, which Papi bought for her. She told him how appreciated she felt when he took her to a Rosarito beach and shucked oysters for her. Papi seemed to soften with each story. But when my sister finished, he stiffened again. The room was silent and awkward. The therapist seemed to be waiting.

"I feel like it's important to mention our mother," I blurted. If this session was supposed to make Papi aware of the pain he had caused people who loved him, she could not be left out. *"Adelante,"* Blanca said, nodding her head.

"You hurt Mom a lot, Papi, but she—"

Papi interrupted me for the first time in the session: "Your *mom*? I didn't hurt your—I didn't—your mom—hurt—I—*no*. I mean maybe, maybe a *little*. But she didn't give a damn about me. She got over it quick. *Real* quick."

I stared at him, speechless with surprise. He clearly believed what he was saying. But there was an effort to his conviction, a corporal one—crinkles and corrugations in his face, crooked angles in his arms, contorted spine. I conveyed the story of my mother as best I could, without letting go of Papi's gaze. I told him what I saw as the blatant truth: that she loved him, that he crushed her, that she forgave him, that she still loved him. I spoke slowly because each word seemed to unfurl him. His fists unclenched; his body uncrumpled. I didn't want to lose my grasp. When I finished, his mouth hung open. He stared at me for several shell-shocked seconds. Then he came loose. His catharsis slammed into me like electricity. His body shook with sobs. He coughed and convulsed. My father was cracking open.

I walked over, tentatively, and kneeled. I grabbed his arm. Heat radiated from his quaking body. His shirt was soaked with tears. "It's okay, Papi," I said, because I didn't know what else to say, and because it was true. "It's okay."

When he looked at me, his irises seemed flecked with embers. Beyond the dying light was a man I'd never known.

CAXCAN: AN EPILOGUE

I ask my father to name everything—his mouth, his nose, his eyes, his heart, blood, skin, fingers, dreams, feet, navel, ears, memories, tongue, guts, neurons. "Thus was their counsel when they had defeated all of Xibalba," reads the *Popol Vuh*. Our tangled tale is done. Clocks no longer rewind. The roads are not conch, cobblestone and *caracol*. Interstate 5 stretches before me, all asphalt and lines. I pass the green sign that reads "Mexico Only" to interview deported migrants who live in sewage tunnels under the border—men rejected by two nations—for my job with a public-broadcasting outlet in San Diego. I head back home, their stories in my pockets. "Anything to declare?" ask the U.S. customs agents. "Nope," I say, and drive back to my country.

•

As I finish this book, I click through folders on my computer and pull up one of my scanned photographs of Juanita—the black-and-white one in which La Adivina rests a hand on a tree branch in front of crumbling adobe walls. I recall chalking pentagrams on the sidewalk as a Wiccan child, but I don't remember why. I am suddenly curious about them again. I turn to the works of Éliphas Lévi and rediscover their purpose: pentagrams invoke the power of the human body with its five senses, the mastery of the human spirit over the material world. It is important to draw pentagrams with a single point toward the sky. "A reversed pentagram, with two points projecting upward, is a symbol of evil and attracts sinister forces because it overturns the proper order of things and demonstrates the triumph of matter over spirit. It is the goat of lust attacking the heavens with its horns, a sign execrated by initiates," Lévi writes. My heart drums in my chest. In the photograph of Juanita, the pentagram of twigs and leaves hanging from a branch is upside down. I never noticed.

•

I contact my cousin Eddie. It is December 2016. He has joined a secret group for sorcerers in Mexico City and is studying neuroscience at Mexico's prestigious public university, the National Autonomous University of Mexico (UNAM). A few days ago, he called to tell me that his dead grandmother, Maria Antonieta, visited him in a dream, saying he needed to travel to northern Mexico to speak with a clairvoyant relative who can help find our kidnapped cousin, Diego. Eddie said: *By "clairvoyant relative," I'm certain she meant your father. If not him, then another one of Juanita's descendants in Tlaltenango. We need to go to Tlaltenango, the three of us.*

When I first learned about Juanita, I called two distant relatives in Tlaltenango, asking if I could come learn more about her. They both said similar things: *Do not come; nobody remembers a thing about her, not even where she was buried or where she lived. More important, the road from Zacatecas is extremely dangerous; there are constant kidnappings; we rarely leave the pueblo anymore. It is not worth the risk.*

Traumatized by repeated encounters with death, I decided not to go. I pieced together the story of Juanita with the few documents I could find online, the recollections of her grandchildren and a few photographs and letters they possessed. She remained a mystery. But the discovery of Juanita's inverted pentagram in conjunction with Eddie's dream renews my desire. I send the photograph to Eddie. *What does it mean?* I ask.

My cousin gasps as he sees it. *A sorceress would never allow her symbols to be seen without a reason. She wanted you to see this.*

Eddie, what if this has been inviting sinister forces into our lives? What if Juanita left open a door to the underworld?

He is silent awhile. Then he says: *You're the first person to find her story, to notice the pentagram in the photograph. If you think she left a door open, she did—and she did it on purpose, for you to find it . . . and close it.*

I persuade my father to come with us. Eddie sends me instructions for a spell he wants me to conduct the night before our departure: "Light a candle and as you light it you are going to say this: 'Marvelous light, symbol of our love, present yourself. FIAT LUX.' So that your soul will be balanced with your mind and we can follow our intuition when we arrive in Tlaltenango. If you start to feel afraid, blow out the candle and start again. Pray three Our Fathers in Latin, you can find them on the Internet. Then finish by saying: *Hecho está en el aquí y en el ahora.*"

I carefully follow each step. In the morning, I pick up Papi from Abuela Carolina's. We take an Uber vehicle to the cross-border bridge, walk into Tijuana, fly to Zacatecas and drive a rental car to our hotel. We plan to stay in the state capital until the next morning, when Eddie's flight lands, then drive to Tlaltenango. My father and I arrive at sunset. Zacatecas is gorgeous, cradled in mountains, colorful old houses and ancient doors on clean, cobblestone streets. Murmurations fill the orange sky like tornadoes, thousands upon thousands of birds undulating like a single mass. *Wow,* my father says.

•

In the morning, Eddie arrives. We drive to Tlaltenango. Eddie talks excitedly in the back seat, arguing that kabbalistic calculations regarding my birthday reveal "a straddling of spirit and human worlds." He has a hypothesis: I am the reincarnation of Juanita. The magic spell he had me conduct was meant to awaken her spirit inside me—so I would show us the way in Tlaltenango. I roll my eyes, unconvinced, though I do think it would be fascinating if true. My father starts to believe him. Eddie says: *Did you know that tonight is a full moon?* I shake my head. *Well, Juanita, you planned the trip, without even realizing it, for the exact day the moon is going to be 100 percent full,* Eddie says. *It's the perfect conditions to encounter a door to the underworld, and close it.* We arrive in the town, which looks like a typical urban neighborhood of Mexico, with trash strewn on the sidewalks lined with stores and stands of street food. It doesn't resemble the mystical rural pueblo I envisioned. The date is January 12, 2017.

We meet Wilfrido, the grandson of Juanita's last son, *El Doctor,* Felipe. Wilfrido looks a lot like the Juanita in the photos, but a chubby, male version, friendly as a teddy bear. His warmth contrasts charmingly with the sharpness of his canine teeth, and I love him right away. He has an elfin tip on his ear like I and my father have, though less pronounced. He shows us Felipe's grave, saying Juanita was buried in the same cemetery, but the bones were later removed, like all old bones, and placed in a mass grave at an unknown location.

Wilfrido invites us to his home in the attic of his motorcycle-repair shop. He laments that he has none of Juanita's belongings; he was a child when she passed away. He once had Felipe's old spell books, but they were destroyed in a flood. While browsing the motorcycle-maintenance manuals on Wilfrido's bookshelves, I notice four volumes of *Grandes Temas de lo Oculto y lo Insolito,* three volumes of *Grandes Enigmas* and eight books on *medicina natural.*

I ask, with a smile: *Are you hiding something, Wilfrido?*

He chuckles and shakes his head. *These questions have always intrigued me. I wish I had Juanita's gift, but I do not. I would tell you if I did.*

•

We head to the Palacio Municipal for information about my great-great-grandmother. They have none. We cross the main plaza, El Jardín, to La Parroquia. The priest, Padre Gabriel, agrees to speak to us. I ask if he has any information about Juana "Juanita" Velasquez, born in the spring of 1880. I have a citation about her baptism certificate from the Internet. She was baptized in early April 1880, which means she was probably born around that time. He tells me he can try to dig up the original baptism certificate.

While we wait, we wander the streets interviewing *ancianos* about La Adivina. Some of the oldest people have vague memories:

"People came from out of town to speak with her," one says.

"She was very serious," says another.

"She wasn't like other people; she rarely socialized."

I show the *ancianos* the photographs I have of her, surrounded by crumbling adobe walls. I ask if they remember where she lived. No one can orient me. The town has changed too much, they say—their mental maps are scrambled up. We return to the church. Padre Gabriel gives me a scanned copy of Juanita's baptism certificate. It reads, in Spanish: *I, the father Juan Montes Casas, solemnly baptized Juana, who was born . . . on the thirty-first of March at five in the afternoon."*

Eddie's jaw drops. *I knew it.*

Juanita was born on March 31—like me.

•

Eddie, my father and I tour the town with Wilfrido. A car-repair shop catches my attention. I shout at my dad to stop driving. He parks. Crumbling adobe walls, like those in my photographs of Juanita, are visible behind the shop, beyond a dirt lot. My dad sighs. *Every house was made of adobe back then,* he says, rolling his eyes. *You'll find those walls everywhere.* I ignore him. I walk into the shop. Wilfrido follows. We approach the only person there, a man in his fifties with a gray goatee. He is repairing a car. *I think my great-great-grandmother used to live here,* I say in Spanish. *Can I look at the walls over there?*

The employee has a friendly smile and vibrant black eyes. He introduces himself as Carlos. *It's all just ruins, but go ahead and take a look,* he says. I compare the walls to the photographs I printed out. They are the same, with similar bases of cobbled stones. But surely my father is right. These adobe walls existed throughout the town. Both he and Eddie are still in the car, engine running.

Carlos approaches me and Wilfrido from behind and says: *You know, it's funny, a man came here a long time ago, from the border, just like you. . . . He walked in here saying he wanted to see the place. He said this house used to be a single property, that it belonged to a woman who cured—with herbs and cleansings, something like that, and—*

I interrupt him, heart pounding.

Did you say a woman who cured? Did he tell you her name? Was she La Adivina?

I don't remember if he told me her name.

Do you mind if I turn on my recorder?

He gives me permission to record his voice. Carlos explains that he was a little boy when the man from the border came, maybe five years old. The car-repair shop didn't exist back then, but his family rented a room on the property.

The man from the border told Carlos that the old woman who once lived there was his grandmother, and that she had lived alone. "He said she was from a ranch across the river over there," Carlos says, pointing north.

Earlier in the day, the townspeople had told me I could find the ruins of Encinillas—the ranch where Juanita lived before moving to Tlaltenango—somewhere in the desert, across the river.

I'm almost certain I've found Juanita's old house. I wonder who the man from the border could have been. If Carlos was five when the man came, it must have been the late 1950s or early 1960s. My great-grandfather Antonio died in 1961. Perhaps he came to say goodbye to Tlaltenango.

Carlos continues: "There is a weird energy here at midday, from 11:30 a.m. to around 12:15 p.m. or 12:20 p.m. Often, *ancianos* arrive and sit on that bench right there for no reason. They sit there while I'm working and they just sit. They say, 'Hey, you know something? There's a vibration here.'"

I show Carlos a photo of Juanita. "This is my great-great-grandmother." His face turns white. He stumbles backward as if I've shoved him. "You're not going to believe this," Carlos says, his mouth agape. He shakes his head, then continues: "There was a little garden here, with avocado trees, orange trees, lemon trees and the *guayaba* tree you still see right there. . . . One day when I came to close the shop, I felt someone throwing dirt on me here. . . . I turned around and there was nobody there. I kept working and I felt it again. I turned around and—with all the fear in the world—I beheld that woman . . . the woman in the photo."

Carlos thinks the woman he witnessed was the ghost of La Adivina.

"She was old, skinny, wearing that gray rebozo, but it had black stains on it," he says. "She just disappeared in the direction of the river."

•

Wilfrido, my dad, Eddie and I cross the river the next day. We want to find Encinillas and are following vague directions from those who say it is "somewhere in the mountains beyond the river, west of town, through a black gate off a dirt road." The road branches several times. I have an eerie sense that I've been here and that I know where I'm going. Each time, I tell my father where to turn. The development ends, and we follow a dirt road through the mountains. Wilfrido's truck gets a flat tire. He doesn't have his toolbox, and he needs a special wrench to remove the spare. We have no phone service. My father improvises tools out of rocks and knives and removes the spare. We fix the truck and continue driving. We find the black gate and park. We walk. Horned cattle crowd around us. We discover Encinillas just as the sun begins to set: a desolate collection of crumbling walls. Towering piles of tree stumps rise in the abandoned rooms. A stone well and two reservoirs are full of silver water. Eddie finds a reddish rock indented with what look like little ouroboros shapes: a fossil. He puts it into his pocket. It may prove useful later.

•

On our last day in Tlaltenango, my father, Eddie and I conduct a spell to close what we suspect is Juanita's open door. It is partially improvised but also uses Eddie's spell books. The three of us take the spell very seriously, sobered by the strange town. The details must remain a secret, to ensure the spell's integrity. But it ends like this: *Hecho está en el aquí y en el ahora.*

ACKNOWLEDGMENTS

My sister, Michelle Guerrero, journeyed through the past with me and helped me find some of the most vital gems in "The Road to Xibalba."

Thanks to the teachers and mentors who lit the way. Steve Brown told me I could write a memoir; Jervey Tervalon told me to throw in as much eye of newt and fairy dust as I desired; Suzannah Lessard brought my feet back to earth and helped me make it true; other faculty in the nonfiction MFA program at Goucher College—Diana Hume George, Madeleine Blais, Dick Todd, Patsy Sims, Leslie Rubinkowski—provided wise guidance; and finally, Gabe Kahn and Anthony Harrup opened the door to my father's birthplace.

I am beyond grateful to the One World team, particularly my editor, Chris Jackson, who gave chase with me upon the sea, keeping me on course through rough winds with his compass, and Nicole Counts, who lives in the lines as well. David R. Patterson believed in this book when it was still a thesis and I am very happy to call him my agent. The recognition from PEN America and FUSION, via the 2016 Emerging Writers Prize, was an unexpected gift. My team at KPBS gave me the time off and flexibility I needed to edit the manuscript even as the news coming out of my beat—immigration—was incessant.

My best friends Sam Oltman, Faith Gobeli, Bonnie Sweet, Lizz Huerta and Ana Vigo kept me sane with their love and ideas. Thanks to my childhood friends Victoria Harper and Elizabeth Baber for showing me the worlds of fantasy and science fiction. And Paul Kiernan for pulling my body out of the ocean so that I could write this. Other friends and family provided invaluable support: Memsy Price, Neda Semnani, Ginny McReynolds, Rachel Dickinson, Theo Emery, Rae Gomes, Anita Huslin, Porscha Burke, Daniel Thiemann, Logan Sullivan, Rodrigo Delgado Calderón, Sophie Cohen, Timmothy Doolittle and Zerina Kratovac. Rob Waller taught me to think of writing as a physical art instead of a mental one—requiring practice to build muscle. The role of my *hermanito*, Eddie Rojas Rosas, is explicit in the pages.

In particular, I am thankful to my friend and *ex novio* Leo Carrión, who moved to the Yucatán Peninsula with me and provided crucial companionship while I was writing much of the manuscript. Although he does not appear in these pages, his joy dwells in them; this book might have withered on the vine without his love and exuberance.

I stand in awe of the courageous collaboration of my family, above all Papi and Abuelita Carolina, who revisited their most painful memories for this book, and my beautiful, extraordinary mother—Mami, Mommy and Mom—who in spite of her private nature always supported this project in every possible way. My gratitude to them is eternal.

ABOUT THE AUTHOR

JEAN GUERRERO is an investigative reporter focusing on immigration and the U.S.-Mexico border. She works for KPBS, with stories airing on NPR, PBS and other public media. She previously reported for the *Wall Street Journal* in Mexico City as a foreign correspondent. She graduated from the University of Southern California in 2010 and has an MFA in creative nonfiction from Goucher College. Guerrero was the 2016 recipient of the PEN/FUSION Emerging Writers prize. She lives in San Diego.

jeanguerrero.com
Facebook.com/jeanguerrero
Twitter: @jeanguerre
Instagram: @jeanguerre

ABOUT THE TYPE

This book was set in Dante, a typeface designed by Giovanni Mardersteig (1892–1977). Conceived as a private type for the Officina Bodoni in Verona, Italy, Dante was originally cut only for hand composition by Charles Malin, the famous Parisian punch cutter, between 1946 and 1952. Its first use was in an edition of Boccaccio's *Trattatello in laude di Dante* that appeared in 1954. The Monotype Corporation's version of Dante followed in 1957. Though modeled on the Aldine type used for Pietro Cardinal Bembo's treatise *De Aetna* in 1495, Dante is a thoroughly modern interpretation of that venerable face.